Advertising
with
Small Budgets
for
Big Results

How to Buy Print, Broadcast,
Outdoor, Online, Direct Response
& Offbeat Media

How-to, where-to, how-much-to advice

from

Linda Carlson

Barrett Street Productions
Seattle, Washington

Copyright 2014 by Linda Carlson
All rights reserved
Printed in the United States of America

Library of Congress Catalog Card Number: 2013916376

ISBN 978-0-9627122-9-6 (paperback)

No part of this book may be reproduced in any form or by any means without the prior written permission of the author. The only exception: brief quotes used in reviews. Send copies of reviews to the author at:

Barrett Street Productions
P O Box 99642
Seattle WA 98139
www.lindacarlson.com
Facebook: Advertising with Small Budgets for Big Results
Twitter: @carlsonideas

Use this same information when contacting the author regarding presentations on small business marketing communications.

Although this book has been carefully researched and the contents are accurate to the best of the author's knowledge, neither the author nor the publisher can accept responsibility for any errors within.

Acknowledgements

Many thanks to colleagues, clients, and friends who suggested what should be included and read drafts. With special gratitude to Jenny Porter, Laurie Forsberg, Lisa Poelle, Kirk Potter, Amy Fass, Larry Howard, Katherine Evanson, Sue Ferguson, Myra Dittes, Marva Pelander, Kent Sturgis, Carolyn Threadgill and Lilian Yetter.

This book is for you if

☐ You run a small business and you're struggling to promote your products or services;

☐ You're responsible for promotion in a larger business and you want to supplement traditional advertising with offbeat or locally-targeted marketing; or

☐ You're part of a startup and have no idea what you can do to make potential investors, customers and employees aware of your operation.

This book is also for you if you

☐ Work or volunteer in a nonprofit, striving to do outreach or create a donor base on the proverbial shoestring;

☐ Handle recruiting for employees, volunteers, association membership or school admissions, and you're ready for some new tools; or

☐ Run a marketing communications or sales promotion agency that wants to help clients explore guerilla marketing.

What you'll find in the pages that follow are the basics about dozens of ways to promote a product, service, event or ongoing need. No hyperbole, no sales pitches, no long-winded theories or research reports: just what, how-to, when-to, and how-much-to to help you decide what is appropriate.

To help you brainstorm a coordinated promotional campaign, there's a checklist starting on page 230 you can duplicate. To make you a more knowledgeable purchaser of advertising time, space, production and printing, there's a detailed glossary. To find a specific advertising tool, turn way back, to the even more detailed index.

Share your triumphs and opinions on the Facebook page, *Advertising with Small Budgets for Big Results*, at Twitter, @carlsonideas, and with "Your Turn, " the final text page.

Contents

How to Use This Book...6

Advertising Explained..7

Advertising Novelties..34
Advertorials...35
Affiliate Marketing..43
Alumni Publications/Websites..43
Apparel 45
Automated Telephone Systems/Voice Mail............................46

Bags..48
Banners...49
Bathroom Advertising...49
Blogs...50
Business Stationery...55
Bumper Stickers...55

Carriage and Pedicab Advertising.......................................56
Catalogs and Sell Sheets..56
Characters in Costumes...59
Cinema Advertising...60
Colors..60
Concert and Theater Program Advertising............................61
Contests as Lead Generators...62
Cooperative Advertising...62
Coupons...65
Crowdsourcing...72

Databases...73
Directory Advertising...74
Direct Response Advertising..75

Elevators and Lobbies..86
Email...87
Endorsements, Testimonials and Review Sites........................96

Ferry System Advertising...102
Free Shipping..105

Game Ads..105
Gas Pump Advertising...108
Giveaways and Samples...109

Inserts..114
In-store Advertising/Point-of-purchase...............................116
Invoices..118

Loyalty Programs...119

Magazine Advertising...120
Maps and Tourist Brochures..128
Naming/Sponsorships/Donations.......................................130
Networking..131
Newsletters...135
Newspapers...137

Out-of-Home Advertising..148

Postal Regulations 156
Posters and Postering...159
Product Placement...161

QR Codes..161

Radio..163

Shopping Channels...174
Signs...174
Social Media 182
Swag/Goodie Bags...192

Television...193
Trade Shows and Conferences...203
Trailers 206

Websites 207
Word-of-Mouth...220

Appendix A: Media Releases..221
Appendix B: Periodical Publishers......................................224
Appendix C: Northwest Public Radio Stations.....................226
Appendix D: Model and Photographer Release.....................228
Appendix E: Advertising and Promotion Checklist...............229
Appendix F: For Additional Help..242

Glossary..244

Index..267

Your Turn!..**274**

How to Use This Book

Advertising with Small Budgets for Big Results is intended as a reference to pull off the shelf when you need definitions, or examples of a medium, or sample rates. It's a mini-encyclopedia of the most affordable promotional tools, not a book you're expected to read from start to finish. (Although, if you do, I guarantee it'll give you dozens of ideas for whatever product, service or campaign you work or volunteer on.)

Written for those with limited resources, this book identifies options appropriate for tight budgets, and explains where you can obtain detailed information. It discusses creating an ad—the copywriting, the design, the physical production—and the cost of media, the printed space, broadcast time or online exposure you buy so that the public can see or hear your ad.

Advertising with Small Budgets for Big Results is also written for those who want to explore what's called "guerilla marketing." Maybe you have a decent budget, and the help of an advertising agency, but you're looking for ways to extend the impact of magazine, newspaper, broadcast and online advertising. Here you'll find dozens of possibilities, many of them possible with software you already have, online sites, your office printer/copier or the print shop down the street.

Whatever your situation, use this guide to brainstorm promotion possibilities. Read the descriptions of advertising types and determine which of these are available in your market area, or which you could create yourself.

Just to clarify what are advertising media and what are not, this book provides brief overviews of media that look like advertising but aren't, like home shopping networks.

Linda Carlson
Seattle, Washington, Spring 2014

Advertising Explained

Advertising is when you pay to develop awareness of a business or organization, or to promote a product or service. It's that simple.

It's the same whether the product or service is provided by a business, charity, government agency, school, trade or professional association, by a campaign or a special event.

Advertising is one form of marketing communications, which also includes public and media relations, and customer service. What makes advertising different from any other marketing communication is *direct cost* and *direct control.* With advertising *you* control what's said, who it's said to, where and when it's said.

Advertising can be inexpensive and simple:

□ handwritten "Garage Sale" signs

□ the "2-for-1 today only" on a readerboard

□ a real estate broker's ad in a concert program

□ the cardboard table tent at a coffee shop

□ a Craigslist or Google AdSense listing

□ a homemade video on YouTube

And, as we all know, advertising can also be costly and complex to create:

□ a commercial airing during national news or a Major League Baseball game

□ the sponsorship of a charity marathon

□ a full-page ad in *Sports Illustrated* or *Martha Stewart Living*

Advertising can be offbeat: T-shirts worn by window-washers to reach executives inside skyscrapers, posters above urinals in sports bar restrooms, costumed characters waving signs on street corners.

Today advertising can also be a means of financing your operation. Ads are a familiar part of fund-raising campaigns for nonprofits and now both traditional and quirky ads can publicize some share offerings and such funding efforts as Kickstarter and Indiegogo.

This is thanks to the Securities and Exchange Commission, which in 2013 ended a ban on publicizing stock offerings not registered with the SEC.

What Should an Ad Say?

Tell prospects what you're offering, and tell them where to get it, or how to get more information about it: it's vital that an ad say at least these two.

In formal marketing talk, these are two of the four classic "p's" of marketing: product and place.

Taking the earlier examples, "Garage Sale" tells people *what*. Add an address or arrow and you're telling them *where*.

The other two "p's" of marketing are price and promotion. That readerboard spelling out "2-for-1 today only" announces the price, and when it's available. Because the readerboard is on a storefront, the prospect knows *where* the sale is, and for *what* kind of merchandise. The Realtor's name, contact information and business name in the concert program also answer the questions of *what* and *where* to get more information.

The fourth factor in marketing, *promotion*, is what this book is about: how to communicate about your business or program. I'm emphasizing advertising, but you'll also find information here about public and media relations, customer service, and sales—all important tools in creating an effective, well-coordinated message for the people you want to reach.

Now, besides the basics, what should your ad talk about? An old public relations maxim is that if something is better, faster and cheaper than what others are doing or making, you've got a story.

The same goes for advertising. Your product or service may not be all three, but you'll have a tough sell if it's not a significant improvement over the competitors in at least one, and preferably two, ways. Communicating those advantages is the ad's job.

Exactly how you describe these advantages—the advertising copy—depends on your goal, your offer, your target market, your medium (e.g., newspaper, radio, direct mail, search engine ad, banner ad) and how much space or time the ad has. For example:

☐ Using a billboard or bumper sticker? Your message must be short and easily read in seconds.

☐ Writing a search engine text ad? You've got one tiny square image and no more than a couple of dozen words.

☐ Sponsoring a public radio program? You'll be allowed about 15 seconds for name, contact information and a very brief description of your business, agency, school or nonprofit.

Ideally, most ads screen prospects and include a "call to action"—clicking through to your website, filling out a coupon, placing an order, visiting your store. The garage sale sign that's large enough to say, "Kids' clothes & toys" and "9-2, Saturday only," targets parents and tells them when to stop by. The elementary school readerboard that says, "Kindergarten tours every Tuesday," narrows the screen to parents of 4-year-olds. If your goal is to sell a new product, say, "Free samples of locally-made blueberry jam Friday" or "Now on display: collages by 3 local artists;" if you want to sell off outdated merchandise, "Lawn furniture now 50% off."

Simply want to get people through your door? Create a reason and announce it: "All red fabric 40% off today only," "Free skin cancer screenings Mondays, 4-6 p.m.," "Get to know us: door prize drawing, must be present to win."

Communicating Your Message

Now, *how* do you communicate advantages? A vintage brainstorming technique is to ask your team what each member would do if the budget was unlimited. Then ask what each would do with a fraction of that budget—say, with $10,000. The next step: "How can we do something similar with $1,000 —or $100?"

Sometimes, even if you have $10,000 or $100,000 for advertising, you'll start with a far less expensive option as a test: 15 percent of a mailing list, or a three-week search engine ad for a single product. Maybe you'll take a small portion of the budget for a specific ad campaign and divide it, so you can test different creative, or different media, or different timing, or all three.

Image and Direct Response Advertising

Some marketing communications are designed to create awareness. Usually called image, institutional or corporate advertising, this may be nothing more than your company or campaign name—say, as a sponsor of a PBS program or a fund-raiser. It may have your logo, URL, a toll-free number, a motto or slogan, but it will not have a specific sales message.

Direct response advertising, by contrast, is intended to sell. It almost always has contact information, and refers to a specific promotion: the Nordstrom anniversary sale, a concert series, a candidate's campaign, a new product.

Although some advertising is clearly one or the other— creating visibility or soliciting a sale or contribution—many marketing communications are more accurately described as being on a spectrum, with "image" at one extreme and at the other, "sell," or what in advertising jargon is "a call to action."

"Support our sponsors: Avia Tours, Barrett Street Productions, and Thistle Press."

Direct Response vs. Direct Mail

Although you may hear the terms used interchangeably, it's important to understand that direct response advertising is not necessarily direct mail.

Direct response refers to what the ad says. *Direct mail* is a medium, just like radio, television, or banner ads.

Advertising with Small Budgets for Big Results 11

"Save on freezers today: up to 30% off."

"Call now for a free SEO consultation."

The focus in this guide is *how* to advertise: the methods and media described can be used wherever your message falls on that image-direct response continuum. Usually, most of a small advertising budget is spent on direct response advertising.

Creative vs. Frequency

What your ad says and what it looks like are called the *creative*. Creative is all about the message conveyed. *Frequency* is how often your ad appears.

A poorly written ad that appears many times may not attract as many customers as you'd like, but a fabulous ad that

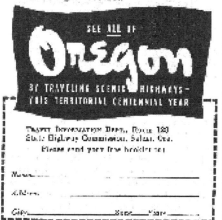

Opposites in advertising: the cocoa image ad and the travel ad with its "call to action," suggesting tourism information be requested via the coupon.

appears only once or twice is almost guaranteed to be ineffective — unless the ad is seen or heard by an extraordinarily large audience, such as that of the Super Bowl. And even that game is typically seen only by about a third of Americans.

(An aside: much of the effectiveness of Super Bowl ads results from advance publicity generated by advertising agencies about the commercials their clients will air, and by the buzz that follows the game broadcast. This publicity creates awareness among those who don't see the game, even those who don't watch television. Read about a few similar — and less costly — examples later.)

As you use this guide, you'll find examples and some how-to's on creative: the most visible colors for billboards and signs, how you acquire photographs for ads, what it can cost to get a television commercial made.

My goal, however, is to introduce you to advertising media and provide an overview of each medium and its costs. For sophisticated copywriting, follow the example of ads you like or hire a professional who has a portfolio or reel that impresses you and references you can check for such important considerations as attention to budget, schedule and your values.

The Importance of Impressions

An adage that's very important: "Half of all my advertising dollars are wasted; I just don't know which half."

Attributed to John Wanamaker, the early-day American department store founder, it refers to the difficulty of tracking what single promotional effort results in a sale — in the unlikely instance that a sale *was* prompted by a single promotion. And remember, when I say *sale*, I also mean donation, enrollment, or commitment to volunteer. Impressions are just as important in the nonprofit arena as they are in the corporate world.

Rather than resulting only from a newspaper ad, blog post, "sale" sign in your window, or the satisfied customer/parent/volunteer who made a recommendation, a sale may have taken all of these and it may have taken more than one of each.

That's why there's another common marketing adage: that it takes at least six to eight *impressions* before a purchase decision is made.

Impressions are the ads, signs, blog posts, tweets, coupons, salesperson's pitch, or someone's recommendation: anything that brings the product or service to a prospective consumer's attention. Advertising media, publicity and sales promotion create the impressions that help a consumer recognize a need for the product or service, or develop a desire for it.

Frequency

Frequency in advertising lingo refers to how often your ad appears in a given medium in a given period. In most cases, a campaign will be more successful if you create several impressions in each of several media during the same period. That's because not everyone sees or hears the same medium—we don't all read the same papers (or read a paper at all), attend the same special events, visit the same websites, see the same billboards or bus cards, or hear the same television or radio broadcasts. Even if we did, we would not all see or hear an ad if it only appeared a few times.

Advertising as Part of the Purchase Process

The steps in the purchase process move a consumer from recognition of need or desire to:

☐ Gathering information.

☐ Evaluating alternatives.

☐ Making the purchase (or commitment) decision.

☐ Post-purchase behavior—a repeat purchase, product return, writing a review online or discussing a similar purchase or contribution with a friend.

These steps can be compressed into a minute or two: you're at a cash register and you see a magazine that looks interesting, or you remember you want chewing gum for your upcoming flight. The process also can take months or even years: going through the interviews, background checks and training to be a Big Brother, making a college choice, or planning the purchase of a car or vacation home.

Advertising can be more effective than publicity in helping a prospect recognize the need or develop the desire for two key reasons.

First, good advertising copy is designed to touch you emotionally: it can scare you into buying insurance or new tires or getting a mammogram. It can create empathy for families displaced by hurricanes or burned out of their homes or grieving the loss of a soldier. It can make you aspire to look as good as the model in the designer suit, the Weight Watchers ad, or at least on the Frost & Tip box. And it can make you yearn for the stimulation of an educational program, or the luxury of a beach vacation in winter.

Second, good advertising provides detailed information: product specs, options, where to buy, how much to pay and how to finance the purchase.

Advertising can also be effective in post-purchase behavior, in reassuring the customer that this was the right choice, in eliminating buyer's remorse, and in helping retain the customer. If you consider the purchases, contributions and commitments you've made in the past few months, you may have experienced such efforts:

□ The grocery cashier who hands over your receipt, cheerfully announcing, "You saved $12.59 today."

□ The telephone salesperson or online retailer's Live Chat representative who concludes the conversation with, "Is there anything else I can help you with?" and "Thank you for choosing..."

□ The thank-you note from the blood bank, or the school board candidate who received a cash contribution.

□ The invitation to a VIP event sponsored by the alumni association you volunteer for.

□ A survey from a car dealership regarding your recent visit for service or your experience with sales personnel.

Impressions Possible on Tight Budget: Zero Landfill

To demonstrate the number and variety of impressions possible, let's take a real event, the Seattle design industry's Zero Landfill giveaway.

Architects, interior designers, apparel buyers, graphic designers and industry vendors bring outdated samples of fabric, leather, wallpaper, flooring, acrylics, paper, and paint chips to a central location one Saturday morning and then in midday, the doors open. Anyone who can use the materials is invited in to take whatever they like—free.

Part of a national movement, the third such Seattle event is scheduled for late 2014. Information about it needs to reach four audiences:

☐ Sponsors, those companies who provide funding, either in-kind or cash.

☐ Local trade and consumer media.

☐ Donors, the designers, vendors and showrooms that have samples.

☐ Art teachers, artists, crafters and other members of the public who take the samples.

At a minimum, the information needs to communicate:

☐ The "green" aspect of the project, important in a region with one of the highest rates of recycling in the U.S.

☐ The need for funding for such expenses as site rental and disposal of leftover items.

☐ Recognition of sponsors and donors—as a thank you, to encourage them to help again, and to create visibility of their

A screen capture from the event's Pinterest page.

community service for current and prospective clients.

☐ Awareness of the event, to encourage participation by donors and attendees.

Here are examples of what can be done by the volunteers who organize this event, who have Facebook and Pinterest pages both for the event and for themselves. Because registration at the door has been required at the 2012 and 2013 events, the volunteers also have a database of attendees.

☐ Email to attendees within a few months of the 2013 event, asking for photos and descriptions of what was made with the donated materials, and asking that photos be posted to the individuals' Pinterest and Facebook accounts and that comments be posted on their Twitter accounts.

☐ Posts with photos to the Zero Landfill Facebook page.

☐ Eblast to sponsors and donors, detailing how many people attended, and describing some of what has been made with the donations.

☐ Emails with some of the best photos and most interesting projects to local monthlies and the alternative weeklies in the spring, asking that editors consider stories that recognize these projects and publicize the 2014 event.

☐ Contacts to past and prospective donors, describing the projects and asking that they consider participating in 2014.

Many design profession associations are involved in Zero Landfill, so the associations can be contacted regarding:

☐ A Zero Landfill volunteer's presentation at a chapter meeting.

☐ Publicizing the event in the associations' newsletters, websites, and blogs and in communications done by members.

By late spring, a date and location will be confirmed for the 2014 event, and this can be announced to sponsors, donors, industry associations, and showrooms at the Seattle Design Center (which often have samples to discard).

Advertising with Small Budgets for Big Results 17

The Facebook and Twitter pages and the attendee database can be used for "save-the-date" publicity, and attendees can be asked to forward information to art teachers, coordinators of child care programs and crafters. Starting in summer, other possible promotions:

☐ YouTube and Vimeo videos made from photos of samples, what's been made from them, the names of previous sponsors and donors, and the date and location for the next event.

☐ Media releases to broadcast stations and daily papers with photos of projects.

☐ Media releases to neighborhood weeklies, tailored whenever possible with information about attendees, sponsors or donors. (For example, "Ravenna Etsy crafter Sissel Sorensen used obsolete wallpaper samples from last year's Zero Landfill event to create...")

☐ Announcements with photos to crafters' blogs.

☐ Requests to sponsors and donors to publicize the event in advertising, social media, employee and customer email.

As the event nears:

☐ Announcements to media for their calendars.

☐ Signs at the site to recognize both sponsors and donors.

Tighter Budget: Food Driving Box

How impressions can be created with even fewer resources, both financial and personnel, is demonstrated by a Seattle entrepreneur who balances a charity with her own business and family life with a busy husband and two young children.

Aware that many of us intend to support food banks, but sometimes pass up opportunities to buy needed items when they're on sale, she created the Food Driving Box program. It's a simple concept: keep the box in your car so that you remember food banks when you're shopping. Add contributions to the box as you can, and when it's full, donate it to one of the food banks listed on the box side.

Besides starting by asking a few hunger-related non-profits to support her cause, this young woman uses the calendars of Seattle's daily paper and the monthly parenting papers to find family-friendly events where she can pass out boxes.

She publicizes the program and has boxes available for pick-up at her own church, at community centers operated by the city parks and recreation department, and through women's groups, including her friends' Bible study and book groups. She and her children even occasionally go door-to-door in their neighborhood and those of friends to explain the concept and hand out boxes.

Her goals include more publicity through parenting publications, neighborhood blogs, scout and Campfire groups, Lions, Rotary, Kiwanis and other civic clubs, and possibly through fund-raising or food collection competitions at schools. She's designing seasonal campaigns—"Fill Your Heart" for February as a Valentine tie-in—and striving to do more with social media, and by asking friends and colleagues to use their social media.

What other tools from this book could be used to promote the Food Driving Box?

☐ Posters. Artwork like that for "Fill Your Heart" could be printed on letter-size sheets and posted (with permission) on bulletin boards in churches, schools, community centers and post offices—even on the "Around our community" bulletin boards some banks have. Locally-owned groceries and specialty food stores could be asked to post them, too.

To work through schools, a poster design contest could be sponsored for students at all levels, perhaps including community colleges and art schools.

□ Public service announcements and pro bono ads on broadcast stations and in newspapers and local magazines.

□ Networking through local organizations such as the Northwest Development Officers Association and chapters of nationals such as the Association of Fundraising Professionals.

Campaign for a Micro-Business

As an example of how other low-cost promotions can be combined to move a prospect from awareness to purchase, suppose a blueberry farmer is introducing a new jam at local farmers' markets. The farmer can:

□ Ask market organizers to announce the jam on the market website.

□ Post a sign about the jam in the market booth.

□ Create T-shirts advertising the jam for booth employees to wear.

□ Offer samples in the booth.

□ Hand out coupons for a discount on purchases or offer a jar of jam and a half-flat of berries at a combination price.

□ To encourage a repeat purchase, offer a discount to anyone who returns a jar when making another purchase.

The Myth of Free Advertising

You've probably heard references to "free advertising." There's no such thing (unless you have friends in the media who are comping you ad space or time). Most often "free advertising" means:

□ Word-of-mouth.

□ Media publicity.

Word-of-Mouth

Marketing experts agree that there is no better advertising than word-of-mouth, the personal recommendation from someone you trust. True word-of-mouth *is* free: you can't buy it, or control it. Usually it's prompted by something done well: you've provided a terrific product or service, perhaps as a sample, or your salespeople have done an exemplary job.

Today, with almost every online retailer soliciting "reviews" and many other organizations surveying customers to get "testimonials," there are questions about the validity of recommendations.

Online retailers are accused of salting reviews with comments from friends, relatives and people they've compensated, and some businesses are known to write their own testimonials.

However it's acquired, word-of-mouth remains a strong form of sales promotion. McKinsey & Company has estimated word-of-mouth is responsible for as many as half of all purchasing decisions. The influence of word-of-mouth is most significant, says the consulting firm, "when consumers are buying a product for the first time or when products are relatively expensive."*

Media Publicity

"We got free advertising from the magazine editor," someone says. Or, "That free publicity from the radio station's restaurant reviewer was great."

Technically, advertising is not free—and publicity *always* is. Publicity means you've been written about or talked about in a media *news* report or review, in contrast to what is said in advertising that you have written, approved and paid for.

Of course there's often a cost to media publicity: you or someone you've hired has written the media release, taken the photos, determined who should receive the material, and actually gotten the release disseminated.

There can also be a direct cost: books and recordings are usually only reviewed if complimentary copies are sent to media reviewers, just as samples of some products and media

---

* Bughin, Jacques, Jonathan Doogan, and Ole Jørgen Vetvik, "A new way to measure word-of-mouth marketing: Assessing its impact as well as its volume will help companies take better advantage of buzz," McKinsey Quarterly, April 2010.

previews of movies, car models, cruise ships and resorts are offered to select reporters and reviewers.

There have always been exceptions to the general practice of not paying for publicity: print publications that wouldn't publish a feature story about your business unless you bought a certain size ad to appear in the same issue, and products, travel destinations and restaurants praised because the reviewer has somehow been compensated.

Another issue today is sponsored content. Some media stories do not disclose that a fee has been paid for the publicity, or use only the vague disclaimer, "Includes sponsored content." Some media now use their advertising rate cards to solicit payment for product placement, just as movies and television programs accept payment for product placement. (For more on this, turn to "Advertorials.")

Publicity often results from a media release (also called a news, or press, release) or other announcement to the media. (Appendix A has examples.)

Publicity can be unsolicited: a reporter doing a story on baby gifts contacts your boutique to ask about new products, or the personal technology columnist calls for tips on trouble-shooting recently introduced software. For a "how-to" story to accompany a report on Internet fraud, a reporter may search websites for advice on detecting phishing; a free-lance writer might contact contractors to learn what winterizing jobs can be handled by a DIY-er.

Although publicity is not the focus of this guide, here's a brief overview of what can result in a business or nonprofit being publicized:

Visibility

An operation has to be easy to learn about, which today usually means an online presence—at a minimum, a website, blog or Facebook page.

The key employees at your business—the owner, the most articulate and knowledgeable technical person, and the marketing communications person—need to have their contact information online.

If you operate locally, it's helpful to be included in your community's business listings or its chamber of commerce. If you operate regionally or nationally, consider participating in the appropriate professional or trade associations, so that someone researching a particular product, service or industry can more easily find you.

Examples of LinkedIn groups.

Key employees should also be on websites such as LinkedIn and should participate in appropriate LinkedIn groups. Many college and graduate school students and alumni, professional and trade associations have LinkedIn groups, and there are countless informal groups as well: language schools, video recording studios, tour administrators, hypnotherapists, product safety specialists, purchasing managers…about 3,000 in all.

Newsworthiness

Issue media releases and post on your blog and all relevant social media sites when you have something that is news: a management change, a new business location, a new product, an award, a major sale.

If your goal is to have daily updates on Facebook and Twitter, also use those sites to

An event which, although promoted in advance with newspaper advertising, probably generated follow-up publicity.

announce last month's most popular products, this month's new products, any product reviews received, schedule changes, and new employees—information that is of less importance to the media and thus may not warrant a release.

Media releases should be written as news, not advertising: only write them for "real" news, and start off with what's most important to the editor and the audience. Present the facts in the traditional "inverted pyramid" used by news writers, getting the *who, what, why, when, how* and *how much* into the announcement by the end of the second paragraph.

How you organize those facts—which comes first—depends on who reads or listens to the medium you're addressing. Each audience is different. Modifying your approach for each audience will significantly increase your chance of getting the release published, or of it prompting a reporter to call for more information.

For example, when Third Place Books announces an author appearance, the release to Seattle newspapers and broadcast stations reads like:

"Third Place Books at Lake Forest Park Towne Center will host Linda Carlson, author of *Company Towns of the Pacific Northwest* (University of Washington Press) on..."

The press release for the *Woodinville Weekly* said:

"Woodinville resident Andy Solberg is among the former company-town residents quoted in *Company Towns of the Pacific Northwest*, written by Seattle consultant Linda Carlson and published by University of Washington Press..."

The press release to the *Shelton-Mason County Journal* about the author's appearance at the local branch of the Timberland Regional Library began:

"Several long-ago Mason County towns and the Shelton-based Lumberman's Mercantile will be described when company-town historian Linda Carlson speaks..."

Accuracy

A well-written press release is fact. That means the information in it can be verified and that it is not opinion.

You can say this is the first product with a retail price of less than a certain amount, or the first service targeting a certain market niche in your city. You can discuss how many products your storefront carries and compare that inventory to your competitors, and you can cite prices.

A good media release will not claim, "This is the best book ever written about..." but it *can* include a review from an independent source, including the reviewer's name, the publication, and how to see the review: "Lee Smith at the *Metropolitan Times*, metro.com, calls this the best book written in the past decade about..."

It is vital that your messages to the media be triple-checked for spelling, punctuation, and accuracy of URLs and telephone numbers. The names of individuals, companies and organizations must be correct and complete. You'll develop more credibility with media if you follow Associated Press style (apstylebook.com), which means spelling, punctuating and abbreviating as newspapers do.

Appropriate Distribution

There's no reason to write a release if it's not going to be received by the right people. Compile a list of the print, broadcast and online publications that can be expected to be interested in your news, and check each one's website or masthead for the most appropriate contact person and his or her email and postal addresses.

In building a media database with the names, titles, and contact information for media in your community and industry, start with the websites of local general-interest and business media and the industry publications you read.

Supplement these with information from newspaper and broadcast professional and trade association directories such as the Pacific Northwest Newspaper Association membership web page, pnna.com, "About PNNA" > "Member Directory." Besides Appendix B, consult:

□ Associated Press bureaus and news correspondents, at "Contact Us," ap.org. (The AP distributes material to 1,400 daily newspapers and thousands of broadcast outlets.)

What Are Writers Looking For?

Complimentary online newsletters such as Wooden Horse Magazine Media News, *woodenhorsepub.com, and* Help A Reporter Out, *helpareporter.com, provide the "who's who" at magazines and alert you to what writers and reporters want for their stories.*

☐ National Public Radio "Station Finder," npr.org.

☐ Public Broadcasting Service "Station Finder," pbs.org.

☐ Magazine Directory, magazine-directory.com, which lists hundreds of general and special interest magazines, from *Acoustic Guitar* and *The Atlantic* to *Working Mother*, *Yoga Journal* and *Young Rider*.

☐ *Ulrich's Periodicals Directory* and the *Encyclopedia of Associations* (for locating association newsletters), often available at public libraries.

☐ Cision's Media Database, us.cision.com, the continually updated successor to Bacon's Publicity Checker, which because it costs hundreds of dollars a month is usually outside the budget constraints of small firms.

For an online search, use the geographic area and such

Media websites often have a "submit news" or "contact an editor" form for pasting in the announcement you've composed. Many conclude an article with the name and email address of the reporter or editor, especially helpful if you want to substitute a note for a media release:

> *"I really enjoyed your story about innovations in prosthetic limbs and want to tell you about how my startup is using 3D printers to create prosthetic fingers..."*

terms as "radio stations," "digital broadcasters," "television stations" or "newspapers."

For example, "San Diego + radio station directory" led to the San Diego Radio Broadcasters Association, sandiego-radio.com, and "Boston TV stations + directory" led to several commercial sites plus the Boston University Information Services & Technology web page, bu.edu/tech/comm/tele-vision/channel-lineup, with links to stations. For newspapers, an online inquiry such as "daily newspaper directory" plus a state name will lead to such websites as that of the New York News Publishers Association, nynpa.com.

Fee-based wire services such as PR Newswire, prnewswire.com, and Business Wire, businesswire.com, will also disseminate your releases. For newly public companies, these services are a convenient means of meeting federal regulations for "simultaneous disclosure" of financial announcements. Charges are based on the number and type of media to which you want your releases sent.

About Price and Place

Besides "product" and "promotion," the four "p's" of marketing include "price" and "place." Neither is the focus of this guide, but here's a look at how each impacts promotion.

First, recognize that what you *charge* for your product or service is seldom the same as what it *costs* your customers or clients. Their cost may include sales tax, interest (whether paid to you or for credit card charges), delivery and installation, transportation and parking, insurance deductibles and even time taken from paid employment.

The parent who volunteers at a school may be taking time off from work. The expectant couple selecting an OB/GYN is probably paying for parking, and the co-pays or deductible.

You can reduce these expenses, perceived or real. Offer volunteers opportunities to contribute after office hours. Offer patients free or validated parking, evening or weekend appointments, and several different payment options for the out-of-pocket expenses.

Reducing the Costs of Acquiring a Customer

As a manager, you have costs associated with each customer, client or volunteer interaction.

Typically, the costs of acquiring and servicing someone new to your operation are far greater than the costs of serving a repeat customer. Including prospecting—which occurs when recruiting volunteers and donors as well as when seeking customers or clients—the cost of developing a new relationship is estimated at five to ten times the cost of retaining an existing account.

What does this mean?

Get the highest, or longest, possible commitment in the beginning. In sales, this means the highest reasonable price for a transaction. A two-for-one sale is more profitable than a half-price sale: for the same amount of customer interaction, you're getting $10 instead of $5. Similarly, the hairdresser who bundles three services for $100 will probably operate more profitably than the one who offers each service at $40.

One strategy: upselling. At the post office today, a clerk may suggest the more expensive options first, or conclude the transaction for a package by asking if you need stamps.

If your staff takes orders by phone or in person, encourage it to try for multiples of the same item, or an additional item—something new, or something you're promoting as the day's special. Program your online shopping cart to suggest additions to an order, too.

At a nonprofit, your time is better spent if you can get someone committed to regular service or contributions. One example: the Puget Sound Blood Bank registrars ask contributors to schedule their next appointments at check-in for the current appointment.

This also means it's more cost-effective to keep existing contacts satisfied. So you may want to create occasional "VIP" promotions publicized only to people who have purchased in the past year or two (see example on page 113). It may mean personalized thank-you notes with coupons to existing customers. It may also mean working harder to create word-of-mouth publicity: say, with "Share this sale with a friend" coupons, "Share this on Facebook for a discount" or two-for-one ticket sales to an event.

Perhaps most important with both storefront and online businesses: keep the prospect from walking out the door, or abandoning the shopping cart.

Most of us are familiar with the salesperson's pitch: "What will it take for you to make this purchase today?" The online version is an automated message that pops up when someone clicks on "purchase now" and, after seeing prices (say, for membership or a subscription), navigates away from the page. Your message might offer a free trial, a lower price, or a lower unit price with a multiple-year purchase.

A variation on this is the automatic email sent a day or so after someone abandons a shopping cart. "Have you forgotten something?" (See the screen capture below.)

You could also program in a new incentive: "Finish your purchase today and we'll ship it free," or "$10 gift card if you buy more than $50 in merchandise today."

Another issue with price: sales. Today a popular promotion is the flash sale, when a reduced price, special service or certain product is available only for a brief period, perhaps only a few hours. This strategy can work if you have a desirable product or service and even more important, if you have a way to advertise the flash sale to a large number of potential customers.

It seems like you tried to create an ad but didn't finish setting it up. To get your first ad, we're offering you a free $50 advertising coupon.

Create an Ad and the coupon code: VWRM-5G6N-8PWO-RJEX will be applied to your account. The expiration date of this coupon is 10/22/2013.

There are lots of reasons to advertise on Facebook:

- Reach your target audience using location, age and interests
- Deepen relationships with your customers by encouraging people to like your Page
- Define your daily budget to avoid any billing surprises

Email requires a good email database and probably an eblast program. To use Twitter or Facebook, you need both a high number of "followers" or "friends," and the confidence that these people read your messages promptly.

Other price promotions will require either a large online community or time-sensitive advertising that reaches the right audience. In the pages that follow, you'll find many forms of advertising that may be ideal for your sales.

Distributing to Customers

How you get your product or service to buyers, volunteers, or recruits is the subject of "place," or distribution. If you do not have distribution in place, if you do not have your product or service readily available to customers, there's almost no reason to advertise.

What's the exception? Why advertise if you have nothing to deliver? Occasionally it makes sense to tease the marketplace. In most such situations, this assumes a generous budget so you can continue advertising and sustain potential customer interest until the product or service is available.

This also works when advance orders or reservations can be taken, especially if there's perceived value to being the first to have the product, or when supplies are perceived to be limited. If you can generate advance orders, these may help you better manage your initial inventory or staffing, and thus do a launch more profitably.

Lead Time for Product Distribution

Getting distribution set up for a new product can take a surprisingly long time. Even if you're delivering to a neighborhood store, the shopkeeper may have to create shelf space, label the packages, get product information in the inventory and invoicing system and add this new product to a website catalog or promotion.

Any product being shipped, especially to a central warehouse for distribution to outlets, or being sent to a distributor or wholesaler and then made available for retailers, will require several weeks' lead time to be available. For those of us in book publishing, it's a shock to learn how long it takes to get a book available to booksellers after stock arrives at the wholesaler's loading dock (and then how long it takes booksellers to learn of the title and place their orders). Libraries also take weeks to process new books and get them on the shelves in branches.

Lead Time with Services

Making a service available should be a quicker process than getting a product on a shelf, shouldn't it? That's often true. But the customers selecting certain services—school assemblies, say, or speakers for a conference—often work months in advance. This is especially true if offering a program depends on grant funding.

Services necessary for a conference or trade show, including the actual venue, the program printers, booth vendors, caterers, tour guides for the optional recreation, and online reservations system, are sometimes selected years in advance. Even the local chapters of professional and alumni associations often plan their programs in the spring, so that an entire season can be promoted prior to regular meetings starting in the fall.

Finally, there's another simple reason that distribution must be in place long before you finish your ads: so the ads can say how to obtain the product or service.

About Advertising Sales Representatives

As you may have already discovered, good salespeople are always prospecting.

Identifying possible new customers is an important part of their job, and as soon as your business becomes visible—when your business license application is filed, when your name appears in the chamber of commerce directory, when you run your first ad in any media—you're likely to be contacted by representatives of media, search optimization specialists, bankers, accountants, publicists and anyone else who perceives that you might need his or her products or services.

Handling emails and postal mail from these sales reps is reasonably easy. Handling phone calls can be much more time-consuming, especially when the conversation takes a few minutes to get to the sales pitch, or if the sales rep tries to keep you talking after you've said your budget is limited. Four common situations:

☐ "I'm calling to offer you an opportunity to be part of…"

It may sound as if you're being offered publicity. My very blunt response is, "If this is something that requires a payment, I must tell you I have no advertising budget at this time." The variation on this: being "offered the opportunity" to make an in-kind donation.

☐ "I noticed your ad in the [medium] and because the [publication/broadcast station/website] that I work for serves the same demographic, I'd like just 15 minutes of your time to tell you…"

I don't work a 25-hour day, so my goal is to keep out everyone I don't need to see. Even if a sales call did take only 15 minutes, which is unlikely, studies show that such an interruption can cause any of us to lose concentration on a project for almost an hour.

My response usually is, "You're welcome to email me the link to your media kit and I'll let you know if I need more information." The usual follow-up question is, "May I call you in a week or so to answer your questions?" to which you (if you're like me) will say, "No, I'll call you."

□ "Well, if you don't advertise, how do you attract customers?" is sometimes the question that follows a refusal to buy advertising.

If you care to respond, your answer might be, "We have commissioned sales reps," or "We have retailers," or whatever is accurate.

□ "I'm sure we can work something out. All I need to customize a package for you is a few details about your business…"

My experience has been that this can lead to several minutes and either a proposal that is inappropriate due to budget or audience, or being asked for an appointment so that the proposal can be made in person. If you truly have very limited funds or you're not interested in purchasing anything from this vendor, cut the conversation short by explaining you're too busy or by pretending that you have another call coming in.

If these responses sound cold and unfeeling to you, I won't disagree. I am well aware that most salespeople have sales call quotas. But I'm not a qualified prospect for most sales reps, and I believe it wastes their time and mine to have a lengthy conversation or any kind of meeting.

Now, what if you're the person prospecting? You'll have a better chance of getting past the roadblocks I've just identified if you:

□ Carefully research each prospect, to ensure you can offer it something it needs, or in the case of a nonprofit,

Advertising with Small Budgets for Big Results

that there's a benefit to it working with you. *Know the prospect's business.*

☐ Be direct and concise so that no one's time is wasted: "I'm calling about advertising in…" immediately identifies why you're calling. So does, "If you have a budget for…"

☐ Offer a free or low-cost trial if you can afford to, or ask if prospects would consider buying close-outs or at reduced prices when they're available.

☐ Be pleasant. Is there anything worse than an antagonistic salesperson or one who is condescending because someone can't afford or doesn't see the value of his or her product or service?

As Simple As...

Advertising—as simple as A to Z? That's what I've tried to make marketing communications and sales promotion with this guide.

Think of it as an encyclopedia with how-to's: hundreds of forms of advertising are defined with an overview of production requirements, schedules and costs. Advertising and sales promotion terms are in alphabetical order, followed with appendixes, worksheets and checklists, a glossary of advertising and printing terms, and a detailed index to make it even easier for you to find answers about specific ad formats or media.

I'm a do-it-yourselfer, and I believe that much advertising can be created in-house. Some requires only word processing. Some can be lettered by hand. Wherever possible, suggestions and sources of help and material are provided. When vendors *are* necessary, you'll see tips on how to find them, usually via the applicable trade or professional association or an online search. Occasionally, usually because I've had experience with a vendor or because it's the only one or best-known of its kind, a vendor will be cited by name.

Note: many images are screen captures and thus lack ideal resolution.

Advertising Novelties

Balloons, key rings, pencils, pens, calendars, card cases, golf balls, adhesive note pads (as shown on the right), license plate frames: a few examples of the dozens of low-cost items

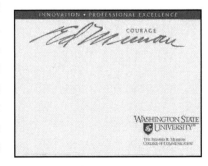

you can personalize with your business name, or the name of a product or event. Use them for giveaways, customer thank-you gifts or premiums.

The pens and note pads are among the novelties (also known as advertising specialties) that you can use in your business as well. Give customers the imprinted pens you hand them to sign a credit card charge slip or order form. Put your business name and photos of your products or people using your products on the calendar hanging in your office. Put the company or product name or motto on the license plate frames on your company vehicles and on the Post-Its or note cards you attach to material being sent to a prospect.

Some of these items can be produced in-house. Note cards and magnets with pictures of your products or quotes from satisfied customers can be created as PDFs and run off on your printer as you need them. Screensavers and games can be offered as downloads. Calendars can be designed with your software's templates, at drugstore photo kiosks or quick-print shops and with online vendors.

More Information
Promotional Products Association International, ppai.org, is the trade group representing the firms that manufacture such items and the sales reps who sell them. Although many regional affiliates do not make their membership lists available to nonmembers, check lists of trade show exhibitors for sales reps who handle products you're interested in. An online search will bring up contact information for sales reps in your area. Also see "Apparel" and "Bags."

Advertorials
Editorial and advertising departments in reputable media always have claimed to have the same kind of separation as church and state, with those who purchase advertising not supposed to receive special treatment in the news pages. That

separation has eroded rapidly in recent decades in even the most respected publications and broadcast stations. Even when news and advertising staffs do not work closely together, it's common to see:

- Advertorials.
- Special sections.
- Sponsored content.
- Product placement.
- Infomercials.

"Advertising Publications Department" signals that this is not written by reporters.

Advertorials

Typically created by an advertising staff or by a free-lancer, an advertorial is usually a page or more—often an entire special section (such as the example above)—that promotes something with news-style articles and photos: a newspaper's special section on traveling in Hawaii, or a magazine feature on the advantages of doing business in Ohio. Advertorials are created in different ways:

- With text written by the publication that highlights products and services being offered by those businesses advertising in the section.

- With text provided by those businesses.

- With both of these, plus press releases from affiliated businesses or industries.

A special section on home improvements might include promotional material from the headquarters of paint and flooring companies, information syndicated by national home improvement and decorating magazines and stories provided by local kitchen cabinetmakers.

Print and web publishers can also receive free content—in fact, entire page layouts—from businesses that specialize in producing stories and photos that feature certain brands.

As one such firm describes itself, "Your one-stop resource for high-quality editorial content…We work with nationally-recognized sponsors to provide timely and professional content at no cost to you."

Today advertorial space is available in a surprising variety of publications—including college alumni magazines. At the University of Utah, for example, alumni can showcase their businesses in *U-News & Views* for a $350 fee.

Special Sections

Special sections are typically financed by advertising. Supplements such as a pull-out guide to a home show may be produced with the assistance of the show sponsors, who may solicit ads for the guide or provide media salespeople with contact information for the businesses exhibiting at the show.

Guides like a county fair special can be created by a local newspaper, which sells pre-designed ads, each featuring a fair princess or fair attraction, to different businesses.

Example of a special section calendar.

To maintain the appearance of a separation between a publication's newswriting staff and its advertising department, some special sections use only text created by free-lance writers or from press releases. Often the articles use different type fonts than the news sections.

To develop relationships with the free-lancers or advertising staff members who create this text and determine if it's possible to contribute information, check the publication's editorial and advertising schedule for references to special sections so you'll know the topics to be covered. Then watch for bylines on advertorials and contact those free-lancers, the advertising manager or the "special sections" editor.

Sponsored Content

"Sponsored" text, typical in some blogs and newsletters, means the writer or publisher has received compensation—cash, products or services—for a positive description.

Today such a blog post is legally required to be identified as sponsored, although language such as "Some content is sponsored," as shown above, is occasionally all you'll see. (For specifics, see the Federal Trade Commission's ruling in October 2009 regarding its "Guides Concerning the Use of Endorsements and Testimonials in Advertising," ftc.gov/os/2009/10/091005revisedendorsementguides.pdf.)

In 2013 the *Washington Post* became one of the major newspapers to allow "sponsored views," content on its online opinion pages that is paid for by special-interest and advocacy groups. The *Post* staff was quoted as saying that "sponsored views" would allow these groups to respond to points made in the newspaper's editorials.

In late 2013, the *New York Times* described sponsored content as "'native advertising,' which is to say advertising wearing the uniform of journalism, mimicking the storytelling aesthetic of the host site." At the time, even such respected publications as *Forbes, The Atlantic* and *The New Yorker* had all developed their versions of it, said the *Times*.

Online sponsored content is only effective if it's shared via social media in significant numbers: in other words, if it "goes viral." Too often, however, that doesn't happen. As a *Wall Street Journal* story reported in fall 2013, "Marketers view sponsored content as a more effective way to reach consumers than traditional forms of advertising, because it appears less overtly promotional...But to work best, the content has to be shared...And to do that, marketers have recognized they can't just rely on consumers..."

To ensure adequate distribution of content with brand names embedded in them, some companies are now buying space on websites and blogs to guarantee placement of these articles on multiple sites.

Sponsored content is different from sponsorships, which often apply to events. See "Naming/Sponsorships/ Donations." For more information about sponsored content, see "Websites," and in the Glossary, "Native Advertising."

Product Placement

When you watch television or a movie, you can't tell whether the heroine is drinking Coke because she likes it, or because a fee was paid to ensure that only Coca-Cola products be shown. Similarly, when you're reading a magazine article on cars, you don't know if the photos are of Fords because those were the best examples the art director could find—or if Ford was invited to submit its photos in return for a fee. These are examples of placements that enhance the visibility of brands.

Product placement is a growing business because an estimated third of television programs are not viewed when broadcast, which makes time-specific promotion difficult and increases the chances that commercials will not be seen. As a result, manufacturers often prefer to have their products embedded in a program or film.

If you're paying for product placement, you'll want to know how long and in what context your product will be shown as well as what the target audience for the program or movie is. A flash in an action flick of the handbag you designed or a 10-second look at your book cover in a thriller may have no impact on sales, while the heroine shuffling through that same handbag or book on a sit-com targeted at young women can create a sales spike, especially if you're tweeting about the show at the same time.

For small businesses for which national broadcast advertising is cost-prohibitive, product placement can be more cost-effective than advertising, although placements do not provide such purchase information as website addresses, toll-free numbers or names of retailers. (No TV character is likely to say, "I got it at Nordstrom!" when showing off a bag.) That information must be provided by manufacturers or retailers in promotions scheduled at the same time as the television broadcast or movie debut.

To attract attention to products, designers and manufacturers and their publicists send information or samples to wardrobe managers, set designers, location scouts and others involved with television and films. Such contact may result in your product being purchased for use. In other cases, you may be asked for samples that can be used, or for samples in addition to a fee.

To promote a location for fashion or other product

Product Placement Help

Professional and trade associations that may provide valuable leads with product placement are listed in their websites' "find a...," "club services," or "local chapters" options:

American Society of Media Photographers, asmp.org

American Society of Picture Professionals, aspp.com

American Advertising Federation, aaf.org

Arizona Production Association, azproduction.com

Photo Assistants Association, facebook.com/photoassistants

American Photographic Artists, apnational.com

photography, start with the marketing departments of manufacturers or retailers who do catalogs as well as with advertising agencies, photo stylists and commercial photographers who specialize in fashion or product photography.

For locations appropriate for television commercials, television programs and movies, contact state film and video offices. In the Northwest, these include Washington Filmworks, washingtonfilmworks.org, Oregon Film, oregonfilm.org, Idaho Film Office, filmidaho.org, and Montana Film Office, montanafilm.com.

For more information about product placement in general and the agencies that specialize in it, check the Entertainment Resources & Marketing Association, erma.org.

Product placement is also available for print publications, even books: for example, the website for the Dummies guides explains in "In-book Advertising" that businesses can "Deliver your message to readers who are attached and engaged by advertising in the For Dummies reference guide most closely aligned with your product. Our marketing and editorial team will work with you to develop placements which make your message stand out from the crowd."

Both in books and magazines it's common for those who provide products and settings to be credited. Occasionally this occurs in the text. More often the credits appear in a section headed "Sources" or "Buyer's Guide." (See below.)

Infomercials

The trade association founded to support infomercial marketing tells us that more than $300 billion dollars is spent worldwide each year on direct response purchases via television, online and on radio.

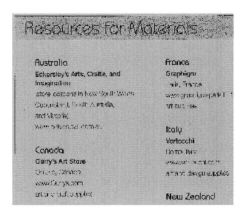

If you think you

can sell your products or services with infomercials, it doesn't take a billion-dollar budget. Once you've outlined a script and determined how you'll get the program filmed or taped, all you have to do is buy air time. That's usually either on a broadcast station or with an online program. A video is another option—on your website, as a video ad or on YouTube.

Typically, infomercials are either very short—30 or 60 seconds—or very long—almost 30 or 60 minutes.

Although they can be filmed with the same equipment used for homemade YouTube videos, industry experts warn that "tacky" and "amateur" are unlikely to create the image or the sales you want.

For extremely tight budgets, consider contacting a local film program regarding instructors, recent graduates or even advanced students willing to free-lance behind the camera. If you're promoting a location such as a resort or restaurant, that's where you'll have the video shot. Otherwise, consider renting studio time at local broadcast stations.

Time can be purchased on local network affiliate stations or on cable stations. What it costs depends on your city, the time of day (obviously, midnight is almost always less expensive than noon) and the station's own pricing.

More Information
Electronic Retailing Association, retailing.org.

Air Time Rates
In Phoenix, airing a 28-minute infomercial on one network affiliate station on a Saturday afternoon will cost about $3,000. On another, it could cost more than double that. In Sacramento, you can buy the 4:30 a.m. slot on a Friday for $700—or the same amount of time on a Sunday afternoon for about $13,000. In Seattle, there's no network affiliate station time available for less than $1,100, and it's around $10,000 for any daytime slot.

Affiliate Marketing

Popularized by websites, especially Amazon.com, affiliate marketing involves a website or blog receiving a commission for sales made as a result of referring customers to a retailer's site. This may be an online retailer (Amazon) or a retailer with an online presence (Nordstrom).

For the referring website, it's a passive means of generating a small percentage of the purchase price; it usually requires nothing more than a special link from a "place your order" button on the host site to the retailer's online page for a given product.

A commission is typically paid when a customer makes a purchase directly after being referred to the online retailer. If the customer leaves the product page and then returns—even directly—to make a purchase, no commission is paid.

A disadvantage if yours is the site providing the referral: you retain no information regarding the purchaser or what was purchased, so you cannot make follow-ups or contact the customer when a new product is available.

To invite others with websites and blogs to become affiliates of you, and thus earn commissions for promoting your products, it's preferable to install software that can track the referring websites and blogs.

A low-tech, DIY option: a discount for using a special code when placing an order. This has been typical with magazine and newspaper ads for decades; the coupon that appeared in *Sunset* in December would have had a code such as "Sun12" in small type at the bottom so that the advertiser knew the source of the inquiry. Such a strategy requires only that you assign a different code to each of your "affiliate partners" and that you track source codes.

Alumni Publications/Websites

Type "alumni magazine advertising" into a search engine and you'll see publications from Cornell and Dartmouth to Georgia Tech, the University of Virginia, Purdue and the Colorado School of Mines. Few care if advertisers are alumni.

For $1,000 you can buy a half-page ad in the Oberlin College alumni publication, which circulates to 35,000 alumni, donors, faculty/staff, and parents. A couple of hundred dollars more buys the same size color ad in the University of Kansas's magazine, which is sent to 45,000 dues-paying members of the alumni association. *California*, published by the University of California Berkeley, charges $3,700 for a half-page ad that will be sent to 95,000.

Harvard Magazine is one of several for which advertising is sold by the Ivy League Magazine Network, ivymags.com. Prime Consulting Services, primeconsultingva.com, handles sales for the alumni publications of Virginia Tech and the College of William & Mary. Sagacity Media, sagacitymedia. com, reps for the University of Washington and University of Oregon alumni magazines.

In most other cases, colleges, universities and graduate programs will have to be contacted individually regarding advertising.

Among the questions to ask if considering advertising in an alumni publication are about such demographics as:

☐ Location (for example, an unsurprising 43 percent of the College of William & Mary grads are in Virginia, and 84 percent of the Berkeley grads are still in California, with almost 60 percent of them in the Bay Area).

☐ Age (50 percent of the William & Mary alumni have graduated since 1990, and so are 44 or younger).

☐ Education level (Berkeley doesn't provide graduation dates for *California's* recipients, but the rate card does note that 71 percent have done post-graduate work).

☐ Income level (which is self-reported).

Another question to ask: whether circulation is by graduate or by household. Many alumni mailing lists do not delete duplicate addresses, so multiple copies are sent to households with more than one grad.

Colleges and universities that replace or supplement their print alumni publications with websites and blogs also may offer advertising. At the University of South Florida, for example, a banner ad on the *AlumNews* e-newsletter is $400 a month. At the University of Utah, a similar ad on the alumni website is $200 a month. Readership of these sites may differ dramatically from circulation of the print bulletins: at William & Mary, readership of the website is estimated at 5,000 vs. the 86,000 who receive (but may not all read) the magazine.

Apparel

What people wear can advertise your business two ways: with what your employees wear, and with what other people choose to wear.

What your employees wear can work as advertising for your business, a particular product or service, or for general promotion such as "Like us on Facebook" or "Ask about loyalty programs."

You've seen the supermarket cashiers in T-shirts promoting fresh peaches or the print shop employees in aprons advertising personalized calendars. Inexpensive shirts can be customized by any part-time silkscreener, or ordered online for less than $10 for quantities of three or more. Many apparel retailers (Lands' End, L.L. Bean) also personalize garments as part of their "business" or "corporate" programs.

Online vendors also offer customized aprons, but what's more economical if you only need a few: purchase plain white aprons at a kitchen supply or craft store and personalize them yourself. Fabric, craft and office supply stores sell paper you can use in your computer printer to create iron-on transfers.

Now, about the shirts, jackets, aprons, hats and other garments that you sell or give away to customers, event participants, or winners of contests: think of how many bars, restaurants, amusement parks, and marathons are promoted with attire. People could be wearing advertising for *your* operation, too.

You'll want attractive artwork and items that are both reasonable in quality and in price.

Suppose you want shirts, jackets, smocks or other garments made in fabric that promotes your operation. (And why not on curtains at the window, tablecloths on the tables or chair cushions?) That's possible, too.

Several companies will now print yardage with your design: company name and logo, slogan, pictures of your most profitable or newest products or even customer testimonials in the original handwriting. Spoonflower, spoonflower.com, advertises fabric starting at $15.75 a yard, and Fabric On Demand, fabricondemand.com, as low as $18.25 a yard. Shipping is extra and minimum orders may apply.

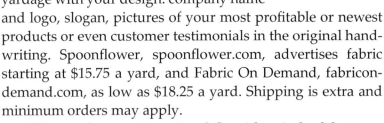

Shirts and aprons too pricey? Consider pin-back buttons. These are something else you can make using inkjet-printed artwork and pinback button blanks available at big-box office supplies stores. The button blanks can be updated with new artwork whenever the promotion changes.

For larger quantities of buttons—especially if you can partner with neighboring or complementary storefronts to promote each other's products or services—have them made locally or with an online vendor. One option for buttons you can use for different promotions: a message such as "Ask me about" and then a blank space where you can hand write the name of the current promotion. For hundreds of buttons, buy a button press and a starting inventory of 500 button components for less than $500 including freight.

Automated Telephone Systems/Voice Mail

Job applicants and salespeople are often told they only have 30 seconds to make a good impression; the same could be said of the staff or equipment that answers your phone.

Especially today, when our first impression of an organization is frequently created by an apathetic employee or

Advertising with Small Budgets for Big Results   47

> *With a phone system that offers many branches ("Press 1 to reach...,*
> *Press 2 to reach,..."), test it often from outside. And ask people*
> *unfamiliar with the system to try it, to ensure instructions are clear*
> *and that callers do not get stuck in an endless loop.*
>
> *Also important: make sure the voice on the system is warm,*
> *welcoming and positive. We've all encountered automated attendants*
> *with crabby voices that appear to chastise us for not providing*
> *information that voice recognition systems can process, or that hang*
> *up because we've missed a key command.*

confusing automated system, distinguish your operation with informative, easy-to-understand phone service that makes callers immediately feel positive.

If phones are answered by an employee with a strong accent, encourage this staff member to speak slowly and as clearly as possible. Listening to recordings of conversations with volunteers or with real customers may help all of your staff recognize the value of professional vocabulary and good diction. One old tip for ensuring that you sound good when answering the phone: smile as you pick up the receiver or click to receive the call.

Frequently check your phone system from outside your building to ensure recorded messages have no background noise or static and that whoever recorded the messages spoke directly into the phone.

A simple answering machine or voice messaging system can provide your open hours and the URL of your website as well as instructions for leaving a message. More sophisticated systems can have brief promotional messages—as well as tips on how to bypass them and go directly to the desired extension. It is vital that you also check these systems occasionally; nothing is worse for customer service than automated systems that put callers in an endless loop or do not permit them to quickly reach a person.

When Callers Are on Hold

Use the few minutes when callers are awaiting help to tell them about specials, new branches, new products or new employees. What's ideal: a pleasant, soothing voice that can exude enthusiasm with a soft sell about your operation. For example,

"Thanks for calling All-Town Florist. New hydrangeas are in stock now, ideal for Mother's Day gifts. For information about these gorgeous potted plants and the decorative pots and baskets they can be delivered in, press 1 now. To reach other extensions, press 2. To bypass this message in the future, press 3 as soon as your call is answered. To reach our receptionist, press 0 now."

Bags

Shopping bags, tote bags, garment bags—examples of where your business name can appear on items that are used repeatedly. If you don't have a convenient local vendor, use a search term like "custom printed shopping bags" or "custom printed tote bags" to bring up dozens of online merchants.

Prices vary, depending on bag size, material, whether printing is on one side or both, and how many colors are used in the printing.

Budget alternatives for small quantities:

☐ Self-adhesive labels you order or make yourself with an inkjet printer and then apply to blank paper bags.

☐ Name, website URL and phone number on a large rubber stamp you use on blank paper bags.

☐ The minimum quantity of shopping bags ordered from a supplier such as Ulinc, uline.com—either split the order with another organization or label a few dozen bags at a time for a specific promotion or event.

☐ Plain cloth tote bags embellished with silkscreening or with iron-on designs that you create and print several to a sheet and then cut apart for applying (see "Apparel" for details).

Selling apparel or other textile goods? Advertise your commitment to reducing waste by making bags from fabric scraps. JLVelo uses its bags to make a statement: "So, first we make your great cycling gear (much of it from recycled fibers already), and with whatever is left over, we sew these bags up!"

Banners

Stretch a banner across a street to announce the opening of a farmers' market or community festival. Mount one on a storefront to promote a new business. Or suspend one from your showroom ceiling to advertise a sale or attract customers to a new department—even use a banner in lieu of a sign if yours is a pop-up store or a new location waiting for a permanent sign to be finished.

If your inkjet printer accepts roll paper, you can print 100 feet of banners for as little as $20 in paper, or you can email the document to a local print shop for output. Even simpler, the banners that can be created with perforated Z-folded paper from manufacturers like Hewlett-Packard. Office supplies stores and print shops create full-color banners using your artwork at prices starting at less than $100.

Bathroom Advertising

Ads in bathrooms may sound unbelievably quirky, but the companies that broker such ads remind us that they provide a captive audience. They are also ideal for gender-specific messages, especially those of such sensitive nature as date rape and STD testing.

If your business location has public restrooms, mount acrylic frames on the inside of stall doors, or above the hand dryer or urinals so you can slip in letter-size ads for new products or seasonal specials.

If you'd like to attract people who frequent other nearby businesses—maybe pubs, coffee shops, health clubs—contact those business owners about mounting frames in their restrooms. Offer them cash, credit at your business — or similar ads for their businesses on the stalls in your restrooms.

Production can be as simple as a print-out from your office copier, laminated if it's not going into an acrylic frame. To offer coupons via restroom advertising, use Quick Response (QR) codes that can be scanned with smart phones.

If you're a nonprofit with an important message — perhaps about sources of help for victims of domestic violence — ask businesses if your posters can be placed in their restrooms. In return, credit them as in-kind donors to your program.

More Information
"QR Codes"
Indoor Billboard Advertising Association, indooradvertising. org.

Blogs
A blog (a contraction of "web log") is a website that consists of entries ("posts") typically displayed in reverse chronological order. There are hundreds of millions of blogs. Some are diaries, some are diatribes, some are informational. Some have daily posts, others are rarely updated. For details on blogs, this section is divided into:

□ Why blogs?

□ Advertising on blogs.

□ How blog popularity is quantified.

□ The lingo of blog statistics.

□ Buying blog ads.

Why Blogs?
Because there can be no charge to post a blog and the software is typically easier to use than website authoring programs, some individuals, smaller businesses and organizations use blogs as a website substitute. As a result, they may be listed in blog directories but may not sell ads or run guest posts as do some blogs.

Three reasons for you to consider researching blogs:

☐ As a place for you to advertise.

☐ To find media to review your product or service, offer giveaways of it, or welcome a guest post by you.

In either of these cases, check blog content: because some are platforms for people who want to rant, you may not be comfortable having your product or service promoted in such a setting.

☐ As a promotional tool for a business or organization.

A blog can create buzz for you, and if you participate in affiliate marketing or accept ads on your blog, it may generate income in addition to prompting direct sales. Note that some blog hosts (companies which upload blogs to the Internet) do not permit their bloggers to publish ads.

Among the most popular hosts of free blogs are WordPress, Blogger/Blogspot and Tumblr. Some of these have paid options with additional services.

How do you find blogs, and how do you determine which could best publicize your business?

Blogs are categorized and ranked by a variety of directory websites, some of questionable value. Others morph or disappear without warning: the well-regarded Technorati, technorati.com, listed more than 1.3 million blogs and offered a "top 100" list until one day in 2014, when the entire directory was removed. To find current directories, search with a phrase such as "blog directories," which may bring up such sites as blogcatalog.com and blogsearchengine.org.

An example of a blog template provided free by a blog host.

Advertising on Blogs

Many bloggers are anxious to monetize their posts, offering display ads and the opportunity to sponsor content or giveaways. Rates vary wildly.

Independently compiled readership statistics are available only for the blogs with the highest readership, unlike audited circulation or viewer numbers for newspapers, magazines, and broadcast stations. To see what information is available on sites that use Alexa, alexa.com, to analyze traffic, use the example on the next page and readership of The Verge, a top-ranked blog. The results for The Verge at alexa.com in mid-2013:

◻ Rank, based on a combination of visitors and page views: 661 in the U.S., 1,443 globally.

◻ Bounce rate, the percentage of visitors who view only one page: 65 percent.

◻ How many pages on the site the average visitor checks: two.

◻ The average time that a visitor stays on the site ("stickiness"): three minutes.

Alexa uses self-reported information—sometimes scanty—to estimate the genders of visitors compared to Internet users in general. For The Verge, it estimates that far more men visit The Verge than is typical. The education level of Verge visitors is believed to be similar to that of all Internet users, as is the number browsing from home (vs. school or work).

More than 37 percent of Verge visitors come from the

1. CFAgbata.com

Pagerank: 1

Mozrank: 4.41

Alexa rank: 81,000

How to Submit a Guest Post: Articles should be must be relevant to the niche of the blog. Your ar anywhere else. You're allowed one backlink to you the contact us page. More information is available

2. UpAndRunningBPlans.com

Pagerank: 1

Mozrank: 6.05

Alexa rank: 10,000

How to Submit a Guest Post: This blog is geare and entrepreneurs. Read the guidelines to find ou guest post ideas or questions. Posts should be on business audience. Read the author's page. It has posting on this blog.

3. Business-Opportunities.biz

Pagerank: 5

The search for "business blogs + guest posts" resulted in this list on guestbloggingtactics.com.

Advertising with Small Budgets for Big Results

Blog Popularity Quantified

When you advertise on XYZ.com, your ad will be seen by at least 150,000 pageviews per month. The blog has 15,000 fans on Facebook, where the weekly reach is typically about 30%. The blog itself has an Alexa score of 4000. The blog author has a Klout score of 68

Pageviews are recorded by Alexa, alexa.com, if its counter is in place on the blog.

Fan and reach figures available from the blog's Facebook page.

Klout scores are based on how active the author is on social media sites. This score does not necessarily represent blog readership.

U.S. The map on Alexa's page for The Verge shows how popular the blog is in other countries, statistics available because email addresses can be tracked by region.

For contrast, look at readership of Posy Gets Cozy, rosylittlethings.typepad.com, a diary-style blog written by Portland, Ore., craft designer and author Alicia Paulson. In late 2013, Alexa reported its U.S. rank as about 74,000. The bounce rate was 78 percent, no surprise because Paulson's fans visit often and thus don't read more than the home page. Less than six percent come via search engines, which says they've bookmarked her site or are subscribing.

Posy Gets Cozy has a primarily female readership, far better educated than blog readers as a group (most attended graduate school), and extremely involved: more than 3,200 sites link to Paulson's blog. Each post typically generates more than 100 comments and she occasionally has as many as 2,000. Those readers translate into sales, too: in fall 2013, thousands of Christmas ornament kits sold (at $30 each) from Paulson's companion website in a single day.

Buying Blog Ads

As you read at the beginning of this section, some bloggers sell ads directly. Some use services such as exchanges and networks. Others carry text ads sold through programs like Google. A search for "buy ads on blogs" will show you several blog ad brokers, companies that provide links to the blogs they work with. Bloggers who sell direct usually offer display advertising, often in the form of banner ads or small square ads on the far side of the blog text.

Such a search will also provide contacts for companies that match bloggers who want to be paid for their posts with advertisers who are willing to pay for reviews of products or services. (Also see "Advertorial.")

Google's program is the best-known example of pay-per-click text advertising, the ads that usually appear in the right column. As Google defines it, "You decide how much you're willing to pay per day. You then only pay when someone clicks on your ad."

The Lingo of Blog Statistics

Pageviews: information from the blog's own counter, or that provided by its host. Not verified as are print publication circulation numbers.

Facebook Fans: equivalent of "friends" or "likes" for a business site.

Weekly reach: Facebook's total of the people who have been on your page when the post was shown, not necessarily those who have read the post.

Page rank: may refer to Google's 10-point scale. Lower numbers equal a lower number of visitors.

Alexa, alexa.com, ranks blogs as well as sites—but it only tracks the small percentage of sites that have the Alexa toolbar installed.

Klout: ranks people based on how active they are on LinkedIn, Facebook, Instagram, Twitter, Google+ and Foursquare. ("Activity" may indicate only how often someone posts rather than how often those posts are read.) Describes itself as, "Influence is the ability to drive action. When you share something on social media or in real life and people respond, that's influence. The more influential you are, the higher your Klout Score." Uses a 100-point scale.

More Information
"Syndicating Updates" in "Social Media"
"Websites"
Word-of-Mouth Marketing Association, womma.org.

Business Stationery

If you work in design or professional services, you need business stationery that helps you develop credibility. Many consumer businesses also find eye-catching, even quirky, graphics an advantage. In these cases, a designer experienced with identity packages is important in determining how your business is presented in print and online.

What's also important is having a overall graphic style: specifying such basics as type fonts and colors, paper and website colors, and format for all printed and online publications. Even for a one-person business, this graphic identity can be inexpensive and reasonably easy with the use of templates. If you're not working with a designer for custom business cards and letterhead, create the cards, letterhead, envelopes, shipping labels and invoices with the same template so they look similar. At a local or online printer or office supplies store, most standard templates can be modified at least slightly.

With the promotions offered often by online business stationery merchants, it's possible to get cards and stationery for as little as $50 or $100. Or use templates in your word processing or desktop publishing program for letters and invoices. Envelopes can be imprinted as they are addressed in a desktop printer, or you can use labels.

If you do most of your correspondence via email, use the same template for your individual messages as you do for eblasts; that allows your messages to be consistent in appearance and include images and links to product descriptions, your Twitter and Facebook posts, and your blog.

Bumper Stickers

With bumper stickers and window clings, people are volunteering to use their vehicles to promote your business, cause or campaign. You can get a single 3 x 10-inch bumper sticker printed for a few dollars, or 1,000 for about 60 cents each. Both the familiar opaque rectangles and transparent ovals are available.

Or make your own stickers. Office supplies stores and online vendors sell water-resistant and polyester-faced adhesive-backed paper that can be run through an inkjet printer. Use desktop publishing or illustration software to create the artwork for the sticker. Even less expensive: miniature stickers for rear windows: easily made with 2 x 4-inch or 4 x 4-inch mailing labels, these cost pennies each.

More Information
"Advertising Novelties"

Carriage and Pedicab Advertising
Even horse-drawn carriages often have advertising messages, but it's unlikely that you'll find large transit advertising brokers handling such sales. Besides asking carriage drivers for business cards, check with wedding and event planners regarding the carriage services they use, or do an online search for horse-drawn carriages in your area.

Cabs operated by bicyclists—pedicabs—also offer vehicle signs. Cab canopies can be printed with a company name, logo or message, too. One national vendor, Main Street Pedicabs, pedicabs.com, also offers "billboard" bikes. If it does not handle the pedal cab advertising in your area, try approaching the pedicab drivers just as you would a carriage driver.

A quirky variation: a bicyclist with a poster-sized sign who pedals back and forth on Ruston Way during the day to advertise the Lobster Shop, the most distant of several water-front restaurants offering lunch service near Tacoma, Wash.

Catalogs and Sell Sheets
Many businesses and organizations now have catalogs that are online, either on web pages or as PDFs that can be down-loaded and printed. Some also advertise their products in catalogs that include products from many different retailers.

This section covers:

☐ Your own printed pieces, whether printed digital, offset or on an office printer.

☐ the Espresso Book Machine.

☐ Catalogs in which you buy space, like Sky Mall.

Your Own Printed Pieces

If you need to supplement what's on your website with printed pieces, several economical options exist for standard quality product catalogs. High quality publications to showcase art, architecture, fashion, interior design, landscape architecture, custom furniture and woodworking will require a significantly greater investment in graphic design, photography and printing; they are less likely to be produced in-house with standard office equipment.

Regardless of printing method, you can save on photography and graphic design by using the same materials on several pieces. The trio of samples on the next page from online retailer Lands' End illustrates this. The original catalog cover (left) was updated with sale information (center) and then the same photo was used on a package insert (right) with different promotional text. For a low-cost variation on this strategy, update the original piece with labels imprinted with new text, or design your piece with a light-colored portion that can later be overprinted in dark ink.

If you need thousands of catalogs, you'll probably use an offset printer. If you're printing a few hundred copies, digital presses offer reasonable unit costs. Some are local, and some market online, with all work done in a central location in the country. Two other options to consider:

☐ *DIY:* Simple folded pieces can be created as large as 11 x 17 inches (tabloid) using desktop publishing software and office color copiers. This allows you to update the sales piece as necessary and to print a couple, or a couple of dozen copies as you need them. In most cases, you will hand-fold them. (See example on next page.)

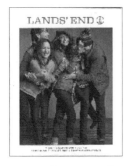  

☐ ***Espresso Book Machine:*** Bookstores across the country are introducing what some people call "book ATMs," machines that combine digital printing, glue-binding and trimming to create books from a PDF within 10 minutes. (In fact, Seattle-based Bartell Drugs began tests of an EBM in its University Village store in 2014, the first drugstore in the U.S. to do so.)

If you're producing vintage-style molding and want 25 copies of a 50-page illustrated catalog of your products, this may be the fastest way to get a professional presentation of your samples. For more information: On Demand Books, ondemandbooks.com.

One side of an 11 x 17-inch piece printed in color on an office copy machine. It will be folded in half twice, once on the vertical white space, and then on the horizontal, to fit into a standard 5 x 7-inch envelope.

Catalogs Published by Others

Catalogs such as SkyMall are made up of ads from retailers and manufacturers. Distributed in seat pockets on many commercial aircraft, in some hotel rooms and on Amtrak, SkyMall describes itself "a landlord to a mall. Companies like yours take space in the mall, in the form of full or partial pages in our quarterly publications. Our rates include printing and distributing the catalog, taking the orders, billing the credit cards, and handling customer service."

Its media kit says that ads are seen in SkyMall "for a minimum of three months 'on-board' and six months online at www.skymall.com." The list price in 2013 for a quarter page advertisement was $11,666 per month, with a three-month minimum. (Prices are subject to negotiation.)

Many associations and business groups coordinate joint catalogs that retailers can buy space in, especially for the holiday season.

For information on catalogs that accept inserts and blown-in cards, see "Inserts."

Characters in Costumes

A form of advertising that can be described as "Outdoor" are the people who wear costumes and wave signs on street corners. They can be hired directly or through temporary agencies.

Costumes are available from display and costume supply vendors, and signs can be as simple as 18 x 24-inch posters on foam core board. More elaborate signs—cut-outs of ice cream sundaes or tires—can be printed on rigid stock and trimmed by print shops.

For more sophisticated marketing, look for the talent agencies that provide models for trade shows. They can contract with you for "street teams" that distribute product samples and flyers or encourage participation in contests and quizzes that showcase your business.

The costumes for copyrighted characters featured on television and in books (for example, the Magic School Bus, Curious George, Pippi Longstocking and Olivia) can be borrowed for school, library and bookstore events. There is a charge for cleaning and shipping. One rental agent is Costume Specialists, costumespecialists.com.

Cinema Advertising
"Big results on the big screen" is what the Cinema Advertising Council, cinemaadcouncil.org, says about advertising in movie theaters. This includes lobby exhibits, concession-stand signage and couponing as well as filmed advertising. Because this trade group has only a few members and doesn't appear to include owners of community or small theaters, you'll want to contact your local theater owners if you're interested only in a neighborhood campaign.

Ads on Rented and Streamed Movies and Programs
Hulu, an online video service that provides television programs and movies, offers both advertising and sponsorships. Information: hulu.com/advertising.

Colors
Whether you're creating a sign for short-term use or something you expect to use for months, maybe years, here are three specifics to consider:

☐ Strong contrast in both hue and value is essential for words to be read from a distance. Clear Channel Outdoor, which creates billboards, lists these as the five best combinations for readability (in descending order):
- Black characters on yellow
- Black characters on white
- Yellow characters on black
- White characters on black
- Dark blue characters on white

☐ Thin, or condensed, typefaces like THIN, Thin, and Thin are often difficult to read. They can be almost impossible to read, regardless of size, if printed in white or pale colors on a dark background.

☐ Red ink fades. So do red paint and the red color in

Advertising with Small Budgets for Big Results   **61**

natural fabrics. If you're using bumper stickers to promote your business, avoid red or any ink color like purple mixed from red; the words printed in that color will fade faster than those printed in black. The red paper you print a menu on and post in your window will fade, and so may the red fabric used in or near your window displays.

Concert and Theater Program Advertising

Got a product that's perfect for opera buffs? Interested in people affluent enough to buy season tickets to the symphony? Want to reach people who attend an occasional theatrical or musical performance?

All good reasons to look into advertising in concert, theater and opera programs. Some program ads are brokered by major firms, others by regional organizations.

The smaller your community, the more likely your symphony, theater and opera groups sell their own advertising. The same is true of school, community college and university cultural events.

Examples of ad brokers for several performing groups:

   □ *Playbill*, playbill.com, the program distributed at Broadway productions, also offers advertising for regional productions. The Dallas Opera, Houston Ballet, San Francisco Symphony, and St. Louis Broadway Series are examples of the event programs for which it provides ads.

   □ *Encore Media*, encoremediagroup.com, handles ads for some San Francisco cultural programs and major Seattle events, including the Seattle Men's and Women's Choruses.

   □ *Southern California Media Group*, socalmedia.com, handles program ads for the major performing arts groups in Los Angeles and San Diego.

Contests as Lead Generators

Getting names of prospects for your sales staff or database can be as simple as the fishbowl by your cashier where customers drop in business cards to enter a monthly drawing. It can be a photo contest with entries that show your product or destination in use. It can be 50–100 words on "what I remember most about…" a historic landmark or product.

If you announce winners with email, entrants will include that with their contact information. If the entry form is designed with a message such as, "Keep me updated about sales promotions and special offers" as the default, entrants will automatically opt-in to your database.

More Information

"In-house Email Databases" under "Email."

Cooperative Advertising

To encourage retailers to advertise their products, manufacturers often offer to defray part or all of the cost of an ad. This is called cooperative advertising.

Here you'll find information on:

□ Cooperative advertising policies.

□ Examples of co-op ads.

□ Whether you should offer co-op funds.

Many co-op programs include the production of complete ads and commercials that require only adding the retailer's name and contact information (circled in the vintage ad on the next page); this significantly reduces production costs and lead time for the retailer and allows the manufacturer to control the design and text of the ad.

Co-op policies vary from manufacturer to manufacturer: some provide funds when theirs are the only products shown in an ad.

Others require only that no similar products be shown (e.g., a store can get co-op funds for a line of cookware as long as the only other items featured in the ad are table linens, wine racks and flatware). A limit on the expense is typical: for example, 75 percent of the cost of an ad that does not exceed $1,000 in space or time costs.

Co-op programs require that copies of advertising invoices and copies of the ad, or affidavits indicating when a commercial aired, be submitted with the reimbursement request in a given time period. Ads must sometimes be pre-approved to be eligible for co-op funds. Some nonprofits and associations also offer co-op funds: for example, for advertising lessons in the activity that the association supports.

Co-op ad programs usually offer fixed dollars or a percentage of the value of purchases made in a previous period, as the following excerpts from real policies show:

Examples of Co-op Programs:

☐ *Truck dealership grand opening expenses:* Manufacturer offers 50 percent reimbursement of first $1,000 of expenses for advertising and invitations (printing and mailing), food/catering and nonalcoholic beverages and rental equipment. No reimbursement for giveaway items, door prizes, raffles or drawing prizes.

☐ *Book wholesaler promotions to retail customers:* Publisher offers an amount for the current year equal to 1.25 percent of net purchases for all titles purchased during the prior year.

☐ *Water treatment process promotion to retail customers:* Manufacturer offers a total equal to 2 percent of net purchases made in the previous year, with co-op available

for 25 percent of the cost of any promotion. In multi-product promotions, co-op is limited to the portion of the promotion featuring company products. No reimbursement for postage for direct mail promotions, prizes and awards for incentive programs and sales contests.

When No Co-op Programs Exist

If your suppliers do not make their co-op programs explicit, ask what's available. Ready-to-use photos, logos and other material may already exist, perhaps on the manufacturer's "press" web page.

If no formal co-op program exists, propose a split of expenses, or ask for in-kind help. The in-kind assistance might be the design and production of the ad at the manufacturer's expense, or hosting a page for your business on the manufacturer's website. It might be free or significantly discounted merchandise for contest prizes. For example, although few book publishers have co-op allowances, many will provide books for a giveaway on request: Seattle's Parenting Press encourages booksellers and libraries to promote a best-selling children's book by offering a free copy of the book as the prize in a related contest.

Should You Offer Co-op Dollars?

If you wholesale products, a cooperative advertising program can make stocking your merchandise more attractive to retailers. If your products are sold on consignment or on a returnable basis, any co-op funds should be based on past sales, net of returns. (See the actual book wholesaler co-op policy earlier for an example.)

Given a tight budget, it may be easier to control your costs with such in-kind alternatives as listing merchants on your website in a "Where to buy…" section, doing Twitter and Facebook posts about retailers taking on your products, and featuring merchants in your newsletter or blog on a rotating basis. You can also encourage retailers to run contests focused on your products by providing free merchandise as the prizes.

Even if you do not offer co-op funds, you can help

retailers and the media publicize your products if you make high-quality images of your logo and products available along with application stories, media releases describing how customers use the products or how your services have helped them be more successful.

More Information
"Advertising Novelties"
"Giveaways"
"Swag/Goodie Bags"

Coupons

Coupons can be created with desktop publishing software and run off a few dozen at a time on your office printer to offer a sample, a discount on purchases or complimentary shipping. They can include a code for prospective customers to use with phone or online orders, and incorporate QR codes that send prospects to a special page on your website for more information.

Coupons can be offered through newspaper inserts, magazines and websites, both yours and those of retailers and coupon sites. To encourage repeat purchases by existing customers, you can hand out coupons valid for a future period, or print them at the bottom of your cash register receipts. And coupons can be offered through online "deal-of-the-day" sites and through coupon books.

This section includes:

☐ Cash register tape ads.

☐ In-store coupons.

☐ Online coupons.

☐ "Daily deals."

☐ Coupon books.

Coupons are an ideal form of direct response advertising because you can test offers by distributing different coupons in different media and watching which generate the most orders or the most profitable orders. Coupons not redeemed cost you almost nothing. (And most are not redeemed: in 2012 only one percent of those distributed were used.)

Even if not used, coupons that are perceived as valuable are clipped and saved, helping to build awareness of your business. To ensure that your coupons *are* saved, the product needs to be something that is frequently purchased.

It's also important that the discount be significant. Today, with price-shopping easily done online and many online retailers discounting products, the coupon offer must be attractive enough that prospective customers will come to you rather than an online retailer. Compare the total price of your offer—product less discount plus any applicable sales tax or shipping fee—with the lowest total price offered online.

If you have a significant advertising budget and want to reach prospects in a very small geographic area, consider coupons on printed cash register tapes. One such provider, Register Tapes Unlimited, requires at least a one-year commitment. A similar firm is Register Tape Network. Catalina Marketing Corp. provides a variation: coupons targeted to a purchase and printed on a separate tape when you check out. (For example, a coupon for baby shampoo if baby food has been purchased or, as shown on page 67, the Staples/Kohl's back-to-school tie-in.)

When evaluating cash register tape ads for your business, be aware that the companies providing these ads are generous in their estimates of readership. You cannot assume that everyone who makes a purchase will turn over the tape and read the coupons. Many customers immediately discard tapes. Although ad vendors provide testimonials on their websites, consider telephoning those who advertise on the register tapes you receive and asking how often their coupons are redeemed.

For information regarding local tape ad providers, use a

Advertising with Small Budgets for Big Results 67

To encourage patronage during the traditionally slow January and February, restaurants often offer December visitors a discount on post-holiday meals. This was delivered with the check.

phrase such as "cash register tape ads" in an online search.

To stimulate impulse or larger quantity purchases, consider coupons by a product display. In your own storefront, hang photocopied coupons on a hook or binder clip on the appropriate shelf. This simple method allows you to limit the number of coupons offered, and to test different offers on different days, or by time of day, or offer coupons only during a certain time of day (e.g., "Early Bird Gets the Coupon" or "Last Chance" for the hour before you close).

Nationally, companies like News America Marketing provide on-shelf dispensers.

Online Couponing

Given the high number of people who do not read Sunday newspapers, where coupons have traditionally been inserted, online coupon portals have become popular. If couponing is a promotion you want to offer, you have several online options.

□ On your own website (see page 68), blog, Facebook, Pinterest, or Twitter accounts, and via eblasts to your own database.

□ On the social media sites for complementary businesses or organizations, on a swap basis.

□ Coupon portals, which you'll find with an Internet

search with a phrase such as "online coupons." Some are coupon publishers that charge fees to participating merchants; others are aggregators of discounts and special offers and may not charge you to be listed.

Most firms that offer newspaper coupon supplements also offer coupons online.

"Deal of the Day" Online Coupons

"Flash sale" websites, where a deeply discounted offer is made available to registered followers, sometimes for as little as 24 hours, have become popular in the last few years. For businesses, participating in these programs should be considered a "loss leader," as you'll see when you calculate the required or recommended discount for customers and the commission charged by the sale site.

Businesses that have worked with such sites recommend that you offer discounts rather than free services and offer these on less popular services. They also recommend that you offer a discount on a series of purchases (say, 50 percent off on an item on each of a customer's next three visits) to encourage repeat purchases.

Another important recommendation: limit the number of discounts available. This will reduce how much you spend (because you are likely to lose money on every transaction), and it will prevent you from being deluged during the period of the deal. That can overwhelm your staff and alienate your regular customers.

Among the best-known deal sites:

☐ *Groupon,* groupon.com, which offers discounted gift certificates for specific products or services from both local

Advertising with Small Budgets for Big Results

and national businesses. Anyone can sign up for free and be emailed about local deals.

Groupon requires that merchants offer discounts of at least 50 percent; it retains 50 percent of the revenue, resulting in a total discount by the merchant of at least 75 percent. There is also a credit card processing fee charged to the merchant.

□ *LivingSocial,* livingsocial.com, which offers deals that are typically for the recipient's local area. Its website says, "No up-front costs to running a promotion." Like Groupon, Living Social usually takes 50 percent of the gross.

Besides allowing customers to buy goods and services at significant discounts, LivingSocial also encourages referrals with "Free Deals." As described on the website: "After you buy a Deal, you will receive a personalized link which you may choose to share with your friends. If at least three of your friends buy the same Deal using your personalized link, you will receive your Deal for free ('Free Deal')." As a merchant, you'll want to know exactly how "Free Deals" affect your revenue.

LivingSocial has also introduced coupons: examples of the offers in late 2013 were free shipping on an order of $99 or more at Carhartt.com, five percent off tile or hardwood flooring at Home Depot, and half off on small Vera Bradley totes.

□ *Gilt Groupe,* **gilt.com,** offers members-only shopping for designer labels with discounts up to 60 percent. It includes apparel, food, home decor, travel and activities.

□ *Google Offers*, google.com/offers. Users receive an email with one local deal per day, with an opportunity to purchase that deal within a specified time period. Google Offers are valid no matter how many people decide to take the deal. As of fall 2013, listing offers was free via Google for Business for storefront merchants.

□ *Amazon Local*, local.amazon.com/businesses, is primarily a deal aggregator that promotes flash sales through LivingSocial and other merchants, both local and online.

Besides the discount you offer, the only other cost is a referral fee for each sale made.

□ *Facebook Offers,* facebook.com. Certain businesses, brands and organizations can share discounts with their customers by posting an offer on their Facebook pages. As of fall 2013, a page needed to have at least 100 "likes" before an offer could be posted there. There's no charge for offers unless you want them promoted beyond your page with ads or sponsored stories. Anyone claiming an offer receives an email to show at the merchant's physical location to get the discount. No minimum discount is required, but the company advises that a discount of at least 20 percent pulls better.

□ *Plum District,* plumdistrict.com. This group buying site offers discounts on merchandise for parents, especially those who have signed up to receive notifications for one new deal every day in their preferred local market (the San Francisco Bay Area, Los Angeles, Orange County, San Diego, Denver, and the New York metro area). In addition, there may be as many as six new deals available everywhere. Offers stay on the website for approximately seven days.

Typically, merchandise promoted via email is discounted 40–60 percent from the usual retail price. Plum District takes 40–60 percent of what the customer is billed. So you could net as little as $16 for an item that lists at $100 ($100 x .4 x .4).

The company also offers email coupons, website advertising starting at $500, and advertorials. Promotions can be segmented by such factors as geography, household income, children's ages and past purchase behavior.

□ *Angie's List Big Deals,* my.angieslist.com/thebigdeal/welcome.aspx, offers discounts of at least 50 percent at businesses which already participate in Angie's List.

A customer service representative reported, "There is [also] a small processing fee when the coupon is purchased by the member...That processing percentage changes based on the coupon, market, and category.... [For more information] eligible businesses may speak with a representative in our Storefront of Big Deal departments."

Advertising with Small Budgets for Big Results 71

The website says that the Big Deals, or coupons, are offered to "Angie's List members [those who pay an annual fee to get recommendations on businesses and services] and nonmembers alike...Members can also forward them to family and friends, too."

Coupons must be valid for at least three months. The website also explains, "After the expiration date, you do not have to honor the discount, but companies are encouraged to work with members and make arrangements both parties find suitable. If you do not wish to honor the expired offer, please have the member contact Angie's List directly. We are able to refund their purchase."

A business can be added to Angie's List easily if a List participant contributes a review of your business: as the site says, "Most companies were added by one of our members, who is also a customer of yours. They told us about their experience with you, and that one review is all it takes to be rated on Angie's List."

However, it continues, "companies can also create a free account and appear without a rating on the List. Once your company is registered, you may log in at any time to review and update your company's profile, check your ratings, and read and respond to new reviews."

Coupon Books

The coupon books often sold as fund-raisers are other opportunities to introduce your business to prospects. Some now also offer online coupons.

Examples are Chinook Book and Entertainment.

 □ *Chinook Book*, chinookbook.net/about-us/criteria/, chinookbook.net/about-us/contact, describes itself as focussing on businesses and activities which contribute to a sustainable and vibrant community, so it is selective in the merchants it includes. Online merchants are eligible if they accept promotional codes through their websites.

Besides the print book's coupon and advertising opportunities, coupons can be offered through a mobile app for Android and iPhone. The print and mobile coupon packages for retailers start at $375–$575, depending on market area; they top out at $1,500–$3,000 for a full page with as many as three coupons. For manufacturers, print coupons are available for $475–$2,500. Ads are also available.

The Chinook Book sales staff recommends a discount of 20–50 percent for the coupons. "Experience has taught us that it takes a 20 percent off offer or better to attract a new customer," reported a staff member.

No information was provided by Entertainment book owners despite repeated requests.

More Information
"Direct Response Advertising"
"QR Codes"
"Websites"
American Catalog Mailers Association (ACMA), catalog-mailers.org
Direct Marketing Association, thedirectmarketingsearch.com/
National Etailing & Mailing Organization of America, nemoa.org
VT/NH Marketing Group, vtnhmg.org

Crowdsourcing
Kickstarter, kickstarter.com, and Indiegogo, indiegogo.com, are examples of the online sites that help businesses, organizations and individuals raise money for business, civic and cultural projects, philanthropy—or personal needs. Creating a crowdsourcing campaign has at least two other significant advantages for a marketing communications program:

□ Forces start-ups to get organized about producing images, advertising text and at least a brief mission statement and business/operating plan.

□ Crowdsourcing also serves as a means of creating

Advertising with Small Budgets for Big Results

awareness of your business, organization or charity and may generate advance orders or donations.

Programs vary in what they permit, the length of campaigns, and the fees.

☐ Yes, I want to receive emails about the latest products and services.

Databases

It's possible to advertise without a database of prospects and customers, but if you compile contact information and sales history on people interested in your products or services, or members of your organization, you'll increase your promotional options.

With your own database, you'll also be better able to determine which promotions are most effective. The databases used for tracking sales leads can be used for tracking who receives which ad, who responds, and when they respond.

A good database includes the company or organization name, corporate website, and mailing address, phone number, and email address for each contact person. You'll also want to be able to track the source of database entries: personal, postcard, catalog, email, etc.

As noted in "Contests as Lead Generators," running contests is one way to develop a database. Collecting business cards in a fishbowl at an exhibit in return for a complimentary download of a white paper or other publication is another method. Every click on your website and every email you send out can offer the opportunity to opt-in to a newsletter or to have a copy of the newsletter sent to a friend. This will also increase your database.

Ideally, the software you use for email blasts (eblasts) reports which messages are opened, and that information can be imported into the database. Even better is invoicing software that can export customer records into your database. Then you can focus later promotional campaigns on prospects who have opened email (as summarized in the example on page 74) or who have a sales history with you.

Federal Trade Commission regulations require that you not email anyone who has asked to be removed from

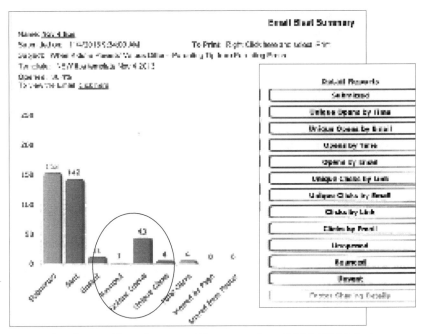

your database. For the specifics on the CAN-SPAM Act, see business.ftc.gov/documents/bus61-can-spam-act-compliance-guide-business.

More Information
"Direct Response Advertising"
"Email"

Directory Advertising
Yellow Pages is the most common directory with advertising, but there are many more, in print and online: church, school, chamber of commerce, trade association, buyers' guide, tourism guide, conference and convention handbooks—and the directories of exhibitors compiled for boat, car, antique, home improvement and other shows.

Given the widespread use of the Internet to find local vendors and repair people, marketers question the value of telephone directories. Some cities also allow residents to opt out of receiving such publications. To measure the effectiveness of directory advertising, especially in guides such as those for tourism and trade shows, use a direct response promotion in your ad: "Visit our booth to enter a drawing for..." or "Mention this ad when you call, and you'll receive..."

Direct Response Advertising

Direct response is advertising that asks you to take action. It is a message, not a specific medium.

You'll see direct response advertising copy on the flyer inviting you to sign up for a study tour; the blown-in card in a magazine that offers a subscription at half-price; on the screen during the PBS pledge drive; and on the instant coupon on the supermarket shelf.

In this section you'll find:

☐ Examples of direct response ads.

☐ Sample rates.

☐ Mailing list rate cards and how to use census data.

☐ How to find, evaluate, test, and rent lists.

Examples of Direct Response Advertising

Before the Internet, direct response marketing was primarily:

☐ Postal mail—postcards, catalogs or flyers—with order forms or toll-free numbers.

☐ Bind-in or blown-in business reply postcards in magazines.

☐ Print ads and broadcast commercials that sought immediate orders, often via a toll-free number.

☐ Print ads in magazines, each with a message such as "For more information, circle [number] on the reader response card," combined with a bind-in card with numbers to circle, or boxes to check by numbers or business names.

The bound-in business reply card went to a service that generated contact information (lead generators) for each business listed and may have fulfilled the requests, sending out packets of promotional literature. Today the bound-in

Reader response or bingo card.

cards still exist; many publications also offer material via a toll-free number.

☐ Coupons, mailed by themselves, or in co-op mailings. They typically offer a discount on a purchase, a giveaway, a premium with a purchase or free shipping. (For online coupons, see "Coupons" and "Websites.")

☐ Statement and package stuffers, promotional pieces inserted in invoices and statements sent out by utility companies, banks, and department stores and in deliveries of merchandise purchased through mail order catalogs.

☐ Co-ops, envelopes or packets with multiple ads, sometimes from noncompeting businesses.

Co-op mailers often include coupons. Some co-ops are run as a business by direct mailing houses. Some are offered by associations, as a means of generating revenue and allowing vendors to contact members.

Some are geographic: a chamber of commerce might organize a co-op for its members. A co-op can be as casual

Blown-in card coded (circled) so that response to the offer can be tracked.

as two or three businesses sharing the expense of an occasional mailing that includes mini-catalogs or coupon offers from each one.

Other forms of printed direct response advertising:

☐ Direct mail wraps, four-page flyers into which other direct mail pieces are inserted. Each piece usually includes a coupon or special offer.

☐ Polybag "outserts," promotional material or samples (sometimes a spin-off publication or special supplement) sealed in a plastic bag with a newspaper or magazine.

☐ Newspaper wraps, usually a sheet of newsprint the length of the newspaper page and a third to a half of its width, which must be removed before the newspaper section can be read. Called spadeas, these also sometimes wrap magazines.

☐ Bellyband, a heavy paper strip wrapped around a periodical and glued at one point, so it must be removed before the publication can be opened.

☐ Stick-on ads, small adhesive-backed pieces attached to the front page of the newspaper.

Direct response advertising can be as simple as campaign

78 — Advertising with Small Budgets for Big Results

These samples demonstrate options that exist with postal direct mail. At top, a university uses information from sales reports to send previous customers a partially completed order form with contact information for those previously sent gifts.

The Crate & Barrel self-mailer has a detachable cardboard coupon and a space that's been imprinted with the names of nearby stores. The same concept could be used by a multi-outlet business, with each outlet offering a different promotion and with adhesive labels instead of imprinting or the coupons.

The restaurant postcard has been preprinted in full-color on the reverse and then imprinted each time a special is offered. Note how the discount increases with subsequent visits.

literature left on doorsteps, flyers on windshields or door hangers on knobs.

Direct Response Advertising Rates

Most publications that accept advertising permit direct response messages. Some alumni publications limit their advertisers to alumni or campus-related organizations. Publications with specialized readership may require that all ads be preapproved.

A publication that offers the inserts, outserts, wraps, stick-on ads and other specialties described above lists costs for each on the rate card. Mailing houses that issue card decks and other co-op pieces also have rate cards. When these are not published, salespeople handle your inquiry.

The Atlanta Journal-Constitution rate card uses this to illustrate a spadea, or newspaper wrap.

Reviewing Rate Cards

Before ordering a list, discuss formats with your mailing house: labeling fees vary depending on label format. Pressure-sensitive labels were traditionally only applied by hand, and so may be the most expensive to use unless the list is so small that manual application is more economical (a few hundred labels) or if the mailer will be difficult to process with equipment (usually because of an unusual shape, such as that caused by an enclosure like a pen).

What other formats cost to apply may depend on your mailing house's equipment and whether the mailing house is combining different purchased lists or combining your customer list with a purchased list.

U.S. Postal Rates

If you're mailing your own direct response pieces, understand that postal rates vary by:

☐ Size and weight of your piece: nonstandard shapes and

sizes cost more, and so do larger and heavier pieces.

□ Postal rate class, either first class or the significantly less expensive Standard (bulk) rates.

□ How many pieces you have, and in what detail they have been presorted.

□ How to handle pieces with outdated addresses.

If you have never done a bulk mailing in-house, check the costs of a bulk mail permit, the indicia permit (which allows you to skip stamps or metering), and, if applicable, the costs of using a Business Reply permit. For information about these and other services, see "Postal Regulations" later in this guide and "Advertise with Mail" on the Postal Service website, usps.com.

If mailing will be done by a mailing house, ask if you can use its indicia instead of procuring your own. If you plan to use the mailing piece for several months after the

> PRSRT STD
> US POSTAGE
> PAID
> SEATTLE WA
> PERMIT NO 2389

initial mass mailing, you can cover the indicia with a first class stamp when mailing one or two copies. (Bulk mail requires a minimum quantity.) If you use a mailing house's indicia, you can use the same indicia with your next campaign if you outsource to the same vendor.

Another option: customizing the permit and imprint with your business name and logo. This is called Picture Permit Imprint Indicia; see "Business Solutions" on usps.com.

Both nonprofits and businesses sometimes prefer to use stamps. Response rates can be better—an envelope is less likely to be perceived as "junk" mail—and with a small mailing, using precancelled stamps can be less expensive than indicia permits and printing. More information about precancelled stamps and their current costs is in "Postal Regulations" and at usps.com.

Mailing Lists
The Postal Service can deliver to every residence in the geographic areas you select, you can create a mailing list from customers and prospects, or you can rent mailing lists from

organizations, businesses and government agencies that maintain their own lists, or from list brokers that handle lists for organizations, nonprofits and publications.

Given postage and printing costs and the number of mailed pieces necessary to generate sales leads or actual sales, addresses should be checked for accuracy and direct mail campaigns should be carefully designed. If you rent a list, have it checked against U.S. Postal Service "address update" databases prior to being sent to you. If you send your own list to a mailing service, the service should have these software products. For information, check usps.com, for "Address Management" and "NCOA."

How Census Data Can Help You Target

A valuable resource for targeting by demographics is the U.S. Census Bureau's online reports, census.gov. The Bureau does not offer mailing lists, but you can use its data to determine which geographic areas to mail to.

For example, if your market is Hispanics, click through to the Hispanic Population: 2010, which lists the 10 places in the U.S. with the most Hispanics and the 10 places with the highest percentage of Hispanics. If you want to know how many people in Washington state speak Russian, see "Language Spoken at Home By Ability to Speak English." Rather know how many women 65 and older live alone in Salem, Ore.? Census data can tell you that, besides how many veterans live in Spokane, Wash., and how many people are raising their grandchildren in Boise, Idaho.

Sources of Lists

Besides the Postal Service, mailing lists are available from magazines, trade journals, membership organizations, state departments of education, school directories, college admission exam registrants, and from list brokers, who compile information from public documents such as voter registration lists, property tax records and business licenses. The more detailed the list, the more information sold (e.g., telephone numbers or email addresses for follow-up), the higher the cost.

List Rental Defined

"Renting" means you have the one-time right to mail a piece to everyone on that portion of a list you select. In some cases, the list will be delivered to you. Often it is sent electronically to your mailing house, or the list owner contracts directly with a mailing house, so you never see the list.

To track use of rented lists, and to catch those who re-use a list without permission, lists are typically "seeded" with addresses owned by the list broker.

Evaluating List Quality

When evaluating the purchase of a mailing list, consider:

□ Whether a subset of the list is available free or for a reduced price for testing the effectiveness of the list.

□ The minimum purchase required.

□ The formats the list is available in, the charge for each format (e.g., adhesive labels cost more), what formats your mailing house or your own mail department can handle, and what the direct or labor costs will be for each.

□ The charge for each select.

□ How complete the addresses are: contact person's name, title only, or business name only.

□ The source of the list: recipients of a controlled (free) circulation publication? Paid subscribers? Members of an association? Names from a directory—school, church, chamber of commerce, homeowners' association?

What Lists Cost

The most accurate and least expensive mailing may be the Postal Service's Every Door Direct Mail program, which promises a mailer to every address in the area you select for as little as 16 cents a piece in postage and handling. As with other extremely economical lists, pieces are mailed without names, like the "Occupant" mailings you've received, which may cost seven or eight cents per address (plus postage and mailer). What you have to determine is whether this eco-

5,433,030 TOTAL UNIVERSE / BASE RATE	$95.00/M
3,148,849 12-MONTH BUYERS	+ $5.00/M
1,300,809 6-MONTH BUYERS	+ $10.00/M
681,435 3-MONTH BUYERS	+ $15.00/M
224,624 30 DAY BUYERS	+ $20.00/M
INQUIRIES BASE RATE	$80.00/M
336,249 12-MONTH INQUIRES	+ $5.00/M
152,005 6-MONTH INQUIRES	+ $10.00/M
59,435 3-MONTH INQUIRES	+ $15.00/M
24,123 30-DAY INQUIRES	+ $20.00/M

This catalog company rents its mailing list with many options. Most expensive is contact information for the most recent buyers. Some databases are also available sorted by amount of purchase.

nomical list is cost-effective: whether a piece without a name will be read.

When you rent a list from a mail order or catalog company, the list *will* include names and your options may include selecting names based on how recently they were added to the database.

The more recent the inquiry, the higher the price (the base rate plus the additional fee per 1,000 names). The names of those who have made purchases in the past month are the most expensive. Buying all or a portion of the unsorted list is the least expensive. It includes people who have requested a catalog in the past as well as those who have made purchases.

Other expensive lists are those from college and graduate school admission exams, which are opt-in (test-takers have to agree to have their contact information released) and extremely accurate, because the contact information being furnished is used for delivery of test results. Provided only to selected mailers—usually college and university admissions offices and nonprofit scholarship programs—these lists cost about 40 cents per name.

List brokers also offer contact information for high school juniors and seniors, which is often used by senior portrait photographers and similar businesses; these lists are compiled from several years' worth of school directories, subscription lists, online purchases and other sources. They are then "aged" in an attempt to identify the now-current

This portion of a catalog company's mailing list rate card shows the upcharges, by thousand names (M) or for the entire file (F), for coding (in this case, adding a code above an addressee's name), list format (Cheshire, pressure sensitive), and delivery (diskette, email, FTP, rush). Nth name, or nth select, allows a representative sample of the entire database—every 10th name if you want 10 percent of it, for example.

ADDRESSING	
KEY CODING	$0.00/
4-UP CHESHIRE	$5.00/M
CANCEL FEE	$75.00/F
CHESHIRE LABELS	$5.00/M
DISKETTE	$75.00/F
DMA SUPPRESS	NO CHARGE
E-MAIL	$50.00/F
FTP	$50.00/F
HOME ADDRESS	NO CHARGE
KEYING	NO CHARGE
NTH NAME	NO CHARGE
PRESSURE SENSITIVE	$10.00/M
RUN CHARGE	$10.00/M
RUSH CHARGE	$85.00/F
ZIP + 4	NO CHARGE
ZIP TAPE	$8.00/M

school level. (For example, anyone who indicated she was a high school freshman when subscribing to a magazine last year will now be considered a sophomore.)

Although these lists will include students who are not university-bound, they may not be as accurate as the information from the College Board's Student Search Service, collegeboard.com, and ACT, Inc., act.org.

Nixies

"Nixies" are mailers undeliverable because of outdated or inaccurate addresses. Many list sellers offer a nominal refund per returned piece. To obtain the refund, you must submit the returned piece within a short period after renting the list, sometimes as soon as within a month.

When using Standard (bulk) mail, you may not receive any of the returns, and if you do, it may take several weeks for all of them to be received. As a result, it's almost impossible to collect a refund if you're using Standard mail.

Testing a List with Nth Select

Few advertisers regardless of budget would mail to an entire list, especially if it's more than a few thousand names.

Those interested in a list would first test it with a subset, probably created with an "Nth select," or "Nth name." This allows a mailing to be sent to a certain percentage of the entire

Advertising with Small Budgets for Big Results 85

Base rate per 1,000 names.

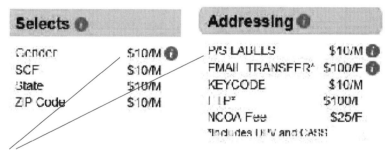

Estimated size of list, and an option to check the exact count.

Extra charges, either per 1,000 names or (F) for the entire file, for such selects (sorts) as gender and geography, pressure-sensitive labels, tranferring via email or FTP, or adding a code above the name that allows for order tracking. NCOA is the change-of-address check.

Source of list, update frequency, preapproval requirement, and amount of commission paid to those who purchase for clients.

database so that the test includes every part of the country, every kind of consumer. ("Nth" means your choice of percentage: say, every 10th or 15th or 25th name.)

Such subsets can also be created after sorts are done: for example, every 10th name on the list of the women who have spent more than $150 at a catalog retailer in the past 30 days.

Approval of Mailing Pieces
Membership organizations that rent lists often require that mailing pieces be approved in advance. Rather than have your piece printed prior to approval, it's wiser to have a rough, with all text, submitted for approval. Then any necessary changes can be made with minimal expense.

Donations
See "Naming/Sponsorships/Donations"

Elevators and Lobbies
You've heard about "elevator speeches"—being able to pitch yourself or your business in the 15 or 20 seconds you have with a prospect (whether or not you're in an elevator). Advertising brokers offer visual pitches via posters, elevator door wraps and digital displays in apartment and office building elevators and lobbies.

One vendor's website says an apartment building resident or an office building employee averages four elevator rides a day, each ride lasting 30–80 seconds. A visitor sees the ad twice per visit. Lobby signs may be seen by those walking through, taking breaks or waiting, sometimes for several minutes.

Those who sell elevator and lobby ads say they can estimate average income, professional profile, age category and interests of the people who frequent office buildings and to a certain extent, in apartment buildings. Vendors also claim high readership: after all, they say, the alternative is staring at a blank wall.

For a DIY option, contact smaller locally-owned buildings regarding the possibility of posters in elevators. In lobbies, besides easels, consider free-standing cut-outs of figures related to your promotion: a historical figure for a museum exhibit, one of the performers for an upcoming concert, or even a life-size cut-out of you, with a tearaway pad offering a coupon valid at your business.

For a true guerilla marketing effort, seek permission to place a mannequin dressed in a company uniform or T-shirt in a chair in the lobby.

Email

Why email? It's cheap, easy, fast—and often the response is fast, too. I've done campaigns where I began to receive orders before I was finished with eblasts. Being able to send direct response advertising, product announcements and other promotional messages via email has significantly reduced the cost of contacting prospective clients and customers. In this section, you'll find information on:

- ☐ Eblast costs.
- ☐ CAN-SPAM regulations.
- ☐ Eblast services.
- ☐ Postal direct mail vs. eblasts.
- ☐ Building and acquiring lists.
- ☐ Spam filters.
- ☐ The value of images in your email.

For about $50 a month, most eblast providers allow you to submit information to as many as 1,000 email addresses each day. At $1.67 per day, that's almost nothing compared to what you'd pay in postage, labels, labor, printing and possibly envelopes for 1,000 pieces sent through postal mail.

The difference is that while you can legally *mail* anyone, the U.S. CAN-SPAM regulations require that you send email only to those who have chosen, or opted, to receive it, and that if you do send email—solicited or not—you offer the recipients the opportunity to be removed from your email lists. MailChimp, one email marketing provider, offers a brief summary of CAN-SPAM on its website:

If you're sending commercial email (selling or promoting):

☐ *Never use deceptive headers, from-names, reply-tos, or subject lines.*

☐ *You must always provide an unsubscribe link.*

☐ *Remove recipients from your list within 10 business days.*

☐ *The unsubscribe link must work for at least 30 days after sending.*

☐ *You must include your physical mailing address. To learn more, go to ftc.gov.*

See "Databases" for more information.

Eblast Services

The companies that handle bulk email—Constant Contact, SilverPop, MailChimp, for example—include strict "opt-in" and "anti-spam" language in their contracts.

Some will expect you to provide proof that those on your database have explicitly opt-ed in, so save the "subscribe me" reports from website or paper forms as you expand your database.

Eblast vendors monitor how many recipients respond to your email with "spam" complaints, and your service may be discontinued if such reports exceed what the vendor considers typical of your industry.

The use of addresses such as "info@domainname.com" and "webmaster@domainname.com" without individuals' names is also discouraged.

Before you contract with a vendor, evaluate your database and discuss its contents with prospective vendors, to avoid problems once you start eblast campaigns.

Direct Response Email vs. Postal Mail

Is an eblast more effective than postal direct mail?

Because eblast providers report how many recipients open a message each time a mass email is sent, they compile that information by industry. With true opt-in email, especially when the message is informational, open rates can be between 20 and 40 percent. Open rates also increase when messages are sent only to those who have opened previous emails. For messages perceived to be almost entirely informational (newsletters, for example), open rates can reach nearly 100 percent.

What you don't know is how much of the opened message was read. That's why including links is important. Eblast providers report how many recipients click on links, and many website hosts can provide information on how long a visitor stays on any single page and how many pages are visited. (See page 90 for an open/click report.)

The time spent on the linked page ("stickiness") often depends on the content of that landing page. When a link leads to a page relating directly to the email message (rather than to the home page), readership is likely much better.

How email and website readership translates to purchases can only be determined if you sell direct to consumers, and even then, it requires careful comparison of eblast and web host reports and customer databases. No statistics can be more than estimates because while prospects may research products on your site, their purchases are often made from online retailers or in bricks-and-mortar stores. (This is especially true when online retailers routinely discount prices and offer free shipping.)

Statistics have never been available on how many pieces of postal direct response advertising are opened and how well they are read. For decades, a one percent response to postal mail was considered good, and a 2012 Direct Marketing Association report shows that is still common for mail sent to those with whom the mailer does not have a relationship. Responses to in-house lists, especially customer lists, are as much as four times better.

The DMA study estimated that postal mail advertising was far more likely to get a response than email—but that the cost of each response was many times greater. Its surveys also showed that response to postal mail advertising had declined by 25 percent in recent years. (The DMA study doesn't show what earlier response rate it is using in the comparison.) Another important point: many responses to direct mail result only in leads, not sales.

In-house Email Databases

The most effective email advertising goes to people who have asked to receive your messages: those who have chosen to subscribe to your new product announcements, newsletter

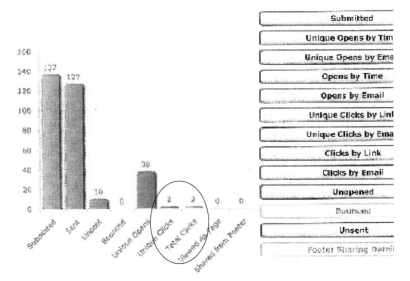

Reports on eblasts typically provide such information as the number of addresses submitted, the number of emails sent, and the reasons some (10, in this case) were not sent (duplicates, incomplete addresses, opt-outs that had not been manually removed from the list). Reports also show the bounces (failures to deliver), the unique opens (for this weekly publication, multiple opens by the same recipient are common, and "forwards" also count as opens), and how many people clicked through any of the links. As the far right column shows, the vendor reports which addresses clicked which links. Such reports allow you to create a new list of those who did not open a message and re-send it, perhaps with a different subject line, or to send follow-ups to those who did click, especially if you know they have not yet purchased. The detail in "unsent" is helpful in cleaning the list.

Advertising with Small Budgets for Big Results 91

Note reference to "other special offers."

or blog. Less likely to respond are those who are opted-in by default because the box by "Yes, send me information on special offers, new products…" or some similar sentence is automatically checked on your website order form.

To invite prospects to be added to your database:

☐ Add subscription options to your shopping cart/order confirmation form.

☐ Include a message such as "Subscribe to our newsletter" on your print and broadcast materials, including ads, catalogs, press releases, packages, product labels, hang tags, shopping bags, invoices and statements—even letterhead and envelopes.

☐ Add "Forward to a friend" on every web page and every promotional email.

☐ Use in-store signs and website messages.

☐ Pass around sign-up sheets when you and your staff members speak.

☐ Offer a "freemium" — a "free premium" such as survey results, product sample, or a white paper to those who opt in. (See example on page 91.)

☐ Ask everyone who visits your office or storefront, or calls for information, for permission to send email.

☐ Run contests everywhere you exhibit, with entry forms that solicit opt-ins.

☐ Run contests online, with entries to be emailed in.

Contests can be product-related, such as pictures of customers using your product, customers' most memorable visits to your resort, or suggestions for naming a new product, menu item or feature of your service.

Contests can also be theme-related: holiday, season, school, career — offer your product or service as a prize for the best DIY gift idea, the most practical tips for getting kids ready for back to school, the most valuable advice from a first boss.

A contest can be as simple as a drawing, with the winner selected at random from among the emailed entries.

Acquired Lists

It's in a legal gray area, but "borrowing" contact information from directories, news articles and even from other businesses or organizations is common. This has less risk if you use these emails for a one-time mailing, and add to your database only those who respond with a "yes."

Besides legal issues, "borrowed" contacts raise the question of accuracy. With addresses you "harvest" from the web (like the school directory on page 93), the published email may only link to an address that changes frequently. The website can say, "Contact our president with your concerns," and the email address may have the president's name, but hover a cursor over the link and you're likely to see someone else's name — a name that changes with personnel changes.

Washington State School Districts: Maps

Educational Service Districts (ESDs)

ESD 101 - Northeast
4202 S. Regal
Spokane, 99223 7738
(509) 789-3800
http://www.esd101.net

ESD 105
33 S. 2nd Ave.
Yakima, 98902-1485
(509) 575-2885
http://www.esd105.org

ESD 112
2500 NE 65th Ave.

ESD 113
6005 Tyee Drive SW
Tumwater, 98512
(360) 464-6700
http://www.esd113.org/

ESD 114 - Olympic
105 National Ave. N.
Bremerton, 98312
(360) 479-0993
http://www.oesd.wednet.edu/

ESD 121 - Puget Sound
800 Oakesdale Ave. SW

Especially if you're working from a printed directory, some contact information is almost certain to be outdated. Even online information is often inaccurate: it takes time for a company or government agency to get personnel changes to the webmaster, and for that person or department to make the necessary updates.

Harvesting addresses for the purpose of writing *individual* emails is not illegal, and can be as effective in introducing your business or service as a personal postal note with catalog or flyer.

Buying or renting email addresses is another option, and if you're exploring it, refer to the questions in "Direct Response Advertising" to help you assess the value of the list. Among the most important questions are "What is the source of this list?" and "How frequently is it updated?"

Most of all, you want to see an example of the opt-in form used by the list owner. If that's not available, you have no proof that this is a legitimate list. If the contacts were not acquired legally, and you email the addresses with your address, you—not the list provider—can be marked as a spammer. This means that any email with your domain name—sent by eblast *or an individual*—will be blocked.

Even if you're shown examples of the opt-in method, avoid lists lacking individuals' names. If addresses are for "webmaster@," "contactus@," "sales@" or "info@," it's unlikely that your message will be read.

Avoiding Spam Filters

Every direct response advertising campaign requires a good message, and your eblast requires even more: it's important

---

Blocked Email

Even carefully composed email messages can be filtered into "trash" or "spam" boxes. Among the situations that can cause this:

☐ *Your intended recipient's server blocks all messages sent in bulk, even when you write a personal email and copy several people.*

Addressing this problem requires finding out how many recipients the server will permit, usually a trial-and-error process.

☐ *Someone whose legitimate email address uses the same domain name as yours (so probably someone in your organization) has offended a recipient, resulting in all messages using your domain name to be blocked.*

Solving this problem requires contacting your intended recipient, determining whose emails have been offensive, and asking that filters be revised to allow your messages.

☐ *Someone is impersonating you ("spoofing") and sending offensive messages that have resulted in your messages being blocked. This usually happens in one of three ways:*

• *With an address almost identical to yours. If my address were* lindacarlson@ix.net, *a spoofer might use* linda-carlson@ix.net.

• *By sending email from an unused address on your domain name. For example, if the legitimate address is* manager@lindacarlson.com, *a spoofer might use* orders@lindacarlson.com.

• *When your email account has been hacked and someone has gotten access to your address book.*

You ordinarily become aware of a spoofing problem when you begin receiving irate responses from strangers or alerts from friends who suspect the offensive messages were not sent by you.

to avoid words and type that can filter your email into the recipient's "junk" box.

Email consultants point out that a word or two typical of spam will seldom block your message; instead, it's the combination of too many suspect terms, too many images and exaggerated punctuation that will trigger a spam label. Test a message by sending it to yourself using whatever email service providers you use (gmail.com, msn.com, and your domain name email address, for example). If the message is filtered as junk mail, check for:

□ Image to text ratio (too many images or very large images can trigger a filter).

□ Number of font colors (too many is a problem).

□ Unusually large type.

□ Excessive use of capital letters.

□ Repeated exclamation points or question marks.

The Value of Images
When a budget is small, and in-house IT and web design resources are limited, using an email marketing service for

An example of an eblast template.

eblasts (mass emails) can be an economical choice.

A significant advantage of these services are templates that make it easy to insert photos and links. You can include pictures of the employee you're introducing, product you're launching, and location being opened.

You also can use multiple columns, bullet points and headlines—all features not available with the plain text emails that many of us send.

Perhaps best of all, eblast templates allow links to be inserted in the messages, and the eblast vendors provide details on which recipients opened which messages and which clicked through to landing pages.

More Information

"Direct Response Advertising"

American Catalog Mailers Association, catalogmailers.org

Direct Marketing Association, thedirectmarketingsearch.com

Email Sender and Provider Coalition, espcoalition.org.

National Etailing & Mailing Organization of America, nemoa.org.

VT/NH Marketing Group, vtnhmg.org

Endorsements, Testimonials and Review Sites

How important endorsements and testimonials are in selling products or services is hard to quantify. With cynicism rampant today regarding celebrity endorsements, comments by customers are known to help make sales, especially when comments are specific, such as those about size, quality, and customer service.

For books, publishers say they believe that favorable recommendations and comments are helpful in getting books reviewed, accepted by wholesalers and distributors, handsold by booksellers, and actually purchased by readers. Positive comments, either from prepublication reviews or about the author's previous titles, are almost always incorporated into book cover design, and often used as front or back matter, too. Similar praise is used on packaging of many products,

Advertising with Small Budgets for Big Results 97

either with specific names or with such general comments as, "Moms everywhere love it!"

This section covers:

- Celebrity endorsements.

- Fan mail as a source of endorsements.

- Ensuring variety in endorsements.

- How to use endorsements and testimonials.

- Endorsing products yourself.

- Federal regulations.

- Review websites.

Celebrity Endorsements

Having a product recommended by Oprah Winfrey is what many consider the pinnacle of success, and it *will* give sales an immediate spike. If you believe a celebrity endorsement will help your sales, go for those experts, elected officials or entertainers who appeal to your market: the more famous, the better. Your request being declined or ignored is the worst that can happen.

What many have discovered is that some celebrities are glad to write brief testimonials—or sign their names to testimonials you have drafted—as a means of marketing themselves. Because some celebrities do not have unsolicited packages opened, it's wise to inquire first if you're sending a product, or manuscript, to determine whether the celebrity will consider an endorsement.

Fan Mail as a Source of Endorsements

Another source of compliments is the unsolicited fan mail you receive. Some businesspeople recommend immediately responding with a thank you note, and asking if excerpts from the message can be used in promotion.

Endorsers who are willing to have their names used can be asked how they'd like to be credited, which makes it clear that they'll receive some publicity from being quoted. Fans can also be asked if they are willing to repeat their praise on your product's Amazon.com page, if it has one.

Ensuring Variety in the Content of Endorsements

One valuable characteristic of fan mail is that people sometimes write more naturally than they do when asked for an endorsement, so selecting phrases from customer messages can provide sincere-sounding and varied comments.

Too often, when asked for a testimonial comment, a customer will speak in such general terms as, "It's wonderful," or "Solved my problem!" Among the ways you can encourage customers or clients to cite different attributes of your product or service are:

□ Brief surveys with open-ended questions such as, "What I appreciated most was…," "What I learned most from this session was…," or "The most important reason I use this product is…."

If you have customer emails, you can run surveys with such online programs as SurveyMonkey, surveymonkey. com, which is free for short surveys that you expect fewer than 100 people to respond to.

□ Personal interviews by phone, when you or someone from your staff identifies specific factors you want to discuss. For example, "We're working on improving customer service and I'd like to know what we do best in that area, and then how you think we might improve."

The phone call can also be a follow-up to a general compliment, where you probe for details: "I'm delighted to hear that our product solved your problem. What I'd like to know is more about the problem you had."

There's no reason why you can't be direct: "Several people have praised the app for being user-friendly, and I'm wondering if you're also willing

An example of how Lands' End uses customer comments as endorsements.

to comment on how comprehensive and accurate its information is."

How to Use Endorsements

Your own website is an ideal place for a "What our customers say" page.

If you have several products, you can also create a different printed page of testimonials for each product—simply word processed on letterhead. When sending a package or an invoice to a customer who has purchased only one product, include a sheet of praise about the other products appropriate for that customer.

Your Endorsements and Testimonials

Obviously, having your name, and possibly your business name, appear in another business's ads, brochures or website is a reason to consider writing fan mail about the products or vendors you use. Create a standard citation that you request be used whenever you are quoted: "Lee Smith, founder, LeeWay Plastics," or "Linda Carlson, author, *Advertising with Small Budgets for Big Results*."

Regulations: Endorsements and Testimonials

How someone can be quoted in promotional material depends in part on whether the endorser actually uses the product or service, and whether he or she has been paid to compliment it. The Federal Trade Commission's detailed regulations can be found on websites such as "Truth in Advertising and Marketing," ftc.gov/opa/reporter/advertising/endorsement. shtml. Here are brief excerpts:

> *The most important principle is that an endorsement has to represent the accurate experience and opinion of the endorser:*
>
> □ *You can't talk about your experience with a product if you haven't tried it.*
>
> □ *If you were paid to try a product and you thought it was terrible, you can't say it's terrific.*
>
> □ *You can't make claims about a product that would require proof you don't have. For example, you can't say a product*

will cure a particular disease if there isn't scientific evidence to prove that's true.

[I]f your ad (...[or] your website) says or implies that the endorser uses the product in question, you can run the ad only as long as you have good reason to believe the endorser still uses the product. If you're using endorsements that are a few years old, it's your obligation to make sure the claims still are accurate. If your product has changed, it's best to get new endorsements.

Review Sites

Yelp, CityGrid and GoodReads are examples of websites that collect and disseminate reviews without selling or lending anything as do Amazon.com, other online retailers and public libraries. Angie's List is a web-based subscription service, with reviews available to those who pay.

Yelp, https://biz.yelp.com/

This San Francisco-based company publicizes reviews in several, but not all, parts of the U.S. It also posts reviews of restaurants, services and retailers in several foreign cities. Businesses can create profiles for free. Yelp then encourages their customers to write reviews, and it recommends that businesses both respond to the reviews and offer discounts (called Deals) via Yelp.

Reviews appear for businesses that have profiles, and a quick check showed some inaccuracies: businesses that long ago closed and incomprehensible price ranges (my neighborhood hair salon's rates are not "$$$").

It's important to realize that reviews are only accepted from people who have opted-in to receive email from other Yelp users, businesses, and Yelp itself. Account holders can opt-out of some of these emails.

If you offer discounts and gift certificates on Yelp, it will collect payment from the purchaser, and retain 30 percent of the revenue for Deals and 10 percent for gift certificates. You can limit the number of Deals available.

Yelp also offers advertising. Its web site says, "Yelp Ads are placed on search result pages, so that users searching in your area will see your business above Yelp's natural search results. Ads are also placed on the business pages of nearby businesses in your category. Advertising on Yelp will remove competitor ads from your Yelp business page." Yelp business advertising packages are priced between $300 and $1,000 per month.

CityGrid, citygrid.com

"Online provider of local entertainment and business listings" is how this West Hollywood firm is described. Its listings are for major metropolitan areas. They appear to be compiled from telephone and other directories. Besides businesses that have created profiles, the listings include those who have not, and if you click on one of those, you'll see an invitation for the proprietor: "Claim your Citysearch profile for free!"

Like Yelp, CityGrid requires that reviewers opt-in to receive e-mail from the company.

CityGrid offers advertising on search engines such as Ask and SuperPages starting at $99 per month. It does not offer advertising on the most popular search sites such as Google and WhitePages.com.

Goodreads, goodreads.com

Now owned by Amazon, Goodreads is a book review site. As it describes itself:

- *See which books your friends are reading.*
- *Track the books you're reading, have read, and want to read.*
- *Check out your personalized book recommendations. Our recommendation engine analyzes 20 billion data points to give suggestions tailored to your literary tastes.*
- *Find out if a book is a good fit for you from our community's reviews.*

Signing up requires providing your e-mail address or, like the other sites, registering with your Facebook information.You can opt-out of having Goodreads post to your Facebook page.

And, yes, Goodreads offers promotional opportunities. For authors, it offers several options. One has no fees, but does require that you give away printed books. For more information on either advertising or the author program, check the bottom of the home page.

Angie's List, angieslist.com
All it takes to be rated on Angie's List is one subscriber's review of your business. However, says the site, "companies can also create a free account and appear without a rating on the List. Once your company is registered, you may log in at any time to review and update your company's profile, check your ratings, and read and respond to new reviews."

For More Information
"Word-of-Mouth" in "The Myth of Free Advertising"
"Advertorials," especially "Sponsored Content"

Ferry System Advertising
Passenger and car ferries operate in several states, some run by state government, others by counties, community associations or private companies. Advertising opportunities on large systems are similar to those offered with outdoor and transit advertising. Examples, in the general order of the advertising opportunities offered, from most to least, are in the states of:

- Washington
- Alaska
- Massachusetts
- New York/New Jersey
- California
- Wisconsin

Washington
Washington State Ferries is the U.S.'s largest ferry system, serving eight counties and sailing in international waters to Vancouver Island, British Columbia, Canada. Twenty-eight vessels serve 19 terminals. All routes except one carry both vehicles and passengers.

Ferry Media, ferrymedia.com, offers advertising on vessels and at terminals—billboard-size posters on terminal walls, small posters on terminal and vessel walls, multi-sign images on ferry steps, and digital ads played in a loop. It also sells ads for the ferry schedule web pages.

Brochure racks, which accommodate brochures folded to letter size and magazine-style tourist and sales publications, as well as small digital displays, are handled by Certified Folder Display Service, Inc., certifiedfolder.com.

Washington's Skagit County Public Works division, which operates the tiny Guemes Island ferry, has no space to install multiple-brochure racks, so it allows businesses to place their own small plastic or cardboard brochure racks on the ferry's window sills at no charge.

In the south end of Puget Sound, the Pierce County Airport and Ferry Administrator handles ads for the small ferries that serve Anderson and Ketron Islands. Contact: Deb Wallace, dwalla1@co.pierce.wa.us.

Alaska

The Alaska Marine Highway System, which operates from Bellingham, Wash., to Alaska's Aleutian Islands, offers brochure racks on its vessels through Anchorage Brochure Distribution, customerservice@anchoragebrochure.com.

The same firm will install digital information systems for another advertising option. Each of the system's 33 ports has a different terminal configuration, so only some provide brochure racks.

At this time, space is free, and advertisers are responsible for keeping racks supplied. Terminal managers check brochures to ensure content is appropriate.

Massachusetts

The Steamship Authority runs the ferries that serve Martha's Vineyard and Nantucket islands from Cape Cod, Mass. It claims more than 2.6 million passengers a year: year-around and summer residents, seasonal visitors and day trippers. Advertising is sold for vessels, at terminals, in brochure racks and on the authority's website, steamshipauthority.com. The rate card is at steamshipauthority.com/ssa/advertising.pdf.

New York/New Jersey

NY Waterway is a privately-owned New Jersey-based passenger ferry system with 33 vessels that serve 21 routes between New Jersey and Manhattan; Brooklyn, Queens and Manhattan; Rockland and Westchester counties; and Orange and Dutchess counties. It offers both static and digital advertising; for information, see nywaterway.com/AboutAd vertisingwithNYWaterway.aspx.

In New York, the Bridgeport & Port Jefferson Steamboat Co. offers vessel advertising through Prestige Media, richconti@prestigemedia-inc.com. Advertising in terminals is handled by Carol Koutrakos of the ferry management staff, Port Jefferson, NY, 631-473-0126.

California

Much of the California ferry traffic is tourists. Most service is via passenger ferry. San Francisco's Golden Gate Transit, which has significant commuter traffic, offers ferry terminal, ferry cabin and ferry schedule advertising. Contacts are CBS Outdoor, www.cbsoutdoor.com/media/transit, for terminal ads; TOPDOG Media, topdogmediaoutdoor.com, for ferry cabins; and the transit authority itself for schedule ads, Alfonso Beasley, Golden Gate Transit, abeasley@goldengate. org.

Another Bay Area company, Blue & Gold, also offers both commuter and tourist services. Information: blueandgoldfleet.com.

Flagship Cruises & Events, which serves San Diego, is introducing advertising on its boats, which carry an estimated 500,000 passengers annually on 15-minute trips. Brochure rack space will also be available. For details: 855-955-9558.

Wisconsin

Wisconsin's Washington Island Ferry Line, wisferry.com, accepts ads only from locals on the 35-mile square island. Hoyt Purinton, hoyt@wisferry.com, is the contact for website ads, brochure racks and the Visitors Center.

A Wisconsin ferry that connects two National Scenic Byways and crosses the Mississippi, the Pride of Cassville, accepts ads from a greater variety of businesses. For information: cassville.org/ferry.html.

The Beaver Island Boat Co., a private Wisconsin service, also sells ads on its boat. For information: Cathy Dewey, cdewey@bibco.com.

Free Shipping

Free shipping is one of the most powerful sales tools, and today it's one of the most important to advertise. In some tests, customers offered their choice of a discount or free shipping opted for free shipping. Given the number of online retailers who ship purchases with no additional charge, you can be more competitive if you offer free shipping on purchases, and possibly even on returns. If you are unable to offer free shipping on all purchases, consider it on any purchase in excess of a certain dollar amount, on new or slow-selling merchandise, or during such important sales periods as back-to-school and holiday.

Game Ads

Computer and online games offer two opportunities for advertising:

☐ In-game advertising (IGA), when a product or service is shown, or must be used, in a game.

☐ Advergaming, when a game is made to promote a product.

Besides these two, this section covers:

☐ Placement of products in games.

☐ Creating games.

☐ Accepting product placement for your games.

In-game Advertising

In-game advertising may be a $1 billion business by the end of 2014, the Entertainment Software Association reports.

It describes the original form of in-game advertising, static ads, as virtual billboards or in-game product placements which cannot be altered once placed by an artist or programmer. This is similar to product placement in movies and television. Examples: building signs, billboards or a character eating a branded snack food.

The newer option, dynamic advertising, allows ad sponsors to interact with game players. Says the ESA:

"Dynamic advertising also allows ad companies to track and receive information from a player's console...Advertisers can record data—such as time spent looking at the advertisements, the most-viewed advertisements and viewing angles...[The] new suite of advertising tools called NUads [launched by Microsoft] in 2011...allow gamers to use voice and motion commands to access additional information about the product or service advertised, post messages about an advertisement on Twitter, and [see] maps of related retail locations nearby."

Advergaming

The product promotion in advergames can be as specific as simulated test drives of a new car model. They can be puzzles, races, or Wii games that develop awareness of the sponsors' products (e.g., movies, beverages or beauty products). Or they can be games, coloring sheets and e-cards that say little about the product or service, but develop awareness of the company name and URL when the activities are shared.

Advergames are typically sponsored by a company or nonprofit, just as promotional videos are. If your budget is very small, you may be able to get a short game created by a student as a project or on an internship. See below for places to network with academic and technical programs and with start-ups, which might produce a game on a contract basis.

Another option, suggested by the Tampa nonprofit Big Cat Rescue: buy commercial usage rights to raw game resource and programing files that can be personalized for your organization.

Placing Your Product in a Game

If you're attempting to place your product in a well-known game, one place to start is with the Entertainment Resources & Marketing Association, erma.org, the professional group for placement specialists and studio representatives.

With a limited budget, consider networking with start-up gaming companies: you may find them in professional associations, gaming groups, crowdsourcing promotions, or through the game development and digital art programs at colleges, universities and technical schools. An online search will turn up such resources as:

□ International Game Developers Association, igda.org, with more than three dozen chapters across North America

□ Ohio Game Developer Association, ohiogamedev.com, a separate organization

□ Casual Games Association, casualgamesassociation.org

□ Serious Games Association, seriousgamesassociation.com

Creating Your Own Games

For organizations without in-house game creators, assistance in developing games may come from members of the associations listed above, as well as schools such as the DigiPen Institute of Technology. Big Cat Rescue, bigcatrescue.org, also recommends building simple games on your own site with Flash, Adobe software used to create what the manufacturer calls "immersive experiences, games, and interactive content."

At Big Cat Rescue, the goal has been to offer child-oriented games—math, science, memory matches—that can be co-branded for use on other sites as well as on the nonprofit's own site. Like many, it encourages teachers to use its games and print-ready materials in the classroom.

Accepting Product Placements

If you are creating or selling games, accepting product placements can be a significant source of revenue.

One estimate is that it will be a $85 billion market in 2014, although the largest game publishers obviously will generate most of that income. As a start-up game developer, consider offering placement to companies on a trade-out basis: for example, to the media in which you'd like advertising.

Gas Pump Advertising

Watched a video while pumping gas? Listened to a commercial? You aren't alone! In more than 150 cities across the U.S., self-service pumps have advertising signs or commercials. As one broker of these ads points out, "Drivers are standing around for an average of five to 10 minutes pumping gas, during which they can view ads, such as those on top of the pump." Visual options at service stations include:

☐ Gas pump topper signs, popular because they reach drivers at eye level, $75–$250 per ad per four-week period.

☐ Digital gas pump television advertising (gas pump LCD displays), $20–30 per 15-second spot per 1,000 impressions (purchases), $30–40 per 30 second spot per 1,000 impressions (transactions).

☐ Nozzle advertising, $45–95 per ad per four-week period.

☐ Ice box/ice chest advertising, $600–$1,200 per ad per four-week period.

These estimates are exclusive of production. There are also minimum purchase requirements, usually 10 and as many as 50 stations.

Some gas station ad vendors also offer audio ("gas station radio") and business card dispensers as part of the displays.

More Information

Do an online search for "gas station advertising" or "gas station radio."

Giveaways and Samples

Why give away anything? Some reasons are obvious: to

Advertising with Small Budgets for Big Results

109

get prospects into your storefront, whether it's physical or virtual. To get people to try new products or services. To create awareness of a business or organization's name or brand.

Two other possibilities: to create goodwill, and to get prospects all the way through your store, or to visit several pages of your website.

This section covers:

□ Examples of giveaways and samples.

□ Publicizing the giveaway.

□ Self-liquidating premiums.

For information on inexpensive merchandise imprinted with a company or product name, see "Advertising Novelties."

Getting Customers through the Store

You probably know why milk is often shelved at the back of a supermarket: so customers have to walk past all sorts of enticing displays to get to this frequently-purchased item. The hardware store in Seattle's Magnolia neighborhood does something similar with its giveaway — the free popcorn is near the back, by the cage of love birds that also fascinate kids. Another way to build walk-in traffic: give away a

I love bookstores. *I love them.* So to support fine bookstores everywhere, I'm giving away an exclusive short story to anyone who boldly ventures into their local bookery and pre orders *Songs of Willow Frost* (or pre orders online from an honest-to-goodness brick-and-mortar bookstore).

Just text me a pic of your receipt or order confirmation, or heck—just send me a photo of you smiling with your friendly neighborhood bookseller and I will be delighted to email you a copy of *Middle, Lost, and Found,* a 7,000-word tale featuring Mrs. Beatty from *Hotel on the Corner of You Know What.* (And if you include a mailing address I'll also send along a signed bookplate).

Author Jamie Ford's giveaway offer.

service, like offering a collection point for used printer cartridges, incandescent light bulbs, packing pellets or, as an occasional event, outdated electronics.

Websites with right columns headed "You may also be interested in..." serve a similar function, especially if some featured pages offer free information or downloadables. (Another way to keep people reading web pages carefully: offer a discount or gift certificate for the typographical errors that are reported. The bonus for you: the proofreading.)

Samples

Physical samples are often distributed in retail outlets, especially supermarket, specialty and warehouse club stores. In small storefronts, the merchandise company owner may offer the samples; in large retailers, samples are usually offered by employees of an affiliated sampling agency or by those hired through temporary agencies that specialize in sampling. For example, Warehouse Demo Services is the independent contractor that has the exclusive on product demonstrations for Costco along the Pacific Coast.

Cosmetics and fragrance samples are offered by demon-

Creating Goodwill

You can create goodwill for your operation on an ad hoc basis with a variation on sampling: by giving selected customers free merchandise.

Depending on your business, it may be appropriate to give employees a small budget for comping. In my neighborhood, the sale of a much-beloved independent grocery set off a jockeying for customers among the two supermarket chains with nearby stores.

After the cashier at one store and I had a friendly discussion regarding combining Nutella and peppermint ice cream, he insisted on comping me a regular-size jar of the store-brand hazelnut spread.

Will I ever buy that product? I'm not sure. But did the free jar and the cashier's interest in me reinforce my loyalty? Many times over!

Advertising with Small Budgets for Big Results

111

> **THIS STICKER IS NOT A LAWYER AND CANNOT PROVIDE YOU WITH LEGAL ADVICE**
>
> **HEMPFEST 2013!** **We thought you might be hungry.**
> We also thought now might be a good time for a refresher on the do's and don'ts of I-502.
>
> DON'TS Don't drive while high. Don't give, sell, or shotgun weed to people under 21. Don't use pot in public. You could be cited but we'd rather give you a warning. DO'S Do listen to Dark Side of the Moon at a reasonable volume. Do enjoy Hempfest.
>
> **Remember:** respect your fellow voters and familiarize yourself with the rules of I-502 at seattle.gov/police/marijwhatnow ♥, SPD
>
> **WARNING: THE CONTENTS OF THIS PACKAGE ARE AS DELICIOUS AS THEY APPEAR**

Months after Hempfest, the Seattle Police Department blog still carried a copy of the label and this post: **How to Be All That And a Bag of Chips In Four Easy Steps,** *written by Jonah Spangenthal-Lee on August 17, 2013: "Didn't make it to Hempfest but still want to own a piece of snack history? Here's how you can be all that and a bag of chips in just four easy steps. Step one — Purchase your bagged snack of choice—Doritos, pork rinds, anything but Bugles. Step two — Print out our sticker (or just find some tape). Step three — ??????????????????? Step four — Rock it."*

strators in storefronts, sometimes by doing partial applications of a cosmetic, or by spritzing a prospect with cologne. Fragrance is often applied to promotional pieces bound in or blown in to magazines or department store catalogs or newspaper inserts. Liquid cosmetics and skin-care products such as foundation or moisturizer can be distributed in a foil or plastic-lined packet on the same kind of piece.

In publishing, it's not unusual for paperback editions of novels to conclude with a sample chapter from a similar book, usually by the same author. (See page 109 for a giveaway on Jamie Ford's blog; it promoted his new title as well as his first book, and supported independent [non-chain] bookstores.)

Trial size packages of food and household cleaning products and new magazines are sometimes delivered to homes, polybagged and hung from door handles; polybagged with newspapers; or sent through postal mail.

How much attention your giveaway attracts depends on such factors as:

☐ Value of the sample or giveaway.

☐ Innovativeness of your distribution method.

☐ Advance publicity.

"Value" may be perceived dollar value, but it can also be how useful or attractive the item or service is at the time: bottled water or five-minute foot massages at a rest stop on a walk-a-thon, for example.

The more distinctive and creative your distribution method, the more likely yours will be the only sample seen at that time and in that place. As an extreme example, consider what Seattle police officers did during the 2013 Hempfest: they handed out 1,000 one-ounce bags of Doritos attached to informational labels about Washington's new legal pot law. The snack food bags were labeled with a link to the police department's online "Marijwhatnow" FAQ. The goal: to get current and potential pot-users to visit the marijuana info website.

To distribute physical samples of your products or coupons valid for free or discounted services, consider:

☐ Local restaurants to distribute your sample with the check.

☐ Restaurant, grocery and other delivery services to include your sample.

☐ Bed-and-breakfasts to offer your sample at check-in.

☐ Housecleaners, gardeners, pool cleaning services and similar small businesses that serve residences to distribute samples, especially if workers would accompany samples with notes of endorsement, printed by you and signed by the service person.

To obtain endorsements, provide potential endorsers with the product so that they can speak knowledgeably about it and be truthful in their endorsements.

What sample distribution costs may depend on whether your product replaces something the partner business would otherwise have to buy.

Advertising with Small Budgets for Big Results 113

Another possibility: trade sample or flyer distribution with a complementary business, or offer to publicize that business. For example, if gardeners hand out your samples, put their business cards on your cashier's desk or distribute them in the envelopes with your monthly statements.

There's also in-kind payment: a start-up magazine can provide free ads for those who distribute samples of the magazine. The soap vendor can run small website ads for the bed-and-breakfasts using its products with links to the lodgings' websites.

Self-liquidating Premiums

Often offered as an introduction to a product or a thank-you for a purchase, a self-liquidating premium can be a means of gathering email addresses if it's promoted online. Often all or most of the cost is covered with the shipping and handling fee paid by the customer.

When estimating the fee necessary to pay for the sample or premium, it's important to include the cost to you of the item, the product package, label, shipping container, shipping label and the actual shipping charge. Ideally, the fee would also pay for at least part of the labor involved.

Publicizing Your Giveaway

Increase the awareness of your product or service by pub-

This was probably designed to create a sense of loyalty as well as generate a purchase. Because almost everything on the company website was priced significantly higher than $10, the amount paid, even with a $10 discount, could cover the retailer's cost for the merchandise. There was no discount on shipping.

> Our gift to you! To thank you for being a loyal Eddie Bauer Shopper, we're giving you a $10 Eddie Bauer Certificate. Outfit all your adventures this season with Eddie Bauer.
>
> Apply your certificate toward your next purchase through our catalogs, online at eddiebauer.com or at any of our U.S. stores, including Outlet locations.
>
> **Hurry – this Certificate expires October 14, 2013. Valid for one time use only.**
>
> Thanks for being a loyal Friend. Stay in touch with us at eddiebauerfriends.com.

licizing the giveaway, especially if you represent a local business, or the local office of a larger operation and you are offering samples or giveaways in a small geographic area—the home-owned gourmet grocery, the neighborhood farmers' market, the local park's summer concert series.

That Doritos giveaway by police, for example? It was publicized in advance, and the buzz continued after the Hempfest when unopened bags were offered on online auction sites for prices as high as $60 and television stations around the region broadcast video of police officers distributing Doritos.

Use Twitter, the company or product's Facebook page, and other social media sites—perhaps even Classmates. com—to make your giveaway visible to even those who do not pick up a sample. For example: "Taste my new almond coffee ice cream at the Magnolia farmers' market this Saturday" or "Come say hello and get a neck rub when I do massages on Monday as a fund-raiser for..." Posters, email, announcements at the neighborhood chamber of commerce and a media release can also generate interest in the giveaway.

More Information
"Blogs"
"Direct Response Advertising"
"Inserts"
"Naming/Sponsorships/Donations"
"Newspapers"
"Swag/Goodie Bags"

Inserts
The flyer in your natural gas bill, the tabloid full of coupons stuffed into the Sunday paper, the mini-catalogs in the package with your order from an online store: all are inserts. This section covers:

☐ Package and catalog inserts.

☐ Insert production.

☐ Alternatives.

When budgets are limited and a campaign has a geographic target, consider single sheets inserted in a weekly or specialty newspaper, especially if you can send the insert only to the zones, routes or ZIP codes in which you do business. This is especially common with newspaper inserts, which are covered in "Newspapers."

Package stuffers, or bouncebacks, can be cost-effective because there's no cost for list or postage. If the packages you ship to customers include a discount coupon or sale catalog, you may prompt a second purchase. If you're doing your own shipping, it's easy to control how many inserts are used.

Package and Catalog Inserts

Promotional material for your business can also be inserted in packages shipped by catalog and online merchants. Sometimes called "package insert programs," this advertising allows you to reach customers you consider good prospects. Some inserts are loose in the box, others are gathered in an envelope. In most cases, yours will not be the only stuffer.

In 2013, costs for package inserts were typically about $60 per thousand inserts. Barnes & Noble, Blair, Day-Timer and Norm Thompson are examples of the retailers who accepted inserts at that price point.

Another option: inserts in mail-order catalogs. To reduce their mailing costs, some catalog companies sell non-competing businesses inserts in their catalogs. The advantages for you: a well-defined demographic with a mailing addressed by name, and savings on postage and handling. In many cases, you can specify that your insert only go to those who have previously purchased from the cataloger, which means the response to your offer will almost certainly be better.

To assess the effectiveness of any inserts, it's important to track how many additional sales result from them. This can be done with different codes for each kind of insert: e.g., P101 for the first insert, P102 for the second, or if by medium, ST1 for the first insert in the *Seattle Times*, and MN1214 for the one in a December 2014 issue of the *Magnolia News*.

Producing Inserts

Inserts can be as simple as photocopies or as elaborate as extra copies of a full-color catalog. For package and catalog inserts, you may be required to have your piece produced by the company doing your insertion. The most obvious disadvantage of this policy is that you're unlikely to see the quality of the finished piece in advance of the mailing.

To update information on a printed piece, imprint it with your copier or at a quick-print shop. For a limited number, apply adhesive labels with the revised information: "Sale Extended to July 30," or "Now 50% Off!"

Economical Alternatives

Companies offering package or catalog inserts, or brokers handling such placements, may offer limited flexibility in geographic targeting, in the length of an insertion contract, or in the cost of the insert. Consider offering a barter arrangement to reduce your cash costs, or work with local merchants.

More Information

"Advertorials," for inserting special sections in newspapers and magazines
"Coupons," for inserts in statements
"Newspapers"

In-store Advertising/Point-of-purchase

In-store and point-of-purchase promotions such as temporary displays at a store entrance, at the ends of aisles (end caps), and at the cash register, are designed to prompt impulse purchases and upsales—and they do. Especially when combined with a special price, an end cap display can at least double sales of such modestly priced merchandise as toiletries. At libraries, displays are responsible for more than 20 percent of patrons' choices.*

With consumer goods and media, many countertop and free-standing displays are provided by the manufacturer

*Library Journal *group publisher Ian Singer, speaking at the 2013 Publishing Business conference, quoted in* Shelf Awareness *Oct. 1, 2013.*

Advertising with Small Budgets for Big Results

Publisher's catalog describing countertop display.

or publisher with a minimum product order, usually enough to fill the display when it's erected. Vendors' sales reps and catalogs explain what purchase is necessary for a free display.

There's nothing complicated about creating in-store displays. They can be as simple as letter-size acrylic easels, with or without a brochure pocket, with a mini-poster inserted. They can be whiteboards with a hand-written discount offer for the current day, or a reminder to return later for a special ("Senior Citizen Day," "Daffodil Special," "County Fair Discount Tickets"). Print your own sign as a header for an end cap or a tabletop display.

If you serve food, turn tabletops into advertising media with:

- Table tents created with acrylic stands or by scoring and folding letter-size cover stock that has been printed in-house.

- Advertising messages inserted in napkin dispensers.

- Place mats, coasters and vinyl table clings.

Other DIY options:

- Floor graphics.

- Photocopied coupons, either hung by a product display or handed out with receipts, to encourage a return to the store.

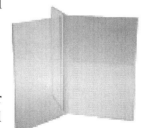

Promotional messages can be inserted into each of the acrylic wings.

☐ Shelf talkers, short reviews or testimonial comments posted on the shelf by the applicable product.

☐ Tearaway pads with recipes, how-to's or coupons by product displays.

Depending on budget, consider shopping cart ads, cash register coupons, in-store demonstrations and sampling.

Gobos
A form of in-store or event image advertising that will require expertise to create in-house is the gobo, a lighting display that uses a physical template in front of a lighting source. This template determines the shape of the light, so it's popular for logos and simple shapes related to a product.

Cardboard self-easel.

Gobo projectors for interior use start at less than $300 and one-color custom templates at less than $100. Projectors appropriate for outdoor or bright environments can cost significantly more, perhaps as much as $4,000.

More Information
"Cooperative Advertising"
"Coupons"
"Direct Response"
"Elevators and Lobbies"
"Giveaways and Samples"
"Signage"

Invoices
Invoices, packing slips, statements and statement envelopes all have advertising potential—at almost no extra cost.

Invoice and statement software is often formatted for a message at the page bottom, a message which can announce new products or special pricing.

Because envelopes are usually printed in large quantities, use a promotional message that won't become outdated

("Ask about our personal shopper services" or "Gift registries for every event in your life").

If you have regular seasonal promotions, have different envelope messages and change envelopes on a schedule. Other options: imprint the envelopes using your office printer or copier (assuming it doesn't skew artwork or jam); add a promotional message with a rubber stamp; apply labels made with your printer, or add a message to your postage meter imprint.

Loyalty Programs

Anything that keeps customers returning to your storefront or website can be described as a loyalty program:

- A "buy 12, get one free" card that's stamped or initialed with every purchase.

- Shoppers' cards that make customers eligible for special pricing (and usually are coded so that information regarding their purchases goes into your database).

- Discounts on the next purchase when packaging or the receipt from a previous purchase is returned

Some of these are easy to implement. In western Washington, Hayton Farms staff offers farmers' market customers $1 off on their next purchase if they return the cartons in which half flats of berries are sold.

The most complex loyalty program is probably the co-branded or affinity credit card. These are issued in conjunction with bank credit card programs. Visa, with which many banks work, suggests such cards for businesses with customer bases of 50,000 or more. Its definitions:

- A co-branded card is typically issued in conjunction with a corporation and offers value to the consumer.

- An affinity card is issued in conjunction with a nonprofit organization, and benefits that organization.

For details regarding co-branded cards, see Visa and MasterCard websites.

Magazine Advertising

Advertising in magazines and trade journals has several advantages: the publications are usually kept longer than newspapers, and each copy may have several readers.

Specialized magazines can target certain audiences better than newspapers and general-interest magazines. Paper quality is almost always better than in newspapers, so photographs look better. Some periodicals have indexes of advertisers in their back pages, to make it easier for someone to find your ad a second time, and some offer reader response (bingo card) devices (see page 76 for an example).

Especially with trade journals, the editorial theme of an issue may reinforce the message of advertisers: if the main articles are on accounting software for a particular industry, ads will be solicited from accounting software firms and it's possible that some advertisers will be quoted in articles.

This section discusses:

☐ Lead time.

☐ Controlled vs. paid circulation.

☐ Design and production costs.

☐ Space costs.

☐ SIPs and custom publishing.

☐ Reader demographics.

☐ Finding appropriate publications.

Lead Time

Few magazines offer the opportunity to do spur-of-the-moment advertising or to make changes near the publication date.

It's not unusual for advertising deadlines to be three or six months in advance of the publication date, which is almost always in advance of the issue "date." (That is, the May issue may appear the first week of April.) Campaigns must be planned carefully, using magazine ads for those promotions that can be scheduled in advance. Or use magazines for image advertising: promoting products or services in general or asking for support of an annual event or fund drive.

Some specifics about timing: ads for Christmas events, gift and decorating items or specialty foods for celebrations often are drafted early in the calendar year, produced during the summer and printed in magazines that land on newsstands in late October or early November. In a recent year, for an ad in a regional edition of the December issue of *Sunset*, all materials were due Sept. 24 and the magazine was on sale Nov. 16.

Free Copies/Controlled Circulation

Trade journals and business publications — *Microscopy Today, Motor Age, Foundry Trade Journal, Attorney at Law, Seattle Business* — are often mailed free to "qualified" members of a periodical's target industry or profession.

A sample issue is sent free and then recipients are asked to "qualify" by answering a few questions about their office or shop. The answers help the periodical's advertising sales staff prepare its rate card, which usually describes the "subscriber" base in terms of education, years in business, size of business and business specialties.

Some controlled-circulation publications are routed in offices; others are discarded without being read. That's what makes estimating the readership of these complimentary publications difficult.

Most publications, whether controlled or paid circulation, are sent free to some people, or they are sold at such low rates (e.g., $5 for a 10-issue subscription) that recipients may not perceive them to be of high value.

Magazines report paid and free circulation, often in the year's final issue.

In other situations, free copies go to medical office waiting rooms and similar locations where they are seen by many people. The number of free copies is noted in an annual statement printed in the publication.

Cost of Design and Production

Small ads can be simple, with a few lines of black and white type, an illustration, logo or QR code. Some publications will create these for advertisers. Larger ads, especially those with color photography or illustrations, will be more expensive to produce.

To ensure the best use of your advertising dollars, ads should always be created by a talented professional with expertise in magazine advertising, someone who understands the publication's audience and its specifications and can submit an ad that will reproduce well.

Magazine ads often require photographs, which should be taken by a commercial photographer with experience shooting for the quality of magazine that you're advertising in. Stock photos, those acquired from a service that licenses photos, can be used, but unless you pay for exclusive use for a lengthy period, you risk having the same photo appear elsewhere—perhaps in another ad.

If you're having photos taken, you'll need model releases from everyone pictured, even if they are your employees, as well as a release from each photographer. To use a portrait of yourself or another individual who was photographed in a studio or even by an amateur, a photographer's release will document that you have the right to publish the image. See Appendix D for a sample.

How magazine ads are to be prepared and submitted is specified in the publication's media kit, which today is often a website. Look for "rate card" or "production specs." Besides specifying ad dimensions, directions may be as specific as:

On bleed ads keep live matter 5/16 inch from trim. Line Screen: 133-line screen. Dot size 5 percent to 95 percent. Density: Overall printing density of all colors cannot exceed 300 percent. PDF files: Ads should be submitted as press-ready

PDF files (PDF-X-1a preferred). Embed all fonts; convert all photos and spot colors to CMYK.

For definitions, see the Glossary.

Cost of Advertising Space

Like newspapers, many periodicals offer both display and classified ads. Display ads are typically available on the inside front cover, inside back cover, back cover and on entire pages within the publication as well as in smaller ads.

Magazine ads are almost always sold in these predetermined modules rather than by the column inch; however, "column inch," if that term is used, means a space that is one inch deep and the width of the column. If the column is 1¾ inches in width, a one-inch ad will be an inch high and 1¾ inches wide.

Some publications also offer "business card" cards which are all the same size and format, with directory-type information rather than product-specific sales pitches.

Besides size and location, another variable in print magazine pricing is color. Ads printed in color will cost more, and some ad sizes or placements (such as the inside front cover) may only be available at the color rate.

The fourth variable: the number of insertions (ads) you commit to. The more insertions, the lower the cost of each ad's space. (An example is on page 127.)

One means of reducing print advertising cost is to participate in group ads. Your chamber of commerce, visitors' bureau or a trade group may purchase space for a large ad, and then divide the cost among every member being listed. Fine Fabric Stores, finefabricstores.com, as an example, is a collective that lists its 29 members in the ads that appear in publications such as *Threads*.

Some publications run ads from similar advertisers together at a special rate: for example, business-card type ads under a heading like "Antiques" or "Women's Consignment."

Classified ads may have colored borders and icons, but otherwise are made of type that runs paragraph-style. The

Excerpt from magazine rate card.

REQUIRED MATERIAL Digital files only - PDF X1A or HIGH-RES PDF (image resolution 300 dpi preferred), accompanied by two SWOP color proofs pulled from the supplied file.

PREFERRED PDF/X-1a DELIVERY METHOD Martha Stewart Omnimedia Ad Portal: adportal Please register an account, wait for an email confirmation, then log on and upload.

LINE SCREEN 150-line screen is preferred, 133-line screen is acceptable. Maximum combin not to exceed 300%. No more than one solid should be used. All material must be prepared to (Specifications for Web Offset Publications) standards. (For more information, visit www.swop.o

PROOFS All final material must be submitted with digital proofs (for color guidance on press) t pulled from the supplied file. All proofs must contain SWOP color bars. We require two digital approvals preferred) pulled on commercial-grade stock. Laser printouts will not be accepted as color. Color on press cannot be guaranteed without a SWOP proof supplied by the advertiser.

UNIT SIZES AVAILABLE

sizes	width		depth	trim	live area	
Page nonbleed	7 3/4"	x	10"			
Page bleed	9 1/4"	x	11 1/8"	9" x 10 7/8"	8 1/4" x 10 1/8"	Live matte 3/8" from t
Spread	16 3/4"	x	10"			
Spread bleed	18 1/4"	x	11 1/8"	18" x 10 7/8"	17 1/2" x 10 1/8"	
2/3 page	5 1/8"	x	10"			1/3 page s
2/3 page bleed	5 3/8"	x	11 1/8"			digest pag
1/2 page horizontal	7 3/4"	x	5"			available i
1/2 page horiz. bleed	9 1/4"	x	5 3/8"	9" x 5 1/4"	8 1/4" x 4 5/16"	
1/3 page vertical	2 3/8"	x	10"			PMS color
1/3 page vert. bleed	3 1/8"	x	11 1/8"	2 7/8" x 10 7/8"	2 1/4" x 10 1/8"	charged a
1/3 page square	5 1/8"	x	4 15/16"			premium

INSERT CARDS / SUPPLIED INSERTS Accepted on a limited basis, specifications and on request. For additional information, please contact Milena Emery.

SHIPPING INSTRUCTIONS All contracts, insertion orders, and printing materials to:

When Adobe Acrobat is used to create PDFs, several options for resolution are available. These specs indicate the required resolution for both the PDF and the images included in it.

Line screen is another measure of resolution. Newspapers ordinarily use 65- or 85-line screens, much coarser than what magazines require.

Laser prints do not accurately represent ink colors as they will be produced on an offset press.

Live area is that part of the page that will show, that will not be trimmed off or hidden in the binding. Live matter refers to everything you want seen.

PMS, Pantone Matching System, refers to colors that must be matched to swatches. Compare to CMYK in Glossary.

number of words typically determines the price. To have responses to the ad sent to the periodical and forwarded to you will cost more.

Print magazines that are available in electronic formats will show prices for the e-published formats on rate cards. Some offer combination pricing; others only offer larger ads the option of being included in digital versions.

To advertise in digital-only periodicals, see "Blogs" and "Websites."

Some publications have special pages, sections or issues for which space is sold by the advertising staff. In *Seattle Met* and similar "who's who" magazines, sections such as "Met Pages" feature photos of local celebrities and the executives of businesses and nonprofits at social events. These can also be described as "advertorial" or "sponsored content;" see "Advertorial" for more information.

Special Interest Publications

Consumer magazine publishers such as Meredith (which owns *Better Homes and Gardens* among many others) and Time (which owns *Sunset* and *Southern Living* as well as the flagship *Time* and *Sports Illustrated*) issue occasional volumes called Special Interest Publications, or SIPs. Examples include *Diabetic Living, Holiday Crafts, Quilt Sampler, Best of Flea Market Style, Do It Yourself Paint Projects*, and *Kitchen + Bath Ideas,* all from Meredith; and *Best Recipes, Summer Travel* and *Backyard Secrets,* all from the Time division that operates *Sunset.*

SIPs allow advertisers to better target prospective customers, and because they are infrequently published (often annually), these issues are sometimes kept longer. They are usually sold on newsstands rather than by subscription, so circulation will be lower, although publishers often pay for premium placement by supermarket and drugstore cash registers to create awareness and generate impulse sales.

Custom Publishing

The monthly you receive from your insurance company, the quarterly from a local hospital, the supermarket magazine: these are often produced by national companies for distribution by sponsors like the insurance company or supermarket.

The publications are sometimes created by major magazine publishers through such "custom publishing" divisions as Time Inc. Content Solutions, Hearst Integrated Media, and Meredith Xcelerated Marketing. Other such publications are written and designed by companies that do only "branded content."

If your budget permits custom publishing, research the cost-effectiveness of such a publication by contacting members of the organization for branded content and content marketing in North America, the Custom Content Council, customcontentcouncil.com/publishers. Or look into whether any of the publications listed on the CCC website accept ads or "advertorial" content from businesses or organizations like yours.

Reader Demographics

Periodical publishers, like publishers of online media, typically use surveys to gather information about subscribers or readers. Surveys never provide information about every recipient, and the information that is gathered is self-reported. In other words, it's the income levels, net worth and frequency of travel that the subscriber *wants* to report. Publishers' estimates of readership—the number of people who read each copy—are only estimates, and no explanations of how pass-along readership is estimated are ever provided.

As examples of survey results, here are demographic figures from two western Washington magazine publishers:

☐ *Seattle Met*'s rate card recently said that its readers have a median age of 42, an average household income of $191,000, and an average home value of $875,750. Almost two-thirds are believed to be "executive, professional or managerial," 93 percent have attended college, and 20 percent hold graduate degrees. Perhaps most important to those comparing different advertising media, 79 percent of *Seattle Met* readers say they

Advertising with Small Budgets for Big Results   **127**

BLACK AND WHITE RATES		FREQUENCY DISCOUNTS		COLOR RATES		FREQUENCY DISCOUNTS	
	1x	3x	6x		1x	3x	6x
Full page	$2,304	$2,116	$2,025		$3,156	$2,897	$2,774
2/3 page	1,654	1,480	1,434		2,267	2,029	1,963
1/2 page	1,117	1,015	946		1,530	1,389	1,295
1/3 page	883	836	665		1,209	1,145	913
1/6 page	589	536	508		808	732	695
Inside cover	2,949	2,658	2,551		3,746	3,377	3,241
Back cover*	3,460	3,323	3,193		3,460	3,323	3,193
Business Reply Card	2,418	2,072	1,865		3,314	2,840	2,553

FLORIDA cpa today — 2013 ADVERTISING RATE CARD — effective January 1, 2013

This rate card shows how the cost of each ad is reduced when several insertions are ordered at once. Note that the inside back cover is sold only at the four-color process ink rate. This rate card also shows the cost of a bind-in business reply card.

do not have a newspaper delivered to their home or office and 78 percent say they have a smart phone.

☐ *Alaska Airlines Magazine* uses its airline passenger data, assuming that most passengers look at in-flight magazine. Its rate card reports an average age of 49, 51 percent female, 68 percent married, 90 percent with some college and 66 percent with college degrees. Twenty-three percent are believed to have household income of $150,000 or more and 46 percent are believed to be "professional/managerial."

Finding Appropriate Magazines and Trade Journals

If your budget is tight, high-circulation magazines like *Sports Illustrated, Family Circle* and *Seventeen* are likely out of range. It's also possible that none of them are right given your target market.

To find publications appropriate for your business and budget, start at well-stocked newstands or magazine racks in a bookstore or specialty retailer (the nursery for gardening monthlies, fabric store for sewing magazines, health foods store for organic cooking periodicals).

Another resource: your nearby libraries, public and college. The most comprehensive source of media information is SRDS, founded as Standard Rate & Data Service and now known as Kantar Media SRDS, next.srds.com/home. Subscriptions are expensive, so contact your library to see if it subscribes to the database and if so, at which branches. Such databases are usually only available for in-library use.

Remember that you're not limited to public libraries. In many cases, you can visit academic libraries, especially of public institutions, although you cannot check out material. Some museums also have libraries with periodicals.

Another source are magazine publishing associations with online directories of member publications such as the Association of Magazine Media, members.magazine.org/source/directory/index.cfm. Some states and regions have their own: for example, Minnesota Magazine & Publishing Association, mmpa.net; Florida Magazine Association, floridamagazine.org; and the Western Publishing Association, wpa-online.org.

Specialized magazine publishers also have associations:

☐ City and Regional Magazine Association, citymag.org.

☐ Association of Business Information and Media Companies, abmassociation.com.

☐ Association of Medical Media, ammonline.org.

☐ American Horse Publications, americanhorsepubs.org.

☐ Evangelical Press Association, evangelicalpress.com.

Such organizations as Association Media & Publishing, American Society of Business Publication Editors, and Magazine Association of the Southeast restrict their directories to members, but you'll find some titles in the information on board members and award winners.

Yet another source are the websites of magazine publishing companies. See Appendix B for examples.

Maps and Tourist Brochures

Informational brochures and maps, often listing tourist attractions or shopping locations, can be sponsored by one company, which includes its locations among the sights to

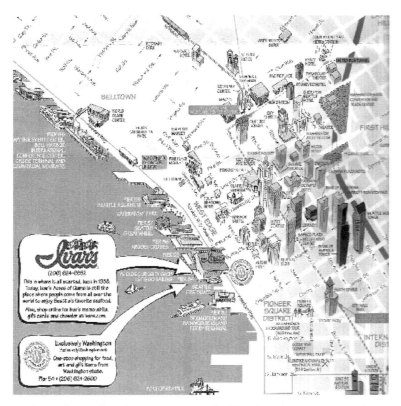

see (see above for the map provided by Ivar's restaurants), or it can feature ads from several businesses.

The brochures distributed to tourists, if they offer enough valuable information in a convenient format, may be used several times during a short visit.

Others—say, a map of a county's wineries or a city's consignment shops—will be used only occasionally, but over a period of several months.

Maps are sponsored by historical societies, business districts, shopping centers, chambers of commerce or trade-specific groups (e.g., antique dealers, quilt shops, used bookstores). A single business also can underwrite the project, selling ads to others to defray costs.

An online search for "advertising map publishers" will show firms that sell ads on existing maps and customize maps for chambers and other community and business groups. Because most maps are three inches wide when folded, ads are typically three inches wide. The vertical measurement varies. Some publishers advertise that a small ad can cost as little as $100.

Are maps and such brochures cost-effective? Undoubtedly many are never read. One way to measure effectiveness is with a code: if you've paid for distribution of brochures on a ferry, the brochure text can say, "Be sure to ask for the ferry discount on any purchase of $10 or more."

Coupons on brochure and maps are common ways to measure effectiveness; if possible, code them by distribution site. Another method: ask customers how they heard of you.

More Information
"Catalogs and Sell Sheets"

Naming/Sponsorships/Donations

Paying for naming privileges is a form of image, or institutional, advertising. Although it gets your company name on a space on a permanent basis, and every reference to an event in that space should use your name, there is seldom an opportunity to advertise a specific product, service or event.

Sponsoring an event, publication, cultural appearance, or website is similar, although such sponsorships occasionally include a newsletter or website advertorial and an ad.

One option that small businesses can use to showcase their products or services: in-kind contributions. Examples are catering, floral centerpieces, photography, graphic design, printing, quick on-site massages for attendees, costume design, web design and media advertising. Some nonprofits such as public broadcasting stations provide only in-kind services (in their case, on-air publicity), never cash.

Many fund-raiser organizers ask businesses to donate items for auctions or raffles without naming these businesses as sponsors. When donations are sought from you, consider how to create a gift certificate, gift basket or other donation that promotes your business or expertise while limiting the direct cost. A hair salon or spa, for example, can combine close-out merchandise with popular products and discount cards, one for the first visit to the business and a larger discount for the second visit. The business name should appear prominently on the basket. A tour operator can offer guest passes for the least popular day in the schedule, perhaps with a sign attached to a toy boat.

Because sponsorships and donations so often do not provide the direct response advertising options that are more cost-effective for small businesses, those with tight budgets should negotiate carefully to ensure they are being adequately recognized. Ideally, the organization asking for your help can provide in-kind compensation, perhaps as complimentary exhibit space at a conference, or your catalogs or coupons in the "goodie" bags distributed to attendees.

If you represent a nonprofit or event, and are seeking sponsors, carefully outline what you can offer that will benefit them before you approach potential donors.

More Information
"Giveaways and Samples"
"Swag/Goodie Bags"

Networking

Networking is not technically advertising, but it's always been one of a salesperson's best tools. Today we do it both in-person and virtually, through blogging, LinkedIn and the other websites in "Social Media." This covers the importance of personal networking and how developing a network will enhance your ability to use other options in this guide:

- ☐ Where to network.

- ☐ How to make contacts.

- ☐ How to sustain a network.

- ☐ How to use your networking contacts.

Where to Network
If you're not a natural at sales, you may shudder at the thought of reaching out to strangers at professional and alumni association meetings, conferences and conventions. It can be hard

to think of PTA events, neighborhood association gatherings and even church coffee hours and the sidelines at kids' sports events as places to network. But they can be!

Suppose you've never been a joiner, but there's a topic that looks interesting scheduled for the next meeting of the local chapter of the American Society of Whatever that you are eligible to join: architects, booksellers, photographers, project managers, social workers, spa owners. Go early, so you won't walk into a room where everyone is already bunched in conversations. Chat up the person at the registration desk, and peek at the pre-printed name tags, to seek if you recognize individual or company names. If it seems appropriate, offer to help set up the registration desk, explain that you're new — and take the opportunity to introduce yourself to the first few people who arrive.

Among the comments to use to start conversations:

☐ Do you come regularly or did you come today because of the speaker?

☐ Do you find the association helpful in business development?

Suppose you are a member, or you've visited before. Then your openers might be:

☐ I haven't been a regular, and I'm wondering if being more active would be valuable in business development.

☐ What do you find valuable about membership?

☐ I'm not a member, but now that I'm launching/opening [product/service/new location], I'd like to know what the local chapter and the association as a whole can offer.

Whatever your position, comments like the following are almost always appropriate:

☐ What brings you here today?

☐ What do you do?

Of course, have a stash of business cards in your pocket for when it's appropriate to exchange contact information.

Another important source of contacts: events that attract prospects. If you're an architect or interior designer, introduce yourself at the local home show, or at a how-to remodeling workshop sponsored by a community organization. If you're a bookseller with how-to books and organic gardening magazines, attend garden club meetings and get to know the staff and volunteers at the tool lending library. You're a commercial photographer? Attend meetings of architects, designers, builders and graphic designers. You're skilled at sewing and would like some paid projects? Sit in at the fashion shows at local fabric shops, where some attendees may be enthusiastic about new patterns, but lack your expertise.

At such events, take every opportunity to identify yourself without being pushy.

You're standing by a display at the home show with someone who looks friendly? Break the ice with, "Thinking about this for your home?" If the response is "No, are you?", you can say, "I'm an architect, I'm always interested in..."

You're attending the garden club meeting? Open a conversation with, "What kind of gardening do you do?" and follow up with a comment about a new or classic book your store has on the topic.

At the fashion show, consider telling your seatmate, "That would be perfect for some of my clients."

Pushy is also something to avoid when networking at alumni, civic, school, church and social events. If you join other volunteers on a one-time project or long-term volunteer commitment, it's natural that people share some personal information.

Even on the sidelines at kids' soccer matches you'll get to know people who can be sources of valuable information if you initiate contact or respond to others.

Alumni groups—for sororities, fraternities, dorms, college bands, high schools and even elementary schools as well as colleges and graduate schools—seem to be more common now with social media.

Some are informal, like Facebook pages or LinkedIn

groups. Others have blogs or newsletters, regular reunions and directories. Some offer business development and job-search programs; others provide options for polling classmates on a question (e.g., as I did regarding advergaming for this book).

If you attended a school or participated in an activity for which there is no local alumni group, consider trying to establish one: there's no better excuse for cold-calling people. (And it's possible that your college or graduate school has a database of alumni in your area that can be used.)

Sustaining Your Network

Networks need maintenance. This can be simple: call a contact to say you enjoyed taking that continuing education course with him, and how about coffee sometime soon. Or it can be emailing someone an article with a note such as, "Thought of you when I read this. I remember you mentioning…"

Using Networking Contacts

☐ "I've always wanted to know more about [company/industry/market]."

☐ "Where do you perceive the market going for [the product/service you're selling]?

☐ "Would you be willing to…?"

All are examples of comments you might make to people in your network. With the first, you could get general information about an industry, or specifics about those who make purchasing decisions at a company you're targeting.

With the second, you could be doing informal market research, and possibly setting up your contact for a sales pitch, on how you can meet the anticipated needs. With the third, you're making a request:

"May I use your name when contacting…?"

"Would you be willing to explain the buying process at…?"

Or, as I did with this guide when it was in manuscript form: "Would you be willing to critique this?" This question can result in constructive criticism and in comments that

Advertising with Small Budgets for Big Results   **135**

can be edited into endorsements. (See "Endorsements, Testimonials, and Review Sites.")

How else can you use contacts?

□ Add them to your database for newsletters, announcements and invitations (media stories, awards, product launches, open houses, your booth at fairs and shows). (See "Databases.")

□ Connect with them using social media such as Facebook for your business and LinkedIn. (See "Social Media.")

□ Use them as resources when you need product testing, feedback on advertising campaigns you're considering, references, testimonials—even models for product shoots.

What's vital in networking?

□ That you be respectful and able to identify why you believe a relationship will have value to both of you. (For example, it was after my hairdresser said her business had declined that I asked if she'd critique this manuscript.)

□ That the association be reciprocal, that you help as well as ask for help in making professional contacts. (This assumes that you are not expected to reciprocate with action that is costly, unethical or illegal.)

□ That you be courteous. Express your appreciation promptly. Even if the information you received was not helpful, follow up with a written or emailed note of thanks for the contact's time and interest in your project.

Newsletters

Newsletters are published by neighborhoods, homeowners' associations, church congregations, professional and trade associations, alumni groups, sororities and fraternities, medical centers, retailers, hobbyists—almost every possible business, individual and group. Your business or organization may be able to buy ads in newsletters, provide an insert, or sponsor issues—or it may choose to issue its own newsletter as a promotional tool. Among the topics covered here:

- Newsletter advertising.
- Newsletters as advertising.
- Content sources.

Newsletter Advertising

Newsletters are specialized in either topic or distribution, or both. Although many are online today (see "Websites"), a wide variety remain available in print.

You can spend $30 or $40 on a ad in the quarterly *Bone Yard Boats*, boneyardboats.com, or Baton Rouge's *Garden District News*, gdcabr.org. An ad in West Central Wisconsin's *The Bottom Line* business newsletter, tblnet.com,will cost you a couple of hundred dollars. Or spend many times that for space in the publications issued by the New England Journal of Medicine, jwatch.org, the Independent Book Publishers Association *Independent*, ibpa-online.org, or the infertility information and advocacy group Resolve New England, resolvenewengland.org.

Newsletters as Advertising

Run an online search for "newsletter advertising" and up will come dozens of links to articles about the value of newsletters as a promotional tool: "Keep your name foremost in previous customers' minds;" "Increase loyalty;" "Enhance your credibility;" "Create material so valuable that it'll be kept or passed on." Those are among the reasons you'll see for creating a newsletter of your own, either print or email.

Obviously, newsletters are convenient for announcing new products, services and sales to people already aware of you, and delivering class and special event schedules. Perhaps most important, offering a complimentary newsletter allows you to build a database of prospects and customers.

A newsletter can be a photocopied sheet, or it can be email, sent out in an eblast program that makes it easy to include photos. (See "Email.") It can be a full-color magazine created entirely for you or a combination of stock and original images, your own articles and a few copyright-free pieces gathered from online sources.

Content Sources

To find websites that provide copyright-free material you can use on a complimentary basis, search online with a phrase such as "copyright-free newsletter content" and your topic. For example, "home improvement."

Run an online search for newsletters, and you'll see many companies that create partial or entire newsletters. "No canned material," they insist, but if you look at samples, you'll see that often most of the text is…well, generic. One source said that all its customers have to do is provide a couple of photos for each issue, to ensure that it looks "personalized." Some newsletters come with stock photos and articles in place, ready for your business name or logo to be attached.

Other content providers sell articles and images you can add to your own material. One example is The Parent Institute, parent-institute.com. Besides providing newsletter masters for schools to duplicate and printed newsletters to mail, it offers four of its articles from each issue for a school's own publication.

For larger budgets, custom publishing is an option. Often used by insurance companies, packaged goods manufacturers and medical centers, custom publishing usually results in a well-designed publication that appears to be produced by the organization it discusses. In some cases, all content is specific to the sponsoring organization. For more information, see "Custom Publishing" under "Magazine Advertising."

Newspapers

Among the original media for advertising, newspapers are published in print on daily, weekly, and monthly schedules. Many "non-dailies" publish two or three times weekly, and today, as traditional dailies struggle financially, some publish online part of each week and in print on the days most popular with readers and advertisers.

In evaluating newspapers as a medium for your advertising, be aware that daily and community ("non-daily") readership has plummeted in the past few decades, especially among younger adults.

In late 2013 the trade journal *Editor & Publisher* cited an Oxford University study that showed that only five percent of those younger than 45 use print newspapers as their primary source of news. Even among those older than 45, only 10 percent identified newspapers as their first choice for news.

This section starts with information about the advertising common in major daily papers. Following that will be:

☐ Alternative papers.

☐ Community papers.

☐ Special interest papers.

☐ Business papers.

☐ Campus papers.

☐ Military publications.

What Newspapers Offer

Besides display and classified advertising in their regular sections, newspapers offer:

☐ Special sections (Also see "Advertorials").

☐ Special publications.

☐ Inserts.

☐ Adhesive note ads.

☐ Wraps (Spadeas).

☐ Bags.

☐ Ride-alongs.

☐ Website advertising.

General/National vs. Retail Rates

Daily newspapers typically differentiate between national (or general, or "non-local") advertisers and those that are local (retail). General rates are higher. Local businesses—not franchises or dealerships—probably qualify for local/retail rates.

Print Advertising

Like magazines, newspapers sell ad space with frequency discounts for those advertisers who make up-front commit-

DISPLAY RATES

(all rates are per column inch)

OPEN/AGENCY $11.75
Applies to non-local businesses and any business in which payment is made by a non-local office.

LOCAL $10.25
Applies to businesses in Pullman, Moscow, Lewiston and outlying areas.

UNIVERSITY/NON-PROFIT $7.75
Applies to WSU departments and organizations and to local, non-profit clubs and organizations that can show proof of non profit status with a copy of their 501 c3.

This campus paper's rate card shows how its Agency (also called General/ National) rates differ from Local (Retail) rates. Some metro dailies also offer nonprofit rates.

ments. These may be based on space, which is the number of column inches of ad space purchased during the contract period, or for the number of ads purchased.

Unlike magazines, which usually sell ad space in standard modules such as quarter, half or full pages, newspapers sell space in column inches. Because most newspaper columns are more than an inch wide, a one-inch ad will be one inch high, and in width, 1¼, 1½, 1¾ or even two or more inches. So if columns are two inches wide, a one-inch ad would actually be two square inches.

At the Tacoma (Wash.) _News Tribune_, there are two rate cards for local advertisers. One shows the "open rate," the price paid by one-time advertisers or those who have not contracted for space or number of insertions, as well as discounts for commitments ranging from 50 to 5,000 inches, with prices for black and white and for full-color. A second rate card shows the discounts for number of weeks that ads are run, starting with four and topping out at 52.

At the Wenatchee (Wash.) _Daily World_, the cost per column inch declines by the dollar amount spent in a year: from $30 at the open rate to $18.08 if $15,000 is spent. An advertiser who commits to 52 insertions annually will save even more: at that point, the charge is only $12 per column inch, regardless of ad size.

Different policies apply to political ads; it's common for media to require payment in advance of publication.

Premium Placement

A newspaper rate card will show the cost of premium placement, such as the front page, second page or opposite editorials, and for guaranteed placement, which means a certain section and possibly a specified page.

Special Discounts

Slight discounts are sometimes available when several retailers in a shopping center purchase ads for the same page or section of a daily paper.

Many papers offer discounted rates to nonprofits. Media like the *News Tribune* and the *Charlotte (N.C.) Observer* offer discounts of as much as 15 percent off the contracted rate for nonprofits' ads. For example, if you contract to buy 1,000 inches annually, you'll receive that rate plus the additional 15 percent discount.

PSAs, public service ads, are sometimes available on a space-available basis. These are typically for charities and are inserted at the last minute when a "hole" exists.

Commissions

"Commissionable," "Net" and "Noncommissionable" refer to whether an advertising agency or media buyer will receive a better rate than a business working directly with advertising salespeople. Most discounted ad rates are non-commissionable (net); in other words, no further discount for agencies or media buyers is available.

Classified Advertising

The ads that run in narrow columns at the back of a paper, usually in very small print, have for decades been the way to attract local buyers for real estate, cars, pets, livestock, and used goods. "Help Wanted" ads were also a mainstay of classified sections. Rates were low, and because ads were usually only text, they were quick and easy to place. Today, however, classified sections have shrunk, with many of their former advertisers using the merchants' or employers' websites (in the case of real estate, car and personnel ads, for example) or such online classified sections as Craigslist, eBay and Etsy. If you do buy a classified ad in a newspaper, you'll probably have the option to have it also appear on the paper's website.

Special Sections

Special newspaper sections are typically financed by advertising. As described in "Advertorials," these sections may use stock photos and syndicated text or material from manufacturers and retailers. Some are directories or maps for a special event—county fair or RV show, say.

Others are regularly issued supplements such as *Explore the Pearl*, the *Oregonian's* bi-monthly guide to Portland's Pearl District, published in partnership with the Pearl District Business Association.

Special Publications

The special publications issued by newspapers are often compilations of previously published material, made available either in print or as a downloadable epub. In many cases, these are marketed as references and expected to have a long life.

One example is the Books of Lists produced by such American City business journals as the *Puget Sound Business Journal*. These include the lists of local leading firms in each industry that have been published throughout a 12-month period. The "books," sent to subscribers and sold at a premium price to non-subscribers, carry ads.

Newspapers also issue special publications that cover major events—photo books that chronicle a natural disaster or a professional sports team's championship season, for example. These are expected to be keepsakes so advertising, if accepted, may be more expensive than that sold for regular issues. Some such publications are financed with "sponsorships" rather than ads.

Shoppers

Often published weekly, shoppers are heavy on ads, especially classified ads. Some carry a small percentage of editorial material; others are all advertising. Because they don't have enough "editorial" text (news or feature stories) to meet postal standards for newspaper rates, shoppers are distributed in racks, or by carriers. Today they also often publish online.

If the rate card says that circulation is "guaranteed," the paper is sent or delivered to every address. Recognize that "circulation" does not equal "readership." Many shoppers are discarded by recipients. Others, of course, are like Craigslist.org—read enthusiastically. For shoppers distributed in racks, the number cited as "circulation" by publishers may be the number printed rather than the number picked up.

Although the cost of an ad in a shopper will be less than a similar ad in a daily newspaper or news-filled business weekly, ads created for shoppers should have strong direct response "calls to action" and response to the ads should be tracked carefully so that you can determine if they are cost-effective in generating sales.

Shoppers are sometimes owned by newspaper publishing companies. For example, Iowa-based Lee Enterprises publishes the *Magic Values Shopper & Auto Trader* in Twin Falls, Idaho. Others are the only papers issued by their publishers.

More Information

Two trade organizations that include shoppers (as well as editorially stronger publications) are the

☐ Independent Free Papers of America, ifpa.com

☐ Association of Free Community Papers, afcp.org

Inserts

Material that is not part of the newspaper but delivered inside it is called "inserts" or "preprints." The pieces are printed in advance of the paper, and they are inserted between sections of the paper.

These are usually also sold with frequency discounts: the more often you advertise with a preprint, the less you pay per time. At the Tacoma daily, frequency discounts start with ads that appear six times. That paper's insert rates are quoted per 1,000 copies, so the total price depends partly on how many copies will be delivered in the zone or other option you

Advertising with Small Budgets for Big Results   143

select. (The other part of the cost is the creation and production of the insert itself.) Some papers deliver preprints and coupon pages inside a special wrap. With major dailies, you can also arrange to have these sections delivered to non-subscribers.

Adhesive note ad.

Adhesive Note Ads

Typically three inches square, "sticky note" or "peel off" ads often replicate the look of a Post-It. Others are designed as coupons. They are usually attached at the top of a newspaper's front page. They can be sold by zones. At the *Atlanta Journal-Constitution*, production and advertising rates for a note applied to 10,000–49,000 papers start at $100 per thousand. The rates per thousand drop as the circulation increases.

Wraps/Spadeas

Like magazines, newspapers can be wrapped with ads. Called spadeas, these are usually printed on the same newsprint as the paper. Some cover the entire front and back of the first section; others cover only half of the front page.

Bags

Want to advertise on the bag that covers a daily paper? In Atlanta, the cost starts at $57 per thousand; the minimum purchase at that price is 100,000 papers. At most papers, you can have your ad printed on a bag by the newspaper, or provide your own bag (perhaps through your vendors' co-op program). Some papers will also print your business name on the rubber bands that fasten the papers.

Above, spadea. Below, delivery bag printed with advertising (in this case, for a different newspaper).

Ride-alongs

With newspapers, a ride-along

is a promotion—often a sample or magazine-style advertisement—that is inserted in the delivery bag with the paper.

Website Advertising
All major newspapers have websites, and many offer print advertisers combination newspaper-website ad deals. Some offer web-only classified advertising.

Alternative Papers
Mostly established in the 1970s and 1980s, alternative papers and their websites range from the *Arkansas Times*, which calls itself central Arkansas's "most trusted source for news and views on politics, culture, events and dining," and Buffalo's *Artvoice*, which says it offers "in-depth coverage of local politics, event information, and art critiques," to *DigBoston*, which claims, "We cover local news, arts, music, sex, food, movies and shopping in a lively, funny, incisive and, most importantly, dead honest style."

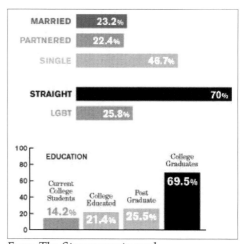

From The Stranger rate card.

There's also *Metro Silicon Valley* ("news, arts and lifestyle features,...and comprehensive entertainment and dining listings") and the *San Francisco Bay Guardian*, which says it "employs dedicated people of all ages, racial backgrounds, and sexual orientations...to help us print the news and raise hell."

These, like Seattle's *The Stranger*, are among the 124 members of the Association of Alternative Newsmedia, altweeklies.com, which cover every major metropolitan area of North America. Many describe themselves as "left-leaning" and some have significant GLBT readership. Contact information for each is on the AAN site. The association also offers an advertising buying service for 100 of the members; you can place ads in multiple papers with one AAN purchase.

Other weeklies also provide entertainment listings and restaurant descriptions but not enough news and commentary to be AAN members. (They are distinguished from "shoppers" because they do provide some editorial material.) Most are distributed free. For the names of those in your market area, check newsboxes outside coffee shops and near college campuses or do an online search for "Alternative newspaper" plus the name of the city.

Community Newspapers

Papers that serve neighborhoods are often referred to as "community" papers and "non-daily." Many were originally weeklies and are now published two or three times a week or monthly. Some are sold, others delivered free (guaranteed circulation). Most have small staffs; when several papers have a common owner, the same articles will appear in all or most of the papers. Some articles (Little League sports reports, say) are often contributed by volunteers.

Membership in the National Newspaper Association, nnaweb.org, is open to community papers in the U.S. with an editorial content of at least 25 percent. Publications with less than 25 percent editorial content may be members of the organizations listed under "Shoppers" earlier in this section. The Local Media Association, localmedia.org, formerly Suburban Newspapers of America, says it represents more than 2,000 community and suburban papers. Neither of these organizations has an online directory open to everyone.

For directories and detailed information on papers that serve the small town or neighborhood in which you do business (sometimes including big-city papers), check state newspaper associations such as the Washington Newspaper Publishers Association, wnpa.com; Oregon Newspaper Publishers Association, orenews.com; and Newspaper Association of Idaho, newspaperassociationofidaho.com.

For others, search online with such terms as "weekly newspaper association" or "community newspaper association" and a state name.

Special Interest Newspapers

Besides the daily and community newspapers which have a geographic focus, there are newspapers that serve ethnic and religious groups, and people with such special interests as rural life. In Minnesota, for example, the special interest newspapers include *Feedstuffs*, which covers agribusiness; *The Land*, rural life; *Gente de Minnesota, Heraldo Pages, La Prensa de Minnesota*, and *Latino Midwest News*, all directed to Hispanic readers; and *Korean Quarterly* and *Kurier Polski*, for Korean and Polish immigrants respectively.

If you're unfamiliar with special interest papers in a market, try a search for "special interest newspapers in U.S.," which will show such resources as Carnegie Mellon University Libraries, search.library.cmu.edu, or "ethnic newspapers in U.S.," which leads to the Center for Research Libraries, catalog.crl.edu.

Legal Papers

Larger cities have papers that focus on legal advertising, including calls for bids on publicly-financed projects and probate notices. (See right.) The news stories cover the same topics—construction, architecture, engineering, government. Examples:

WEST SEATTLE RESERVOIR PARK DEVELOPMENT

Bid Opening: November 6, 2013 @ 2:00 PM
PW #2012-048
PROJECT LOCATION: West Seattle Reservoir, 9000 8th Ave SW

PROJECT DESCRIPTION: Development of new park area over a covered SPU reservoir. Includes installation of pathways, parking lot, entry plaza with prefab restroom, pre-fab maintenance shed, play area, site furnishings, utilities, earthwork, landscaping

☐ Seattle-based *Daily Journal of Commerce*, which covers Washington and Idaho.

☐ Portland OR-based *Daily Journal of Commerce*, a different entity which covers Oregon and Idaho.

☐ Tucson's *Daily Territorial*.

Business Papers

Besides papers that serve business communities with RFQs, RFPs, and lien bankruptcy notices, most cities have weeklies that publish news about regional business and industry, including new business launches and individuals' promotions. Most advertising is display. Many of these publications issue such special publications as annual Books of Lists, which also accept advertising. You'll find examples of these papers on the websites of:

- Alliance of Area Business Publishers, bizpubs.org.
- American City Business Journals, bizjournals.com.
- Crain Communications, Inc., crain.com.
- New England Business Media, mainebiz.biz.

Campus Papers

Most colleges and universities also have newspapers, sometimes one for students and another for staff and faculty. If advertising is accepted in the student paper, it's usually handled by students, often because the school offers advertising courses. Larger papers will also have national sales reps.

From the Washington State University rate card.

At Washington State University, which claims to have a larger circulation daily paper than any other campus in the state, several rates and ad formats are available. Like many campus papers, the *Daily Evergreen* is produced in a daily paper's printing plant, which makes such specialty ads as "sticky notes" possible.

Military Papers

Many military bases have their own papers, with advertising handled by a civilian vendor. Near Washington, D.C., a division of the *Washington Post*, Comprint Military Publications, dcmilitary.com, handles ads for such base papers as the Joint Base Andrews *Gazette* and Naval District Washington's *Waterline*.

In the other Washington, *Northwest Airlifter* and *The Ranger* are published for Joint Base Lewis McChord by

Swarner Communications, northwestmilitary.com. Sound Publishing, soundpublishing.com, publishes the papers for U.S. Navy operations in Kitsap County, Washington.

To buy advertising in several papers at once, use a broker such as Military Media, militarymedia.com, which handles 174 base papers.

Stars and Stripes, stripes.com, has published a newspaper continuously since World War II. Weekly and monthly publications and special supplements also are published.

Each branch of the military also has national publications: *Navy Times, Army Times, Air Force Times,* and *Marine Corps Times,* with advertising sold by Gannett Government Media, militarytimes.com. MilitaryShoppers.com sells ads for the giveaway advertising circulars with coupons that are inserted in base papers.

Out-of-Home Advertising

Blimps, billboards, park benches, bus cards—what we usually think of as "outside" or "outdoor" advertising, is what the advertising industry calls "out-of-home."

This category also includes commercial messages *inside* institutional and commercial buildings such as airports and transit terminals. Many options fit small budgets.

You'll find detailed information at oaaa.org, the website of the Outdoor Advertising Association of America. Its "Find a member" option allows you to search for vendors from Abilene and Atlanta to Yuma and Zanesville. To find very small vendors that are not OAAA members, try an online search in the area where you want to advertise. This is how you'll find those who own only a few outdoor displays.

Blue Line Media, bluelinemedia.com, and Clear Channel Outdoor, clearchanneloutdoor.com, both commercial websites, provide design advice, and show which color combinations for banners and billboards are easiest to read. For example, yellow type on dark blue is very readable, as is black type on a yellow background.

Specifics on different kinds of out-of-home advertising are described in the categories that follow:

Advertising with Small Budgets for Big Results

- Aerial.
- Airports.
- Ballparks and stadiums.
- Benches.
- Billboards.
- Sidewalk, beach and street projections.

Aerial

Seen a skywriter lately? A small plane pulling a banner? A blimp? A giant balloon above the location of a grand opening or special event? They're all aerial advertising.

Skywriting is limited to short words or phrases: eight characters is typical for single-plane messages. One vendor, which says that letters will be visible for as long as 10 minutes or as little as a few seconds depending on wind, quotes rates starting at $1,500.

If you'd like a banner towed over Florida beaches during spring break, over your own state fair crowds or your favorite college's homecoming game, you'll probably pay for creation of the banner as well as an hourly rate for the towing.

Giant balloons, typically five to 22 feet in diameter, can be re-used at different times at the same location or moved between your locations (or the locations of organizations with which you have shared the production costs).

Blimps range in length from eight to 40 feet. Many are filled

Wall mural with embellishment (the "car"). This message plays off its location, across from the Seattle baseball stadium.

OAAA Definitions

Alternative outdoor media: Locations outside the home to reach a localized audience: stadium, airborne, marine vessel, beach, ski resort, golf course, rest area, bicycle rack panels, gas pump panels, parking meter panels, and postcards.

Billboard: Large-format advertising for viewing from more than 50 feet away. Billboard styles include bulletins (typically 14 x 48 feet), junior posters (usually 6 x 12 feet), posters (typically 12¼ x 24½ feet), and spectaculars (usually larger than 14 x 48 feet, positioned at prime locations and sometimes "embellished" as on page 149).

Count station: A section of road with a specific traffic pattern. Offers traffic count estimates and the demographic composition of that traffic.

Digital billboard: Billboards that change advertising content using digital technology. Each message is static (rather than video or electronic) and rotates every few seconds.

Digital place-based media: Screens other than digital billboards that change advertising content using digital technology. Can include static messages or video with an audio track.

Embellishment: Letters, figures, mechanical devices or lighting attached to the face of display to create a special effect (say, mannequins).

Facing: Direction that a unit faces: for example, a north-facing bulletin is viewed by vehicles traveling south.

Mobile billboard: Truck equipped with poster panel units. Can be parked at specified venues or driven on specified routes.

Snipe: Adhesive strip that covers a portion of copy displayed on an unit (for example, to update an offer).

Street furniture: Transit shelters, benches, newsstands/news racks, kiosks, and shopping mall panels.

Transit: Signs installed on the interior or exterior of public transportation or in transit terminals and stations, including bus panels, train/rail panels, airport panels, taxi panels and mobile advertising.

Tri-Vision: Sign with a slatted face that allows three different copy messages to revolve at intervals.

Wall mural: Painted or attached directly to a building exterior surface.

Advertising with Small Budgets for Big Results   151

with helium. Some vendors offer rentals as well as sales. For what's available in your area, search online for "giant balloons" or "advertising blimps."

Airports

Like train, bus and subway stations, airports offer many advertising options. The most common is signage, often backlit or as enormous banners.

Besides this signage, which is expensive to produce, ad space is sold on luggage carts, at taxi stands, in terminal and rental car facility shuttle buses, and at TSA security checkpoints. At Seattle-Tacoma International and other large airports, the bins by the TSA often are lined with a sheet advertising online shoe retailer Zappo's.

Some transportation authorities sell advertising directly; many outsource the sales. If you're not working with a media buyer, obtain rates, production requirements and information on availability by contacting firms listed on oaaa.org.

Another option for reaching pilots and crew is advertising on airport websites. AirNav.com lists dozens of small public airports in each state on its website, and sells both display ads and business listings—for motels, rental cars, restaurants, avionics—for airports ranging from Bremerton and Brewster, Wash. to Atlantic City, N.J., Edgartown, Mass., and Corning and Cooperstown, N.Y. SkyVector, skyvector.com, also lists U.S. airports, and provides contact information for their managers.

Looking for "guerilla" or nontraditional marketing in airports? Check what newsstands, fast food outlets, information booths and other consumer services are located in your geographic target areas. Ask a newsstand to tape up a mini-poster about your business on its check-out desk, or offer a sandwich shop napkins custom-printed with your advertising message.

Ballparks and Stadiums

When a ball sails into the outfield, where do eyes follow? Chances are some of them focus on the advertising signs on the ballpark fence. Big names have the spaces on major league

> **Billboard Design Tips from Blue Line Media**
> 1. Use a maximum of seven words, preferably short ones.
> 2. Letters should be at least a foot tall.
> 3. Use bold, contrasting colors.
> 4. Use a single idea or objective.
> 5. Test your design by simulating billboard viewing: stand 15 feet away and glance at the design for no more than five seconds.

fields sewed up, but to advertise in your community, look at local fields, where an ad may cost as little as $150 a year plus production of the sign.

For farm teams like the Bakersfield (Calif.) Blaze, an outfield sign for the full season is $2,000–$6,000 depending on size and location. Blaze representative Dan Besbris says teams with larger stadiums often charge triple or quadruple that for their signage.

Benches

Get your message on a park bench or at a bus stop for as little as $20 a week plus production costs. The same large companies that contract for billboards and airport advertising usually handle bench ads. Minimums apply: for example, at least 10 benches in the same four-week period. For information, check the OAAA website or use a search engine to locate smaller vendors in your area.

Billboards

Probably the best known form of outdoor advertising, billboards vary in price depending on size and type of sign, traffic estimates, and whether the sign's message is partially blocked on a seasonal basis by trees.

Vendor names are typically on the frame.

With digital billboards, messages can be changed often, even during different times of day (for example, during commutes).

The easiest way to find billboard vendors in your area is to watch signs for the owners' names, which usually are centered in the top or bottom "frame." Major vendors are Clear Channel Outdoor, clearchanneloutdoor.com, CBS Outdoor, cbsoutdoor.com, and Lamar Advertising Co., lamar.com.

Mobile Billboards

Mobile billboards are vehicles with a frame on which ads can be stretched and if desired, backlit. One typical size is 20 feet wide by 10 feet high. Some suppliers can mount billboard frames on a delivery truck you already own. Mobile billboard rates start at $800 per ad per eight-hour period, with minimum purchase requirements, according to Blue Line Media, bluelinemedia.com. For a DIY variation, consider vinyl banners or plywood signs on a frame on your truck or that owned by someone you pay or barter with.

Floating Billboards

Floating billboards are inflatable units or mesh bulletins and banners. They can be mobile or stationary, although some local governments have ruled the stationary forms illegal if installed by bridges because of the distraction to motorists. Boats or personal watercraft such as Jet Skis usually tow floating billboards.

DIY options also exist here, especially for image advertising. Why not fly flags with your business or product name from the stern or mast of a boat? Or suspend a banner on the cabin of a boat that circulates during an event.

Sidewalks

Keep customers' eyes down, with promotional messages on the sidewalk leading to your store, and on the floor inside. On private property, and on public sidewalks where legally permitted, consider vinyl clings/decals. Both they and chalk art can also be used inside a storefront or (if permitted) in a convention exhibit space.

For cling/decal vendors, run an online search for "vinyl clings for floors," and you'll see dozens of options, including yellow footprints that can lead customers into your space for as little as $10 per pair. Custom printed signs for your floor (or tabletops) start at about $10 per square foot.

For chalk art vendors, search for "chalk art as advertising" and the response will include both agencies and individual artists. Or contact your local art school about possible free-lancers.

Beach Marketing

Yet another option for getting ads under prospects' feet: messages imprinted in sand. An online search turned up vendors who offer this kind of outdoor advertising.

It's also possible for DIY-ers to create ads on the beach. Two options: a mold to press into damp sand that you build with a board and three-dimensional letters and numbers that are at least a couple of inches thick and three or more inches tall. Or contact the Etsy shop Impressive Steps, facebook. com/ImpressiveSteps, which customizes flip-flop soles with as many as 11 characters per sandal.

Street Projections

A promotion which may require a permit is the projection of an ad—still images, slide shows or video display—on the side of a building or on a sidewalk or other pedestrian space.

In your own building, images can be projected on floors, ceilings or walls, and in your parking lot or on a garage wall. What's required? Perhaps nothing more than a laptop and projection equipment for your space. For outdoor projection, equip a van with the computer and projector and take a drive around the neighborhoods where you're prospecting. (Or, of course, check into firms that provide such services.)

A variation is the gobo, used both inside and out. (See "Gobos" in "In-store Advertising/Point-of-purchase.")

Transit

Reach those who commute on public transportation with signage inside buses and commuter rail and at transit stations. Exterior signage ("cards") and wraps on buses and trains serve as mobile advertising, visible to both pedestrians and those traveling by car. Traditional bus card formats (sizes are approximate):

- King, on the left side, 30 x 144 inches
- Queen, on the right (curb) side, 30 x 88 inches
- Tailgate, 21 x 70 inches
- Interior cards

Other formats available in many markets include:

- Super king, 30 x 216 inches, on the left side
- Oversized tailgate posters, 36 x 80 inches
- Half side (left), 37 x 312 inches
- Interior ceiling ads
- Transit shelter posters

Rates vary significantly: some transit authorities offer free interior space for public service announcements, while rates for a single outside card can be a couple of thousand dollars, even outside major markets.

Transit advertising is typically purchased in campaigns of at least four weeks. How many vehicles and what combination of formats you buy depends on how many people you want to see your ads, and how often you want the ads seen by the same people. Advertising salespeople estimate viewership by route and format. They can also estimate production costs. Cards are discarded after each campaign except when the transit authority's advertising office or contractor agrees to save them for a future campaign. (For example, if you use the same campaign each quarter.)

In King County, Washington, where Seattle is located, bus advertising is handled by Titan360, titan360.com; it also handles bus advertising for Pierce Transit, which serves the county to the south, and for Community Transit, which serves Snohomish County to the north.

For Sound Transit, which provides express bus, commuter rail and light rail service in King, Pierce and Snohomish counties, advertising is handled by Clear Channel, (206) 494-4242. Spokane Transit Authority's advertising is contracted to ooh Media, oohmediaspokane.com/.

In Oregon, Lamar Advertising, lamar.com/portland, sells the ads for transit in Portland, Eugene and Corvallis.

In central Oregon, where Cascades East Transit, cascadeseasttransit.com, serves the Bend-Redmond-Prineville-Sisters area, advertising on bus exteriors is limited to public service announcements except for Ride the River sponsors, who pay $1,000 per year for logo-only signs. Inside the buses, local agencies and nonprofits can have 11 x 17-inch cards; messages must be public service or educational and preapproved by the transit agency.

Ads for buses and benches are sold for ValleyRide Transit in Boise, Idaho; to contact contractors, see valleyride.org/about/advertising/. In Sacramento, options include both transit advertising and space on vending machines at light rail stations; see sacrt.com/advertisert.stm. For an average of $15 per day per bus, signage is available on Modesto, Calif., transit, modestobus.weebly.com/about.html.

More Information
"Banners"
"Color"
"Signage"

Postal Regulations
Whether you're mailing individual pieces or in bulk, within the U.S., to Canada or abroad, the shape and thickness of your piece will determine much of the postage cost. This section discusses:

 ☐ Format and dimensions.

 ☐ Quantity required for discounted rates.

Advertising with Small Budgets for Big Results 157

☐ Business Reply Mail.

☐ Indicia.

Format and Dimensions

Easily produced four at a time on an office copy machine from letter-size cover stock, postcards can be sent in the U.S. at the most economical rate if they measure no larger than 4¼ x 6 inches. Cards larger than that, or thicker than .016 inch, must carry letter-rate postage.

Letters and flyers can be mailed at letter rates if they are rectangles no larger than 6⅛ x 11½ inches in size, and no thicker than a quarter inch. "Unenveloped letter-size mailpieces," or "self-mailers," must be sealed along all four sides or tabbed to prevent an open edge from jamming processing equipment. Check the postal service website for current requirements regarding tab sizes and placement.

If you are not using a mailing service experienced with catalogs, have a dummy—a mock-up of your planned piece—reviewed by postal service specialists to ensure you understand prices applicable to different sized pieces and the necessary size and placement of the address space.

Surcharges are imposed on pieces that are not rectangles, that are too rigid, that are lumpy due to enclosures, and if the address is parallel to the short side. Among the other reasons for a surcharge are unusual closures such as clasps, strings, or buttons.

Pieces smaller than 3½ x 5 inches or thinner than .007 inch cannot be mailed unless inserted in an envelope that meets the minimum size requirements.

Precancelled stamps. See pages 80 and 158.

Quantities for Discounted Rates

Pieces can be sent at Standard (bulk) rates if you have at least 200. If you're mailing fewer than 200 pieces at a time, first class postage is required.

If you mail only a few hundred pieces at a time, you may prefer to use precancelled stamps for Standard (bulk) postage rather than a bulk mailing permit and/or indicia. These stamps can also be used for certain first class mailings. The postal service sells precancelled stamps in four denominations: five, ten, 15 and 25 cents (examples on page 157). When you deliver mail with these stamps to your post office, the "business mail entry unit clerk" calculates the balance you owe.

Business Reply Mail

To encourage replies, postage-paid envelopes or postcards are sometimes included with advertising. To pay for these responses, Business Reply accounts are set up with the postal service. Envelopes or cards are printed with the appropriate permit number, which is different than a permit for Standard (bulk) mail.

Requirements for Business Reply Mail are quite specific, and the postal service suggests you have your artwork for envelopes or postcards reviewed by "mailpiece design analysts" prior to any printing. See "Mailpiece Design" on the postal service website.

Picture Permit Imprint Indicia

To add a logo, product image or trademark to your indicia, you can use Picture Permit Imprint Indicia. This requires a color image, which may increase the printing cost of your mailed piece. The postal service requires the use of a specified bar code and that its staff approve the piece in advance. You'll also need a permit. Fees, in addition to postage, are one or two cents per piece.

More Information
"Direct Response Advertising"
U.S. Postal Service, usps.com, "Business Solutions"

Posters and Postering

You've seen the signs that say, "Post No Bills"? They refer to playbills or posters, popular in the days of traveling circuses and other entertainers, whose advance crews would paste up signs to advertise the events. Also called bill posting, fly-posting, wildposting, and wheatpaste postering, the posters that are slapped up on vacant buildings, construction sites, and telephone poles are considered a form of "guerilla" marketing. There are, however, legitimate ways to poster. For more information, this section covers:

- □ Poster production.

- □ Postering services.

- □ DIY postering.

Poster Production

Hire a graphic designer, illustrator, photographer, find a printer locally or online—one way to get posters created and produced. But wait! There are many more options—some ideal for tight budgets.

First, consider what you can create with desktop publishing or illustration software and print out on your copier or at the neighborhood copy center. All-text messages, line art, and a photo with name, date, and URL printed across it are examples of what's quick and easy for posters between letter and tabloid size, even if you have no design training. Other possibilities:

□ Photographs or artwork provided by the performers or manufacturers of products you're promoting.

□ Poster contest for high school, college and art school students and/or community members as a means of getting a poster designed. If you don't have funds or in-kind resources for a prize, offer publicity for the award-winner, including the individual's name on the printed posters. For budding artists creating a portfolio, recognition is valuable.

☐ Poster contest for K–8 students, with each poster used in a different location. If you select award recipients in each community or school, you may be able to get school- or neighborhood-specific publicity for your event as part of the recognition for poster artists.

☐ Short-term internship or community service credit for a student creating your poster and possibly other promotional materials such as T-shirt designs and pinback buttons.

☐ Pro bono or sharply discounted design and printing from local businesses.

Besides providing a URL and QR code for more information, consider adding a tearaway pad for those posters displayed on bulletin boards at post offices, in workplaces, and on campuses. The pads can offer coupons, order forms, or other information for following up.

Postering

Legitimate postering businesses obtain permission to put up signs, many in the windows of storefronts or the entries of businesses like liquor and music stores with heavy foot traffic. On college and school campuses, and in government facilities, posters typically must be approved in advance, and what can be advertised is usually limited. Unauthorized posters are removed.

Many poster services specialize: in cultural events, for example, or rock concerts. Depending on your demographic and the size of your market area, postering can be extremely economical. The proprietor of the six-person Seattle business Keeping Posted, keepingposted.com, estimates the Seattle core area could be blanketed with the smaller of his size options for as little as $250 for a four-week display, including production and labor.

Because postering is often handled by one-person businesses, sometimes even as a part-time operation, finding a vendor may require a little research. This can be as simple as

Advertising with Small Budgets for Big Results 161

questioning a cafe manager about the source of the posters in the windows, or running an online search such as "poster distribution [city name]." Some services offer poster production, others provide only specifics on what sizes and paper weights are acceptable.

DIY Postering

Running an event in cooperation with local merchants—a sidewalk sale, chocolate festival, holiday open house? Ask each participant to display posters (and ideally, to ask their colleagues in other neighborhoods to also put up posters). Use a similar strategy when publicizing a charity event.

If you have run a poster design contest, ask the winners— even the entrants—to help procure poster locations, perhaps in the storefronts of businesses run by family and friends.

When you're promoting a for-profit event for your business, consider offering appropriate merchants and offices a trade-out: either promise to display their posters, or offer them tickets to your event in return for putting up your posters. And if you're comfortable with "guerilla-style" marketing, get those posters up on vacant buildings, construction fences and other semi-private property.

Whether you also post them on power poles and other public property depends on what your local ordinances are. In some cases, government agencies take down illegal posters, contact the event sponsors and fine them.

Product Placement

See "Advertorial" and "Gaming"

QR Codes

QR (for Quick Response) codes, black modules arranged in a square pattern on a white background, were created in 1994 by Toyota subsidiary Denso-Wave, denso-wave.com/qrcode/index-e.html. A QR code is considered two-dimensional because its information can be read in both horizontal and vertical directions. By contrast, an ordinary barcode can be read only horizontally.

The result: a QR code (or other two-dimensional code) can carry several hundred times more data than a barcode. Depending on whether characters are alpha, numeric, binary, or Japanese kanji, a QR code less than an inch square can be encoded with as many as 7,089 numeric characters, or approximately 800 words.

They can be read in any direction, and they can be read even if part of the code has been damaged—two significant advantages when compared to the more familiar rectangular barcodes. To see a diagram indicating each functional element, see the Wikipedia description of QR codes. See this page and the next for information on:

- What QR codes can do.
- What they cost.
- Similar codes.
- QR analytics.

What QR Codes Can Do

With a bar-code reader installed on a mobile device, anyone can scan a printed QR code to bring up a website, ringtone, coupon, or transit schedule. With business cards, letterhead, package labels or hangtags, you can use codes to take contacts to your website or Twitter page, a YouTube video about your company or campaign, or a Facebook page. You can sticker a package with a discount specific to that store or the latest review of the product. Use a door or table cling to show a code that leads to an offer valid only for a given time of day.

What a QR Code Costs

A QR code costs nothing. Denso-Wave owns the copyright, but it has made the technology available to everyone. You'll find lots of code generators who want to charge you for creating your actual image, but you should be able to generate codes for free. To incorporate a company name or logo in the middle of the code—yes, it can work!—have an experienced code designer create the symbol for you.

QR Code Competitors

Many similar two-dimensional codes now exist, but several are proprietary, lack the universal applicability of the QR code, and—no surprise—may not be free to create.

NotixTech, notixtech.com, pointed out a few years ago, "No alternatives possess all of the characteristics of a QR code."

NotixTech calls Microsoft Tag (above) the most similar to QR codes. Service for Tag is being transferred to ScanLife, scanlife.com, which also creates codes in QR (plain and "designer"), EZcode and Datamatrix formats.

QR Code Analytics

Which of your advertising or marketing efforts is most effective? Among the ways you can measure this is with QR code analytics. They can provide even more detail than other codes: for example, analytics will report what sent someone to your website: a Twitter post, eblast, postcard, poster, or garment hangtag.

Run an online search for "QR code analytics" and you'll find that most services providing the analytics are based on Google Analytics, google.com/analytics, which is free for sites with fewer than 10 million hits per month.

Radio

Today radio includes:

☐ Network-affiliate or network-owned stations that broadcast on AM or FM bands, and often live-stream as well.

☐ Independent broadcast stations, typically in smaller markets, that broadcast on AM or FM bands, possibly with live-streaming.

☐ Online programming, which is streamed but not broadcast over air waves.

☐ Satellite radio, a subscription service.

Besides describing each of these, this section provides information on:

□ Evaluating radio advertising: does it make sense for you?

□ Audience demographics.

□ How to cut costs.

□ DIY commercials.

□ Public radio audience demographics, what your spot can say, and what underwriting spots cost.

Radio Today

Traditional commercial radio is broadcast, with most programs produced by professionals and supported by 15-, 30- and occasionally 60-second commercials (written as :15, :30 and :60).

Some stations sell blocks of time for paid programming; this is more typical in smaller markets or for such undesirable time slots as early Sunday morning.

Some paid programming is filled with infomercials; some features specialty programming for which the sponsors sell their own ads. Examples of "brokered programming" topics: ethnic music, investment advice, religion and alternative health information.

Public radio stations have traditionally been affiliated with school districts or universities, although today most rely on "listener support" (e.g., donations) for the bulk of their

---

Rate Card Lingo

Share, the percentage of those listening to radio in the metro area who are listening to a particular radio station.

Average Quarter-Hour Persons (AQH Persons), the average number of persons listening to a particular station for at least five minutes during a 15-minute period. In mid-2013, in Seattle-Tacoma, the ratings for this were as high as 6.5. In the Vancouver-Portland area, the highest was 7.3, and in Spokane, 8.0.

Advertising with Small Budgets for Big Results 165

funding. Many, but not all, are among the 900 affiliated with National Public Radio.

Rather than air commercials, public radio broadcasters use "underwriting spots" to thank the day or program sponsors, and provide general information similar to that of an image or institutional ad. Federal Communications Commission rules prohibit direct response advertising for for-profit enterprises on public broadcast stations.

Online programming is provided both by traditional broadcast stations, which live-stream some programs and provide podcasts of previously aired programs, and by such "pay-to-play" options as Blogtalk Radio, blogtalkradio.com, which claims 188,000 radio hosts.

That's 188,000 people or businesses that are paying a minimum of $39 per month to air their own programs. Some online stations have very small audiences and the ads that appear during their programs are sold by the online radio "network," not the program host.

Satellite radio—most notably, SiriusXM, siriusxm.com— is a subscription-based service with dozens of channels, including talk radio and such music genres as the 1940s, '50s, and '60s. Commercials are sold on many of these channels. Among the most expensive programs for a 30-second spot is Howard Stern's, which is approaching five figures for a national purchase. By contrast, for a couple of hundred dollars per spot as part of a package, you can buy time on the Spanish edition of CNN Headlines.

Pandora Internet Radio, pandora.com, plays music based on the user's artist selection. It has a free subscription supported by advertisements, and an ad-free fee-based subscription. Although most ads are audio, and 80 percent of them air on mobile devices, the company also offers video ads, 15- or 30-second spots that take over the entire screen and cannot be skipped.

Spotify, spotify.com, offers users access to play lists made by friends, artists, Spotify—or collections created by users themselves. It offers both radio-style audio ads and visuals on handhelds and monitors.

Do Radio Ads Make Sense for You?

Whether radio advertising will be cost-effective depends on your location, the audience you're targeting, and the demographics and listener behavior associated with stations available to you. Going for professionals or outside salespeople? If you're where people commute by car, broadcast radio—commercial or public—is worth considering.

DIY media buying is tough. In larger markets, most broadcast time is purchased through media buyers, either independent or on staff in an advertising agency. They can help you through the complexities of day parts, estimated audience demographics for each disk jockey, talk show host or program, and such digital "extras" in an advertising contract as text messaging and website ads. Because broadcast time is seldom purchased at the prices posted on a rate card, an experienced media buyer is valuable in negotiating your deal.

Who's Tuned In?

Audience demographics for radio, like much other media, are estimated. Although audience size is monitored by ratings bureaus, listeners' age, income level and other information are always approximate. For example:

☐ In Seattle, which has more than four dozen stations, one of the oldest stations is KJR. In 2013, it estimated its weekly radio audience at more than 770,000 people 12 and older. Two-thirds of those listeners are believed to be between 35 and 64, and slightly more are men than women.

☐ In Portland, Ore., KINK estimates that more than 70 percent of its listeners are between 35 and 64, and that 53 percent of them are women.

The ratings cited in station media kits come from local surveys and from Nielsen Audio (formerly Arbitron), arbitron. com, which reports spring and fall on stations across the U.S. and abroad. Larger markets, including Seattle-Tacoma, Portland, Ore., and Sacramento, are surveyed 13 times a year, once a month and during the holiday season. Smaller markets (e.g., Spokane and Monterey) are done each quarter. Markets like Washington's Tri-Cities, Bend and Eugene, Ore., and Modesto and Redding, Calif., are checked twice annually. Nielsen, a media and marketing research firm, also covers television, cable, out-of-home, and the mobile industry.

Cutting Costs on Radio Buys

Long-term contracts with radio stations will reduce your cost per commercial, but if your business has no experience with broadcast advertising, it's better to test the medium itself and specific stations before making a lengthy commitment. At a minimum, a test should run three or four weeks, with several spots airing each day on each station you're testing.

To test your message and how it's presented, consider using two different commercials so that you can see which approach results in the most responses. One ad can run one week, or on one station, and then the other ad can run on another station, or the next week. If you're reading about radio advertising, you'll see this referred to as an A/B test.

If you know that radio makes sense for your product or service, consider a 13-, 26- or 52-week contract. This is particularly important if you need to advertise during ordinarily busy periods such as the campaign season or the holidays. You'll lock in a rate, guarantee yourself the air time and pay only after the commercials have aired.

Media buyers have other tips for buying on a budget:

□ *Short ads:* 10-, 15-, and 30-second spots instead of the 60-second commercial that was once standard.

□ *Run of station airtime:* Allowing your ads to air anytime between early morning and midnight. If you believe your target audience will be listening outside "drive time," you can save money by not requiring that your ads air during weekday commuter rush hours.

□ *Fringe days and times:* Days or times of day when there are fewer listeners and so lower prices for advertisers. Again, this only makes sense if you are confident the people you need to reach are tuned in during the middle of the day and on weekends.

□ *Sponsoring a program or feature:* "This news report is brought to you by..." is an example of how a business name can be showcased with something that's likely to grab people's attention: most often, news, traffic and weather reports. Sponsorships often include a brief commercial before or after the report. Because sponsorships are sometimes sold at a premium, an experienced media buyer may be able to reduce what you pay.

□ *Station promotional events:* Sponsoring a station-organized event — a winter coat collection, a voter registration drive, a concert — also means that your business name will be used frequently on air as the event is publicized. You may be one of several sponsors, so what you'll hear will be, "Join KXO and the Dravus Garden Center at..." and then later, "KXO and the Ballard Bridge Club present..."

The sponsorship buy should specify the minimum number of times your business will be named. Besides commercials, the buy may include a booth at the event, where you can distribute samples, do demonstrations, hand out promotional material — maybe even sell products.

□ *PSAs, Public Service Announcements:* Some stations will, on a time-available basis, run free promotional ads for charities and government agencies — sometimes even public schools. Because there's no guarantee when these will be used, they are best written for continuing campaigns (e.g., "give blood") or as image advertising.

Another way to create greater exposure for whatever you're advertising, and for your organization in general, is a cross-business promotion. Similar to what is described in "Food Truck Advertising" in the "Signs" section, this involves mentioning another business in your commercial, and it mentioning your special in its commercials. This results in each business name being aired twice as often.

Usually set up by an advertising salesperson for the station, this could involve each offering a coupon valid for a discount at the other's business: for example, a free music lesson offered by an instructor when an instrument is purchased at a music store, or a discount on a sprinkler at the hardware store when a purchase is made at the sod farm.

If the station's website has a lot of traffic, it may be worthwhile negotiating advertising on the website as part of your purchase. First, you'll want to preview the site and see if you'll be comfortable having your products associated with it, and you'll want information on number of visitors, what pages they view and how long they stay on the site.

(Some of this information may be available independent of the station via Internet and blog ratings websites. See "Email" and "Websites.")

What The Station Must Provide

When a station's schedule is made up for the week, it should send you a copy, with the approximate times your commercial will air.

This will help prepare your staff for calls resulting from the commercial, and you can use social media to remind your followers to listen. A message such as, "And if you don't hear the ad announcing today's special, check our Facebook page after noon to see the deal" should enhance the effect of your commercial.

As part of your radio buy, specify what you need to satisfy any cooperative advertising requirements, and that you cannot pay your bill until you receive this documentation.

Creating Your Radio Ad

The most economical way to have a radio commercial created is at the station, with that cost negotiated into your purchase (another way a media buyer can help you).

You or someone from your organization can do the talking, or you can have a station on-air personality do it. You'll have to provide at least a rough draft of the text. This does mean that your commercial will sound different on each station.

Hiring a writer and actors and arranging to have the commercial taped will cost much more—a couple of thousand dollars or more. This will probably result in a more professional ad, and if you can use the same ad for several seasons,

Creating an Ad

A simple ad you record yourself might start out:

"If you're thinking about starting a family, or already expecting a baby, let me tell you why South-North Hospital offers the best maternity care in our area. I'm Amy Smith, and I've spent the last 10 years at South-North, where we on the OB and pediatric staffs..."

It could conclude:

"If you want to ensure that you and your baby receive the best possible care during labor, delivery and recovery, call South-North now to schedule a visit. You can reach me, Amy Smith, at (206) 000-0000. Or email me at amy@south-north.org. Visit us online at www.south-north.org/babies, too!"

the cost per advertising campaign may be insignificant.

How much can be said in 30 or 60 seconds? Experienced professional scriptwriters can help you determine what can be communicated in a commercial. If you're drafting your own text, assume that in 60 seconds you can say at least 100 and possibly 200 words, including teaser, introduction and the contact information that typically closes an ad. To test the length, record yourself reading the text.

In almost every case, an ad that airs on a commercial station will be direct response, with a telephone number or address included. The business or product name should be repeated, and contact information should be provided at least twice or in two or more different ways.

Here's an example for a truly small business:

"[Sound of school bell]

"If your kids are struggling in school, they need help, and they need it right now. That's what Meadowlark Tutors can provide. We're all certified teachers, and we all know how to give kids the training and the self-confidence to get past problems with math or language arts..."

Its conclusion might be:

"Meadowlark Tutors is ready to help your family. Learn

Advertising with Small Budgets for Big Results

more about us and our convenient locations and schedules online at meadowlarksmarts.com, or phone 206-000-0000."

Public Radio

Love NPR? Sure that if you're going to do radio, public radio is the place to be? As you get started, recognize that there are several different kinds of noncommercial radio stations—and audiences.

□ Some serve large areas and are NPR affiliates, with programming that attracts an affluent, well-educated audience.

□ Some have limited bandwidth, are run by students, and primarily serve campuses.

□ Some noncommercial stations, operated by federal and local governments, offer audio of public meetings and services such as the NOAA weather report station.

Public radio stations can, regardless of their network affiliations, purchase content from Public Radio International (PRI); American Public Media (APM); Public Radio Exchange (PRX); and Pacifica Radio.

Who's Listening?

Surveys and data gathered when people donate to stations provide audience demographics. NPR cites such characteristics of its national broadcast audience as

---

Public Radio Audience Demographics

In Seattle, station KUOW describes its listeners as:

- *54.6 male, 45.4 female;*
- *55 percent between the ages of 35 and 54*
- *55 percent with both a college and postgraduate degree*
- *53 percent with a household income exceeding $100,000*

In Denver, stations KUVO/KVJZ say their listeners are:

- *female (62 percent)*
- *25–54 years of age (30 percent)*
- *college-educated (72 percent)*
- *affluent: mean household income in excess of $73,000*
- *travelers (71 percent)*
- *cultural events supporters (54 percent)*
- *online shoppers (69 percent)*
- *voters (64 percent)*

69 percent college-educated, median household income of $91,000 and median age, 49.

What An Advertiser Can Say on Public Radio

The Federal Communications Commission regulates the content of spots on public radio stations that broadcast (vs. those on cable).

KUVO, a Denver-based station, offers these examples of what's acceptable in 15-second underwriting spots:

❑ "Support comes from Second Federal Bank, offering investment CDs and mortgage financing geared to the individual's financial resources. Information is available at (phone) or on the web at … "

❑ "Programming is supported by Hickory Bank, offering

What's OK to Say on Public Radio

Federal Communications Commission rules say that a public radio message may include:

• Address and contact information

• Brief description of products and/or services

• Length of time the business has operated

• The names of affiliated companies, if any

Spots are usually read by a station's on-air staff member rather than being pre-recorded.

Underwriting messages cannot have:

• Information on price (including "free")

• Comparisons or qualitative claims ("best," "biggest," "superb quality," "award-winning")

• Incentives to buy

• Direct response language (such as "Call now" or "Visit our site at…")

• Advocacy of political, religious or other points of view

mortgage loan programs for new homes and refinancing. With locations throughout the tri-state area, additional information is available from Hickory Bank at (phone)."

The ads that appear on public radio stations' websites can be more commercial in language and, like the lists of sponsors, can include links to the businesses' websites.

Another option for underwriters/sponsors: to offer discounts on services or merchandise to "members" of a station's donor community.

Underwriting Rate Examples

WUSM, Southern Miss Radio, charged as little as $100 for 20 spots in 2013 on this University of Southern Mississippi-affiliated station. Besides that bargain for nonprofit events, other tax-deductible rates included:

☐ One-month package: three spots per day, 90 spots at $9 per unit, $810 (new clients' special, $500).

☐ Three-month package: three spots per day, 270 spots at $8 per unit, $2160.

☐ Run of station: $10 per spot.

North Country Public Radio, St. Lawrence University, in 2013 offered spots on "prime-time" programs at $23 per 10-second credit ("Morning Edition," "Writer's Almanac" and "A Prairie Home Companion," regional and national news, and "All Things Considered"). Standard rate per spot was $15.

More Information

"Cooperative Advertising"
"Direct Response Advertising"
Appendix C
Nielsen Audio, Arbitron.com, arbitrontraining.com, and "Arbitron 101"
Radio Advertising Bureau, rab.com
NPR, npr.org, for affiliated stations

Catholic Radio Association, catholicradioassociation.org, select "Travel Guide" for station list
Radio Locator, radio-locator.com, a commercial site that lists radio stations with websites

Shopping Channels

HSN and QVC are examples of multi-channel retailers. They are not advertising media.

HSN, Inc., hsn.com, sells on television, online, via mobile devices, in catalogs, and in brick and mortar stores. It describes itself as offering "a curated assortment of exclusive products combined with top brand names." Its Cornerstone unit owns brands such as Ballard Designs, Chasing Fireflies, Frontgate, Garnet Hill, Grandin Road, Improvements and TravelSmith. "Become an HSN Partner" is the page where you can start a product submittal; it's reached via the home page's bottom menu, "Get to Know Us."

QVC, qvc.com, is a television and online marketplace that compares itself to an upscale department store in merchandise types and prices. To have a product featured on QVC, businesses start by submitting brief descriptions using the online form (see "Vendor Relations"). If your product is considered both appropriate for the marketplace and innovative, a sample may be requested.

It's important to understand that if your product is to be featured on the regular QVC program, you'll be expected to ship a large quantity (say, 1,000) to the QVC warehouse prior to the air date. Unsold product is returned to you.

Signs

Signs can be as inexpensive as the chalkboard in your window, an A-frame sign outside your door, and the highway department-sponsored roadside list of nearby lodgings and food service. They can be as costly

Advertising with Small Budgets for Big Results 175

as digital, neon and mechanical signs, huge readerboards and wall murals. Many different options are discussed in "Banners," "Out-of-Home" and "Posters," and here you'll find information on:

- Sidewalk signs.
- Building signs.
- Vehicle signage.
- Yard signs.
- Roadside and rest area signs.

A-frame Sidewalk Signs

Sidewalk signs can be plywood and painted with a permanent message or, for convenience in changing messages, made with chalkboard paint, a whiteboard, or a frame into which a laminated paper poster can be inserted. Plastic signs can be purchased with chalkboard surfaces and poster frames. Other sidewalk sign options include vertical signs that can swing, some with bases that are filled with water to keep the signs erect. Signs installed in windy areas will need anchors such as sandbags. Cost: less than $100.

Check municipal regulations regarding where signs can be placed. For vendors, check local sign shops or search online for "sidewalk signs."

Building Signs

The signs with your business or organization name may be painted on the building or windows, or built of wood, acrylic, or metal. Some businesses start out with banners fastened over the previous tenant's sign or poster-size clings in the window.

What you choose will depend in part on zoning regulations and the conditions of your lease, if any. If yours is a stand-alone building and you have the right to paint each side, consider well-designed promotional messages that will serve as billboards for you.

Some signs are three-dimensional, with cut-outs of eyeglasses for the optometrist, shoes for the cobbler, cups for the coffee shop, donuts for the pastry shop, and a vehicle at the new car dealership. Others have 3D displays that change: a mannequin who "moves" up the side of a building every week, adding more to the "painted" message, or mechanized figures that wave.

Readerboards can be part of elevated illuminated signs, an expensive and permanent installation, or movable, at street level. Ideally, they'll be constructed of material unlikely to break and easy to clean if vandalized with thrown objects or paint. If the letters on street-level readerboards can be secured behind a lockable frame, there's less chance that your message will be revised by pranksters. (As a laundry in Seattle's Fremont neighborhood was chagrined to learn, when employees arrived one morning to see letters rearranged into obscenities.)

Window clings, available in poster size for as little as $10, can be used to advertise short-term promotions, customer testimonials or quotes from recent reviews.

Roadside Signage

State highway departments offer simple signage for food service, lodging, gas stations, and other traveler services. They also offer "Adopt-a-Highway" programs with signs that credit sponsors, which can be individuals, groups or businesses.

The federal law about "motorist information" programs is described at "A History and Overview of the Federal Outdoor Advertising Program," fhwa.dot.gov/real_estate/practitioners/oac/oacprog.cfm. A few examples of how this is implemented in states:

Advertising with Small Budgets for Big Results 177

- In Washington, those services eligible to have logos on "motorist information signs" are listed at wsdot.wa.gov/Operations/Traffic/Signs/requirements.htm.

A limited number of logos are on each sign, and spaces are sold on a first come, first served basis, so your business may be wait-listed until another business gives up its spot. Fees for a year range from less than $200 to about $900 per sign.

- In Michigan, the web page "Advertising Your Business with a Sign along a State Trunkline," michigan.gov/mdot/0,1607,7-151-9625-53460...,00.html, explains the two programs available: Tourist Oriented Directional Signs, which start at $360 per year, and Specific Services Signing (Logos), which costs $850 per direction.

- The Kentucky Department of Travel outlines its programs at kentuckytourism.com/industry/tourism_signage.aspx.

Rest Area Signage and Brochure Distribution

In many states, contractors handle ad sales for rest area signs and brochure distribution.

The Washington Department of Transportation web page, "Highway Advertising Control," lists its contractor as Storeyco., Inc., storeyco.com. Backlit signs are priced by size and location; they start at $90 per month. Brochure distribution starts at $35 per month per rest area; a 12-area package is $280 per month.

Oregon Travel Experience, ortravelexperience.com, handles signage at the Travel Center at Woodburn Premium Outlets, which has an estimated 4.8 million visitors annually. Its displays are appropriate for travel destinations and tourism businesses. Oregon also has a dozen information kiosks, most at rest areas. Both offer simple brochure and magazine-style distribution and backlit displays. OTE says that information must relate to travel: lodging, food, attractions, events, museums, historic districts, parks, transportation or public service announcements regarding travel.

Idaho Tourism, commerce.idaho.gov/about-us/travel, is less formal, with one staff member reporting, "Generally, the centers are happy to have any materials of interest to travelers." Business owners or nonprofit directors (say, of a museum) can walk into a center and ask that materials be displayed. Idaho Tourism can also provide details on seasonal and year-round centers, contacts and shipping information.

In your state, start with the Department of Transportation; it may take a few phone calls to obtain details about signage and brochure distribution. Another option: when at a rest area, check the displays carefully to see if a contractor's contact information appears anywhere, such as with the number to report vandalism or weather damage.

"Adopt-a-Highway"

Especially along freeways, you'll often see signs recognizing businesses, organizations or families for sponsoring clean-up efforts for a certain area. Programs are organized in two ways:

☐ With corporate sponsors, who in return for fees ranging from $250 to $600 a month and contracting with a maintenance company, are allowed to have their names and logos on signs.

☐ With volunteers, many participating in programs organized by the International Adopt-A-Highway Association, adopt-a-highway.org.

The sponsored "Adopt-a-Highway" programs are described at such websites as:

☐ State of Maryland, roads.maryland.gov, "Sponsor a Highway."

☐ State of New Hampshire, nh.gov/dot/org/operations/highwaymaintenance/sponsorahighway.

Advertising with Small Budgets for Big Results 179

Two approved businesses that pick up litter are:

□ Adopt-a-Highway Litter Removal Service of America, adoptahighway.net/, which works with 15 states.

□ Adopt A Highway Maintenance Corp., adoptahighway. com/, which has an online map showing which areas in its contract area are currently without sponsors. A spokesperson pointed out, "This is one of the few outdoor media that small business can advertise on the same level as large companies. A Disney sign is the same size as that for Joe's Plumber and our programs consist mostly of small businesses."

Washington is among the states that has two programs, one for corporate sponsors, and another for volunteers, who commit to clean a two-mile stretch of highway four times annually. See wsdot.wa.gov/Operations/adoptahwy/information.htm.

Oregon's program for volunteers has two parts: litter pick-up each quarter or noxious weed control twice annually. See oregon.gov/ODOT/HWY/OOM/pages/adopt/aah.aspx.

California's program, adopt-a-highway.dot.ca.gov/, involves a five-year commitment, and one or more activities: litter removal, planting trees or wildflowers, removing graffiti, or controlling unwanted vegetation.

Kentucky's program, transportation.ky.gov/adopt-a-highway/Pages/default.aspx, also involves a two-year commitment for quarterly clean-ups of a two-mile stretch.

Texas, where the volunteer program was created in 1985, describes its program at txdot.gov/inside-txdot/get-involved/volunteer/adopt-a-highway.html.

The volunteer projects are recognized with simple signs that show only the group or family's name. Logos appear only on signs erected through corporate sponsorships.

Vehicle Signage

Attach a sign to your company car door or window, paint a message on the side or back of your delivery van, pay for a poster on a mobile snack truck—or buy time on the rooftop taxi signs in your city.

Even simpler, buy a vanity plate and a customized license plate holder, like the Seattle computer whiz whose "GEEK2GO" plate was framed with "Digital Handyman." They're all examples of vehicle signage. As a business colleague said, "A vehicle with blank space is a wasted asset." Examples of other options:

☐ *Food truck advertising:* Also known as mobile kitchens, mobile canteens, catering trucks and sometimes "roach coaches," these food service vehicles circulate in industrial areas that lack sandwich shops, near stadiums on game days and at fairs and farmers' markets.

Some make 15-20 stops per day. Depending on their size, trucks may offer space for posters on the tailgate and serving side, or full-vehicle wraps. Some companies offer small businesses poster space for as little as $60 per month. Poster production is additional.

The editors at *Mobile Cuisine* recently suggested another way to get food trucks to attract customers to your business: invite those with appropriate menus to park in your lot. This can be especially helpful if the truck operators are among those who tweet their daily locations, so fans can follow the trucks. Another *Mobile Cuisine* tip: pass out coupons—with every purchase in your business, a customer receives a discount coupon for the food truck of the day. With every food truck purchase, the customer receives a coupon good at your business.

☐ *Taxi cab advertising:* Depending on your location, you might pay as little as $200 for a cab-top or trunk sign for four weeks. Other options include "Taxi TV," with 15 to 60-second commercials running on vehicles; and full wraps, where the cab becomes a mobile billboard, at fees starting at $1,000 per four-week period. With taxi cab advertising agencies, often the same companies that provide outdoor, transit and airport ads, minimum purchases may apply. In smaller communities, with owner-operated cabs, try to negotiate a one-cab ad deal.

☐ *Rooftop signs:* Illuminated signs attached to your

rooftop with magnets can be purchased for less than $200. Space is limited, but you may be able to fit your name, URL or phone number on the sign.

❑ *Vehicle signs:* At a minimum, your company vehicles should be painted or signed with the company name, what your business does, telephone number and URL. State regulations may require the addition of your business or contractor's license number.

Small signs for windows can be made as transparent decals or clings for as little as $5. Simple vinyl signs are available from quick print shops like FexEx Office. Or paint the vehicles with a promotional message: "Follow me to…"

❑ *Vehicle wrap:* Turn a company vehicle into advertising with a partial or full vinyl wrap. Vendors say a wrap can last for years. Because each is custom-printed and requires installation, prices vary. Expect quotes starting at $3,000 for a full wrap.

For as little as a couple of hundred dollars, trailer hitch or truck bed signs can be installed on company vehicles. The sign attached to the hitch area is best viewed by the people driving directly behind you, or those that pass your vehicle when it's parked. Truck bed signs can face sideways or back. Check eBay for options.

Another option: advertising wraps on cars driven by others. Businesses trying to attract young customers sometimes pay college students a modest stipend to have their cars wrapped. (You'll want to doublecheck the driving records of anyone you contract with for such a service, and possibly even specify in writing where the vehicle cannot be parked.)

Yard signs

Corrugated plastic and aluminum yard signs for businesses, campaigns and events can cost as little as a few dollars each, or as much as $15, depending on the quantity you order and whether the design is template-based or custom. Sizes start at 18 x 12 inches. They are available at many different sign and print shops and at big-box office supplies stores as well as from online vendors.

Where you place the signs will depend on local regulations and on how many friends and business colleagues will allow you to post signs in their yards or parking lots. Like A-frame signs, these are ideal for home improvement contractors and gardeners to use temporarily outside project sites.

Social Media

Facebook, Twitter, LinkedIn and blogs are among the oldest ("old" being a relative term here) forms of social media still popular. Google, originally only a search engine and an advertising medium; Amazon.com, originally only an online retailer; Pinterest; Google+; Instagram; and Vimeo are among those increasing in value, especially for certain merchants and services. All are online ways to connect: for you with current and prospective clients, and with colleagues and friends who may recommend you.

This is by necessity an overview of the most common and better established social media sites. New ones launch every day, so a search with such terms as "new social media/ social marketing sites" and a date such as "2014" will bring up articles on both new sites and trends. You can also use Google Alerts, google.com/alerts, to monitor online articles on the topic for you.

In this section:

Advertising with Small Budgets for Big Results

- Getting followers.
- Posting without wasting time.
- Syndicating updates.
- Social media sites, for posting and for ads.

Getting People to Follow You

Developing a following—legitimately, not by paying a service to somehow acquire names for you—requires at least:

- Appealing text describing your business or organization, and if possible, attractive graphics.
- Publicizing your social media sites on every ad, every mailer, every email and web page, with the appropriate icons and links to your pages.
- Writing interesting posts of value to followers.
- Re-tweeting others' posts as appropriate.

Social media sites typically show the screen names of the people following you. More information is sometimes available through services such as Twtrland, twtrland.com, which in its free version shows the information your Twitter followers have provided regarding gender, location and profession or interest, as well as what posts have been re-tweeted.

Saving Time When Posting

The most common complaint about social media posting that small businesspeople make: "Don't have time." They're right: it *is* often difficult to remember to make time in a hectic day to post or "tweet" or "comment." For some people, it's intimidating to think of creating daily messages of interest to your market. The prospect of creating that same message in 140 characters can be overwhelming. There are at least four ways to reduce time spent on posts:

Composing Good Posts

Writing posts that make sense given the constraints on character count takes practice. The more readable your post, the more easily your message is communicated, and the more likely it will be forwarded by your followers ("go viral").

Use only standard abbreviations and, whenever possible, punctuation. Facebook allows many more characters than Twitter, but words in excess of about 40 can only be seen if your "friends" click on "See More." On LinkedIn, without clicking on a post, visitors see about 20 words of a headline and about 40 words of a message.

A few examples of Twitter posts, using content from above:

"Writing posts or tweets that make sense given the constraints on character count takes practice."

This post has 82 characters so it'll work as a tweet...except that a recipient has no context, no contact information, no direct response "call to action."

Better: "Writing posts or tweets that make sense given the constraints on character count takes practice, says Linda Carlson in Advertising with Small Budgets for Big Results."

Except this has 141 characters (without the quotation marks), so it won't work. Lacks contact information, too.

One possible solution, with 138 characters: "Writing posts or tweets that make sense given constraints on character count takes practice, says Linda Carlson in Advertising with Small Budgets for Big Results."

Except that this provides no contact information.

Here's a revision that works with exactly 140 characters because the period has been eliminated. "Writing posts or tweets that make sense given constraints on character count takes practice, says Advertising with Small Budgets for Big Results, lindacarlson. com"

Increase your visibility by re-tweeting information from those you follow, adding a word or two so it's obvious who did the re-tweeting.

When your posts are re-tweeted, respond with a thank you to your follower, and then post about the re-tweet: "So pleased that Linda Carlson re-tweeted our post about..."

Advertising with Small Budgets for Big Results 185

☐ Follow on Twitter only those people whose information you need or sincerely want. The more people you follow, the more likely you'll have hundreds of tweets to read each day.

☐ Distribute almost everything created for one social media site to all your sites. Blog or tweet once, and have that message appear everywhere else you're set up to post. Blogging software often offers that option, as do other programs and the social media sites themselves.

☐ Make social media posts part of your regular media release distribution. Use the headline or first paragraph of a media release as your tweet, Facebook post and "What's New" announcement on your website.

☐ Schedule several posts or tweets at once. Once a week, once a month, whenever you have a spare five minutes, set up posts—the teaser for your next sale, the announcement of the sale, a couple of posts on what the sale includes, and then the "last chance" posts for the sale.

Create the announcements of job openings, new employees, new products or services all at once, and schedule each for a separate post.

To schedule posts on Facebook, see the clock face on the lower portion of the block where you type your post.

For scheduling Twitter posts, use a website such as SocialOomph, socialoomph.com, HootSuite, hootsuite.com, or TweetDeck, tweetdeck.com.

Some services also post to Facebook and other social media sites; most have free options. If you always post with these services and seldom check your own Twitter and Facebook pages, you'll save time by not having to read what others have posted.

Syndicating Updates

RSS (Rich Site Summary) and Atom can be added to your website, blog and social media sites to publish updates. Once your customers, prospects or the media subscribe to a website with RSS or Atom or both installed, people's browsers constantly monitor your site and inform users of updates. The

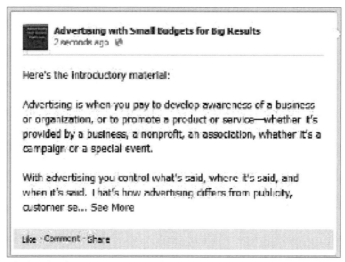

Only the first 40-some words can be seen on a Facebook post unless the reader clicks on "See More."

"feed", "web feed", or "channel" includes full or summarized text, and metadata, like publishing date and author's name.

A website owner who wants to allow other sites to publish its content creates an RSS document and registers the document with an RSS publisher. Syndicated content can be news feeds, events listings, news stories, headlines, project updates, excerpts from discussion forums and even corporate information—whatever the website owner chooses.

RSS is written in the Internet coding language known as XML (eXtensible Markup Language). Some online sites— WordPress, for example—have built-in feeds. If you need to create an RSS feed for your site, it is possible to do from a text editor such as Notepad. For the specific format of tags, check online for how-to's. To make it easy for people to subscribe to your feeds, add buttons for the most popular RSS readers to your sites. (See below for an example.)

For subscribing to feeds, use an RSS reader, software that collects and displays RSS feeds. Some browsers have built in RSS readers. If yours doesn't, an online search will show what's available, either free or for purchase.

Facebook

It's valuable to have a Facebook page for your organization, and if applicable, one for each major product. This is a place where you can encourage satisfied customers to post endorsements or "likes."

Important: only a limited number of words of a Facebook post will show in the feed. So like with Twitter posts, put vital information first.

LinkedIn

LinkedIn started out as a place for individuals; businesses and organizations can now have pages. It's also a place for endorsements. Each executive and manager should have a LinkedIn page, with your organization listed by name on the individuals' employment history. When you receive compliments on your work, or that of your employees, consider asking that the compliment also be posted to the appropriate LinkedIn page.

Even detailed profiles are free on LinkedIn. Strive to keep them updated. If you opt for LinkedIn Premium, a fee-based service, you can see exactly who has checked your profile in the event these are potential customers. You can also see who is connected with your contacts, so that someone you know may be able to provide an introduction for you to a potential client.

For businesses, there are some qualifying factors. One is a domain name for the company website. For details, see "Adding A Company Page" at LinkedIn.com.

Google+

Google+ offers the opportunity to put contacts in different groups, so that you can select who gets which posts, and sees which websites that you contribute to, and what videos you have posted.

Pinterest

Pinterest, pinterest.com/business/create/, can be described as a digital scrapbook of images that "pinners" are sharing with the public and with each other. Or, as the company says, "A pin could be a gift, recipe or even a quote. If you add the Pin It button to your website, people can use it to pin your stuff to Pinterest. Then lots more people can repin those things or click back to your website."

The key word: "image." If yours is a business or organization that can be promoted with high-quality images, consider Pinterest. As the company reminds us, "The very best boards are inspiring, with beautiful images that draw people in."

A few thoughts regarding how to encourage the pinning of your material on pinners' sites on Pinterest:

□ Add the Pin It button to every page of your website with images.

□ Add the Pin It button to your newsletter, if you have one with graphics, and to online ads.

□ Track your pins with Pinterest web analytics and post to Twitter, Facebook and other sites about them.

Instagram

This free application, in early 2014 only available on Apple iOS and Android devices at instagram.com, allows users to upload and share photos and videos. They can also comment on and "like" posts shared by friends. How it can be used by business-to-business operations is demonstrated by an example on the Instagram website:

"[Since September 2011] Maersk Line, the world's largest shipping container company, ...has been using its account (@maerskline) to build awareness and affinity for the brand.

"'Because we are a classic B2B brand, some people just thought of us as another boring, big company,' said Jonathan Wichmann, who manages the @maerskline account."

The Denmark-based company shares images of its 600-plus container ships and ports all over the globe. "Occasionally, @maerskline digs into the past and shares images from the company's photo library, highlighting the rich, century-old heritage of the shipping business...Followers are encouraged to engage as well by tagging sightings of the company's ships…and the photos are shared by Maersk Line on other platforms such as Facebook and Twitter."

YouTube
YouTube, youtube.com, describes itself as "a distribution platform for original content creators and advertisers large and small."

Businesses and nonprofits have two options: one is to upload videos that promote products or business in general. For this, you need a free Google account (Google now owns YouTube) and the simple how-to's for a business account at "Create a new channel." See YouTube > Help > Signing Up.

The other option: advertising. From the YouTube menu, select "Advertising," and with the sign-up instructions for a new campaign, select the geographic area where you want your ad shown (based on where users' computers or other devices are home-based), what devices you want the ad shown on, and many other options.

YouTube offers two advertising programs. One is pay-per-click; you're charged only when a YouTube viewer clicks on your ad. As with pay-per-click ads on Google, you can specify a budget for each day. You also specify the highest amount you're willing to pay for any single click (e.g., $1). With CPM (cost-per-thousand impressions) bidding, you'll pay every time your ad is displayed to a site visitor.

Vimeo
Vimeo, vimeo.com is a video hosting and sharing site. Among the business videos it hosts are trailers for concerts, movies and books. When comparing Vimeo to YouTube, website Mashable wrote: "No distracting banners or 30-second commercials before your video starts…[and] Vimeo allows you to password-protect your videos, so you can share them with friends before setting them as public…you just forward the video to your recipient and make sure they know which password to type in."

Advertising on Social Media Sites
Many social media sites limit ad formats. Headlines on

each site may all be the same size, and the number of characters for both headline and text are limited. Most offer at least two payment options, usually pay-per-click, for each time someone clicks on your ad, and CRM, when you're charged when your ad appears on a site, whether or not anyone clicks on it. Some examples:

 □ *Facebook:* Ads, either all text or a default image, appear in "News Feed," in the right column of any page on the site, or in search results. Among the billing options are pay-per-click, which can easily be $2 or $3 each. See "Create An Ad" at the bottom of your Facebook page.

 □ *LinkedIn:* An ad can have as many as 25 characters for a headline, as many as 75 for a description, company name, a small square image and the URL of the landing page. You can also have "sponsored updates" from a business's page.

LinkedIn requires a minimum daily budget of $10. For pay-per-click, the minimum bid is $2; on the CRM basis, the charge is $2 for each 1,000 times the ad is displayed, whether or not clicked. LinkedIn reserves the right to exceed your

daily budget by 20 percent. See "Business Solutions" in LinkedIn's top menu or "Advertising," the bottom of its home page.

 □ *Pinterest:* It was late 2013 before Pinterest began trying out ads, which initially promoted pins on search results and

Social Media Advertising Reports

Page Likes[?]	Campaign Reach[?]	Frequency[?]	Clicks[?]	Click-Through Rate[?]	Total Spent[?]
16	23,636	1.5	(102)	0.286%	$50.00

Ads, home page, desktops	REACH	FREQUENCY	IMPRESSIONS	UNIQUE CLICKS	COST PER UNIQUE CLICK
Ads, home page, desktops	358	1.31	469	0	0
Ads, desktops	125	1.62	202	0	0
News feed, mobile devices	373	1.02	(379)	(6)	7.77
News feed, desktops	516	1.00	517	0	0

This report on the Facebook ad shown on page 190 indicates that more than 23,000 pages displayed the ad, and that 102 viewers clicked through to the home page associated with the ad. This response rate looks low, but as you'll read in "Websites," this is almost triple what web site banner ads typically pull. On average, people were shown the ad 1.5 times (the frequency).

What this report does not reveal is that most of the page "likes" were for pages other than the advertised book—instead, for the page for my high school reunions and the page for another book, Company Towns of the Pacific Northwest. *What's most significant about this is in the third line, which shows the device used to access the ad:* all *of the unique clicks resulted from people using smart phones.*

Campaign	Status ✱	Budget ✱	Clicks ✱	Impressions ✱	CTR ✱
Advertising Guide	On	Daily 15.00 USD	0	5,216	0.000 %
Total for All Campaigns			0	5,216	0.000 %

Here is the initial report on the ad that ran on LinkedIn (see page 190). The first day it reportedly was shown on more than 5,200 pages, but no one clicked through to the landing page. Subsequent reports showed a similar lack of results. The conclusion: LinkedIn readers are unlikely to be the owners or managers of very small businesses and thus the medium is not appropriate for advertising a book such as this.

category feeds. It had already been offering "rich pins," with metadata embedded in the pins so that additional information (for example, pricing, availability, and where to buy) was available on selected kinds of pins: products, recipes, movies and articles. There's an application process, but as of 2014, no charge for rich pins.

□ *Twitter:* The most common Twitter ad is a promoted tweet—a 140-character message you create and pay to have inserted in Twitter accounts. As on Google, you can define your target audience and your budget, and then Twitter will bid for you for available slots.

You pay only when someone interacts with an ad, which in late 2013 happened 1 to 3 percent of the time, estimated the *New York Times,* which went on to say, "The holy grail for advertisers is an ad that is widely shared by Twitter users to their own followers. To increase the chances of going viral, brands will often embed photos and videos into their ads."

Another Twitter option, simple but expensive: pay for a place on the company's list of trending topics. In the U.S. in late 2013, the list cost for 24 hours was about $200,000. See "Advertisers" and "Businesses," bottom, Twitter home page.

Swag/Goodie Bags

Registrants at many conferences and trade shows are handed tote bags as they check in. Besides being a convenient way to gather the samples and information passed out at lectures, meetings and exhibits, these totes usually hold "swag," and are often called swag or "goodie" bags.

Swag in this case is giveaways provided by exhibitors. Businesses pay to have material distributed in the bags at some events; in other cases, all that is required is the donation of giveaways such as pencils, pens, T-shirts, and note pads.

Says one entrepreneur about what to contribute to swag: "Useful stuff: think of what attendees will need but might have forgotten." Among the suggestions: first aid supplies in a package labeled with your business name, or unusual items that relate to the conference theme or your exhibit: a folding dog dish at a wholesale pet show, for example. If you want recipients to carry your swag home, make it easily packed, and appropriate for airline carry-ons.

Costs for swag bag insertions vary depending on the conference or show, and the size or weight of your piece. One service that inserts material in home school conference and bridal show swag bags has a minimum charge of about a quarter per piece. This is in addition to the cost of producing the piece and shipping it to the swag bag service.

Television

Say "advertising" and most of us think, "television," and for good reason: that's where about 40 percent of advertising dollars is spent in the U.S. For those of us on tight budgets, "television" usually equals "expensive." Certainly commercials on Super Bowl and Oscar broadcasts are more than most people reading this can afford.

To help you determine whether television would be an appropriate means of reaching your market even if budget were no constraint, this section covers:

□ Viewing trends.

□ Creating commercials.

□ Ratings lingo.

□ How to buy television time on a budget.

□ Cable television.

□ Public television.

First, recognize that the television audience is not increasing overall, and because it's become such a fragmented marketplace, no one program or series can attract a significant audience. Today there are far more channels to surf then when three national networks and a public television network dominated the air waves.

Another issue: fewer televisions are on.

In mid-2013 broadcast ratings agency Nielsen issued data showing that in some areas, televisions are on for fewer than three hours a day. In San Francisco, for example, on average, only 2.57 hours of television were watched live (that is, not pre-recorded). In Los Angeles, it was 3.39 hours, in Denver, 3.45 hours, and in Seattle, 3.5 hours.

Data from Nielsen also shows that the more education people have and the higher their income, the less television they watch. Other reasons why television commercials may not make sense:

☐ The number of households with televisions is declining, with younger viewers among those who instead use computers, tablets and other devices.

☐ The number of households subscribing to cable has declined.

☐ Many who do view broadcast television are time-shifting with DVRs, which allows them to fast-forward through commercials or completely eliminate them.

☐ The time spent with video continues to increase, especially among younger viewers (those 18-34).

In late 2013, Nielsen wrote, "Tablet penetration at the household level in the U.S. has already reached 28 percent. In some DMAs, such as New York, San Francisco, Boston and Washington, D.C., the penetration level is over 35 percent. This rapid adoption is likely to continue. In fact, the Consumer Electronics Association forecasts that tablets

---

Decline in Viewers

The February 2014 Super Bowl broadcast was seen by an estimated 111.5 million people, an all-time record for U.S. television. But its rating of 47.7 still represented less than half of households with televisions. By contrast, the previously top-ranked program of all time (still the record for anything other than football), the finale of "M.A.S.H." in 1983, was viewed in more than 60 percent of households. And the number of homes with televisions continues to drop; in early 2014, Nielsen reported 96.7 percent of American households owned sets, down from 98.9 percent previously.

could have a 48 percent U.S. household penetration rate by the beginning of 2014."

Creating Commercials

Although buying television time is expensive, a more serious budget issue can be the creative. Most of us have groaned through commercials with corny spiels, those that use the business owner's grandchildren as spokespeople or are of such low-resolution video that they scream "homemade": advertising that misses the opportunity to enhance the image of the business.

A high quality commercial, especially one that will air on national television, will probably cost $300,000 to $500,000. That's storyboarding, scripting, professional actors, location, filming, and post-production, best coordinated by advertising agencies with extensive television experience.

Must You Spend That Much?

No. Ads don't *have* to cost hundreds of thousands of dollars.

If you're standing in front of the camera in a local studio or on location (say, in your business), you might be able to get a reasonable spot for a couple of thousand dollars. Before you commit to a spot, however, watch dozens of commercials in the length you have in mind (15-, 30- or 60-second) and jot down priorities and concerns to discuss with whoever will be editing your spot. Make sure they acknowledge what's important in creating a positive perception of your business.

Options for a well-made commercial at a reasonable price:

☐ Work with instructors at local art or film schools, either with the instructors themselves or with advanced students who need final projects.

☐ Negotiate production of a commercial as part of your broadcast time purchase at a local television station.

☐ Determine whether a studio-shot commercial (especially if you're not paying for studio rental) can be as effective as a location shoot (which requires that a crew travel and set up either outdoors or in your facility).

□ Have the station or your media buying agency edit footage you've had shot with a hand-held camcorder that can produce high-resolution video (nope, not the time for video from your smart phone).

□ Use still photography, your own or stock images, either alone or combined with video.

□ Use footage available through the cooperative advertising program for the product you're promoting, with your name and contact information added at the end.

□ Use stock footage available through the station, your media buyer or a stock photo service.

Attire and Make-up

Even if those appearing in your commercial want to look casual, both men and women should be made up by a make-up artist experienced in film work (major stations have contact information for free-lancers, and you can use one of those free-lancers even if you're being filmed elsewhere).

Unless people are appearing in uniforms, attire should be carefully selected so that it's not distracting in color, pattern or style. What's best: a flattering dark solid in a flat weave or knit that will not reflect light. Avoid seasonal styles if you plan to use the commercial for several months. Of course, everything should be carefully pressed and checked for lint.

Look Good for the Camera

Avoid cleavage.

Avoid showing underwear, either at the neckline, shoulder, hemline or because clothing is lightweight or semi-transparent.

Wear clothes that are loose enough that shirts and fly fronts don't pull open even when you're seated in a low chair.

Avoid jewelry that makes noise or reflects light.

If your hair is colored, have roots at the part touched up immediately prior to any on-screen appearance, whether for a commercial, a public television pledge drive or a talk or news show.

Because the camera "adds" pounds, dress and be made up to look as slender as possible. Attire is a special issue if those speaking will have microphones attached. You'll want these mics to be inconspicuous, and not obviously pinching lapels or necklines.

What Commercials Can Say

Not everything can be advertised on television. The federal government has certain restrictions (for example, on liquor and tobacco) and stations may have their own prohibitions.

A starting place for information about product comparisons, testimonials, guarantees and deceptive pricing is with the Federal Trade Commission's Advertising Guidance, at ftc.gov/bcp/guides/guides.shtm

Television Ratings Lingo

Both radio and television advertising are sold based on how many people (or households) in your target market see or hear your commercial and how often they see or hear the commercial. These are defined as:

□ *Reach:* the percentage of homes or individuals who see a commercial at least once during a specific period. This figure eliminates duplication.

Nielsen and other ratings agencies will quote this figure in terms of the time periods they use (e.g., "prime time") and advertising salespeople will use the ratings for reach to estimate how many people will see your commercial in the time period you've selected.

□ *Frequency:* of the households or people who are reached, this is the average number of times they will see the commercial during a specific time period.

□ *Gross Rating Points*: GRPs can refer to households within a target audience. This complicated-sounding term is simply a way of combining reach and frequency to compare different advertising options—different day parts, different days, different seasons, different stations. Expressed mathematically:

GRPs = Reach x Frequency
Reach = GRPs/Frequency
Frequency = GRPs/Reach

If 20 percent of the homes in your market area see a commercial, and on average, it's seen twice in these homes, the gross rating points for that media buy is 40: 20 x 2.

Buying Television Time

How much a television advertising campaign costs depends on such factors as:

□ *Location:* A network-affiliate San Francisco channel will cost more than a similar station in San Antonio or Spokane. If your target is one television market (say, Seattle-Tacoma), you'll pay less than if you want all of Washington state, all of the Pacific coast, or every market west of the Rockies.

Television markets are often described with a Nielsen-trademarked term, Designated Market Area (DMA), which refers to the geographic area where residents can receive the same or similar programming and thus the same commercials.

□ *Channel type:* Today most stations operate their original broadcast channels, usually network affiliates, as well as digital sub-channels. (See examples below.) Commercials cost less on these sub-channels. If you're considering a secondary carrier, you'll want to know how much power it has (and thus, how large an area it can serve) and whether it's provided by the most popular cable services.

□ *Time of day:* Prime time, that portion of the evening when audiences are expected to be largest, costs the most. "Overnight," the wee hours, costs the least.

Channel Examples

In Seattle, commercial stations include:

□ KING, the NBC affiliate
□ KING-DT2, a sub-channel
□ KONG, KING's independent station
□ KONG-DT2, a sub-channel;
□ NWCN, a regional news channel
□ KOMO, the ABC affiliate
□ KOMO-DT2, a sub-channel
□ KIRO, the CBS affiliate
□ KIRO-DT2, a sub-channel.

Advertising with Small Budgets for Big Results **199**

> ## Commercial Air Time Rate Examples
>
> In 2013, 30-second spots airing nationwide on ABC, CBS or NBC on popular prime-time shows cost between $200,000 and $600,000 each.
>
> Organizations on tight budgets are more likely to consider local stations and the time slots not committed to national advertising.
>
> In Spokane, for example, an early evening spot on the local CBS station might cost less than $300. In Eugene, Ore., the same spot could be less than $400. In Seattle, an early evening spot on the local ABC or Fox station might be around $800. In Missoula or Bangor, spots could cost $50 to $100. In an even smaller market, $3,000 might buy enough spots for a four-week campaign.

□ *The popularity of the programs on which your commercials air.* High ratings by Nielsen equal high costs, because those shows are expected to deliver the largest number of the most desirable viewers.

□ *Audience:* Programs that attract the most desirable age, gender, income level and race will cost more. In general, viewers between 25 and 54 in age are the most desirable, and women are more desirable than men, because they are perceived to make most of the purchase decisions for a household.

□ *Availability:* High demand—during campaign and holiday seasons, for example—decreases the spots available, and increases the cost.

How much your spots cost also depends on *how* you buy. If you've never purchased television advertising before, and you contact a station, you'll probably be quoted the published rates.

Working with a media buyer or advertising agency may result in a better package. Another option: the firms which buy time in bulk and wholesale rates and then pass it on at "commissionable rates" to customers. ("Commissionable rates" are the discounted prices that a media buyer or agency is quoted.) Such firms will not have time available in every slot on every station.

Saving Money on Your Television Buy

Media buyers suggest several ways to reduce the costs of commercials. These involve trade-offs: less control of time and audience demographic and size.

This means these ideas are best for supplementing an existing schedule. They are unlikely to work if you're testing television as a possible medium for your advertising because you won't have fixed schedules that can be compared.

□ *Remnant advertising.* Remnant, remainder, "fire sale" or "last minute" air time is time that the station has not sold. It's sometimes available at huge discounts, as much as a half or a quarter of an "upfront" price. ("Upfront" is when national advertising time is reserved in huge blocks in advance of the fall season).

Your commercial may be pre-empted, however, if a major advertiser suddenly decides to buy the time. You sometimes get a week or two notice that remnant space is available.

□ *Negotiate added value.* Ask for extras such as advertising on the station's website, either the streaming of your commercial or a banner ad, and being included in any promotions scheduled for the website. If you're eligible, ask for PSAs (public service announcements). One advantage of working with a media buyer or advertising agency is that they will be more aware of what stations have offered other advertisers.

If you've read "Cutting Costs on Radio Buys" in "Radio," you know there are such other options as lower-priced day parts. Of course, this only makes sense if you're sure your audience has access to television at that time of day. If you're targeting professional women, for example, buying midday time slots is not cost-effective.

Cable Television

Think cable, and you may think of the Cartoon Network, or old movies or of the blockbuster cable-only television series.

Advertising with Small Budgets for Big Results

Of the national cable networks that are supported both by subscriber fees and by advertising, the most popular are the USA Network, Disney Channel, ESPN, TNT, History, Fox News, TBS, A&E, Nickelodeon, and Nick at Nite.

A 30-second spot running on CNN in the evening could cost as little as $6,500 and a Saturday afternoon spot on ESPN about $11,000 as part of a multiple-spot package.

But there's more to cable than the national programming. Every community with a cable station can impose a cable franchise fee. This fee is what helps support local access cable television.

Although these stations often do not accept advertising, they may carry programs uploaded by the public. This means that if you have a skill or interest that relates to your business, you could create a program that indirectly promotes the business. Similarly, a nonprofit could create a program about its cause as a means of developing awareness both of the issue and of the nonprofit.

Examples of Local Cable Stations

☐ Seattle Community Media, seattlecommunitymedia.org, is an advertising-free station that encourages members to create programs about their skills and interests. Programs must be noncommercial in nature.

Membership starts at $35 a year, and the classes necessary to use SCM studios and equipment are $50 each. Membership is open to individuals who live in King County and nonprofit organizations, educational institutions, and government agencies.

By contrast, an hour's drive south, Pierce County TV runs only news of the government bodies in its area: city council and school board meetings, for example.

☐ Portland Community Media, pcmtv.org, also offers training courses ($100) for those who wish to use its facilities. Prerecorded programs can also be uploaded to the system. For Oregon nonprofits to publicize their mission or an event in a couple of sentences, there's a free Community Bulletin Board.

☐ Treasure Valley Community Television, tvctvonline.org, based in Boise, says it encourages programs that "provide a forum for debate on local issues; inform residents about community services; expand the audience for a local band, poet or craftsperson; give people a fresh perspective on aspects of our community; follow a subject or issue on a regular basis; present a documentary view of a neighbor, friend or organization in town that's doing something interesting; teach skills ranging from gardening to origami…" Regular individual memberships start at $50. In addition, there are class fees.

PBS Affiliates

The Public Broadcasting System describes itself as "a private, nonprofit corporation, founded in 1969, whose members are America's public TV stations—noncommercial, educational licensees that operate more than 350 PBS member stations and serve all 50 states, Puerto Rico, U.S. Virgin Islands, Guam and American Samoa." A station list is at pbs.org.

> ### Typical PBS Viewers
>
> *Oregon Public Broadcasting describes its television viewers as:*
>
> 73 percent vote
> 33 percent are white collar workers
> 76 percent own their own home
> 18 percent have $100,000+ in liquid assets
> 34 percent have at least one college degree
>
> *Idaho Public Television has similar audience data:*
> 65.7 percent vote
> 15.3 percent are professional/technical
> 79 percent own their own home
> 21.1 percent have $100,000+ of liquid assets
> 36.3 percent have at least one college degree

Like public radio, PBS stations depend on donations and underwriting. Those providing underwriting for programs can be recognized with brief station-produced spots. For example, the website of Seattle's KCTS9, kcts9.org, says, "Market your brand with either a :15 or :30 underwriting spot in a messaging environment free of commercial clutter.…we will produce most spots at no charge with supplied images or b-roll."

In Portland, the rate card for Oregon Public Broadcasting, opb.org, quantifies that clutter-free environment: 3:22 minutes of non-programming time per hour on average compared to 14:49 minutes on commercial TV and 14:23 on cable TV.

More Information

Among resources for identifying stations—network affiliate, public, cable and local—that serve your geographic area:

□ Television Bureau of Advertising, tvb.org, is the not-for-profit trade association of America's commercial broadcast television industry.

Its section for "Markets & Stations" lists stations and provides brief information on the major employers, population, number of households with televisions and with cable service. (My quick look showed that some information regarding employers in a region is incomplete.)

□ PBS.org, which allows you to search for stations by ZIP code or state.

□ Station Index, stationindex.com, an advertising-supported site that describes broadcast stations in each market, including the power of the stations and their corporate owners.

□ Television viewing guides that list channels accessible in your area.

Trade Shows and Conferences

Industry meetings are often an excellent place to network, to display your product, and to demonstrate your expertise. Does it make sense for a small business or nonprofit to attend or exhibit? This section provides information that can help you decide:

□ Costs and potential sales.

□ Networking opportunities.

□ Speaking opportunities.

□ "No-show" promotions.

Costs and Potential Sales

Trade shows can be very expensive, especially when booth rental and registration fees are added to travel, freight and lodging costs. In addition, there may be the costs of door prizes, advertising in the conference's daily "newspaper" or the schedule of events, and sponsorship of a coffee break or lunch.

Many businesses consider participating in such shows a form of image advertising, and do not expect to cover the costs with the receipts for any products sold during the show.

Questions to ask:

☐ What are registration fees? Can you register for the event and pass out information while walking the exhibit floor and while networking?

☐ What does booth rental cost? Are good locations available, or have they all been reserved for long-time exhibitors? What additional costs will you incur for electricity to the booth, furniture rental, and extra badges for the employees, free-lancers or friends you'll bring along to help staff the booth?

☐ How much time do attendees have to visit exhibits? Are important presentations and events scheduled at the same time the booths are open?

Networking

Especially for questions involving attendance, ask for verifiable numbers, not estimates. Consider contacting firms which have exhibited in recent years, and asking two questions: how worthwhile they believe the event is, and what trends, if any, they have observed in number and decision-making ability of those attending.

☐ Are attendees potential customers? If so, will the decision-makers in prospect firms be visiting your booth or attending your presentation? What media are expected? Will you receive a list of registrants for future marketing?

☐ Who can you realistically expect to be able to introduce

yourself to? What value in terms of generating sales or publicity does the networking have?

If this is a new event, those selling exhibit space may speak in terms of how much publicity is planned to attract attendees, or the speakers they hope to confirm. Carefully analyze such plans, and determine how realistic the event sponsors are in predicting interest in the event. This is especially true with such consumer events as "Baby Expos" and "Girls' Night Out."

Among factors that can affect attendance at consumer events are weather, entrance fees, location, the availability of parking, and events oriented to the same audience that occur the same week or at the same time.

Speaking

Submitting a presentation proposal may have to be done several months in advance. It's typical that speakers cannot promote their product or service while speaking or make product sales in the presentation room. Many conferences also require that speakers pay registration fees, especially if they are not exhibiting.

Although keynote speakers are often paid, most break-out room speakers are not; because there are usually several concurrent break-out presentations, sessions are not always well attended. Especially in small or newly-organized conferences, a speaker may be able to negotiate a complimentary exhibit space or a program ad in lieu of compensation.

No-show Promotions

Whether or not you decide to attend a trade show or conference, use it as a reason to contact members of the sponsoring association or others who you expect will attend. Use Facebook, Twitter, direct mail or eblasts to announce your booth location. If you're not going, do a "no-show" promotion: "We won't be at the gift show, but between now and when the show closes, take advantage of our 'no-show' discount of…"

If you will attend, contact the business editors and other

appropriate representatives of local media to ensure they know you're available for interviews.

More Information

In your industry, or the industries of your prospective customers, use the websites of appropriate trade and professional associations to find regional, state and national conference schedules. For information on conferences in any industry in your area, check schedules compiled by local convention and visitors' bureaus and chambers of commerce. An online search for "conventions" or "conferences" with a future date (probably next year's) and your city or region's name will also provide information. Other resources include these websites:

ASAE Gateway to Associations Directory, asaecenter. org/Community/Directories/associationsearch.cfm.

Weddle's, weddles.com, and select "associations."

Available online on a fee-basis are different editions of the Encyclopedia of Associations published by Gale, cengage. com; your library may also have access.

Trailers

Like a television commercial, a video trailer for your business needs to create credibility for you as a professional. Even if your profession is stand-up comedian, everything that presents you to potential clients must attest to your quality and reliability—in short, as someone people can trust. So despite having had 1,000 views of the YouTube video of your cat or dog or kid, or the funny thing that happened in the store one day, get very serious when you're making a trailer.

The first question to ask yourself and those you work with: "What will we use this for?" Perhaps you'll link to it from your website, use it in social media, and show it on a loop at trade shows or meetings. But before you go to the work and expense of creating a trailer, make sure it's something your business or organization truly needs at this time.

Especially if you anticipate using the trailer in noisy

Advertising with Small Budgets for Big Results

settings such as trade shows or career fairs, consider what can be done without sound. You can use silent-film style subtitles or speech bubbles to add dialog or text, either with video or with still photos or illustrations.

If you have good quality images (that you either own the copyright on, or are copyright-free), these may reduce or eliminate the need to shoot video.

Before you start, jot down at least the points you want to cover in the trailer. Storyboarding, creating rough sketches of what will be shown and said in each frame, will further reduce the time you spend in front of a camera or at your keyboard. Be sure to allow adequate time at the end for your contact information to be seen.

Prefer to hire someone to create your trailer? One source of information is your colleagues; they can tell you who they used, and whether that person or firm was reliable, easy to work with and reasonably priced. Another option: check the websites of local businesses for videos and at the end of each, look for the credits. Then contact the businesses to determine if they were satisfied with the work—and for any comments about what they would do differently if making a new trailer, now that theirs are in use.

More Information
"Creating Commercials" in "Television."

Websites
It is possible to be in business today without a web presence, but given how inexpensive a simple website or blog can be, it makes sense to create visibility online for your operation or organization—even if your site is a single page listing only services, location, hours and contact information. So this section discusses:

- □ Creating a website.
- □ Advertising your business online.
- □ Analyzing web traffic.
- □ Accepting advertising for your site.

What a Website Requires

A website requires only three things:

☐ A domain name, a URL, your online address, now available for a few dollars a year. All reputable website hosts and domain registrars work with ICANN. It ensures that a domain name is owned by only one operation at a time.

☐ A website host, similarly inexpensive.

☐ Web authoring software, often available free with the website host.

The easier your site is to use, the longer visitors are likely to stay. This means:

☐ A third-party search feature such as GoogleSearch.

☐ A site index, which functions as an extended table of contents.

☐ Appropriate "alternate text" for images.

For most websites, content would at a minimum have:

☐ A brief description of products, services, markets served, history and location(s).

☐ Contact information—hours, email address and contact form, telephone number, postal and delivery addresses, and if appropriate, physical address with a map or link to a map website.

☐ Media pages, one with examples of product reviews and other publicity, and another with high-resolution images of products, logo and key personnel that can be downloaded.

☐ A sitemap, which is written for search engine spiders rather than for human users as the index is.

Website Design Basics

Web authoring can be a complex task, so here you'll find only a few recommendations. Use these and web templates, or web authoring software, a savvy web design student or a web design specialist to develop a site that both explains and promotes your business or organization.

Advertising with Small Budgets for Big Results

☐ Follow good graphic design principles, limiting the number of type fonts and sizes and the number of colors.

☐ Be consistent in design from one page to the next.

☐ Make the site accessible by the visually handicapped (See "Accessibility," Lighthouse International, lighthouse.org).

☐ Evaluate the site design for the small screens of handhelds.

☐ Create a sitemap to increase visibility to search engine spiders as well as a site index to help human visitors.

Sources of information include Google's Webmaster Tools, "Sitemaps." Some web authoring help sites refer to sitemaps as site indexes, but I'm using the term index here to identify something similar to what you'll find in a book, an alphabetical and detailed list of the site contents, something more comprehensive than a table of contents.

☐ Give pages names that make sense to search engine spiders as well as humans. For example: lindacarlson.com/p/advertising.html rather than lindacarlson.com/ad4smbud.

☐ Add key words to increase the site's visibility in online searches, what's called search engine optimization.

When I created a website using blog software, the key words on the home page were listed as *meta content='Company Towns of the Pacific Northwest, PatternSpot.com, hand-crafted note cards, speech, history, speaker, marketing, book publishing.'*

However, one SEO consultant suggests another way to think of your meta description: "If your webpage were a commercial, this would be its slogan." Given that, perhaps the meta content for the web page describing this book should be: *How small businesses, nonprofits, government can advertise with very tight budgets. Cost estimates, examples, DIY options, checklists, detailed glossary.*

☐ Limit the size of each page so that little scrolling is required on a monitor.

☐ Design a footer with company name, location, contact information, "Return to Home Page," "Forward," and "Print

Friendly Format" that appears on each page of your site along with "Post on..." and the appropriate icons for social media.

☐ Write informative, customer-friendly text for the "Page Not Found" page. Explain why this page may have appeared, suggestions for finding the desired page, a search engine and an email link so that visitors can report the problem.

☐ Test your site on several different browsers.

For both marketing and security reasons, ensure that images and alternative text for images are named the same as in the website text. If I upload photos to my website, the names for each image should be clear: "linda-carlson-author.jpg" and "advertising-with-a-small-budget-cover.jpg."

The alternate text, which shows when the page is loading and the images are not yet visible, and when links are broken, should be something like "Linda Carlson, author, Advertising with Small Budgets for Big Results," and "Advertising with Small Budgets for Big Results by Linda Carlson." This will increase the chance of a search engine finding a site, and it will prevent site visitors from seeing unflattering or unprofessional image names (say, a group photo named "Staff-screwing-off.jpg"). It is safer to not identify children by name in either captions or alternate text unless they are public figures.

On the "Contact Us" page and on any pages that invite visitors to comment using forms, consider adding a CAPTCHA, captcha.net, to prevent spamming.

Most web hosts provide statistics regarding how many visitors your site receives, how many pages they visit, and how  long they stay as well as whether they reached your site via a search engine; a referring website, blog or Twitter post; or by typing in your URL.

Besides a search engine, other third-party software such as Google Analytics can be added. You'll need software like a

Advertising with Small Budgets for Big Results 211

counter and the Alexa web metrics toolbar if you plan to sell advertising on the site because prospective customers will want statistics on your visitors.

Understanding Who Visits Your Site

How do people find your site? Use the "traffic sources" section of your website statistics to review:

☐ Referrals from other sites, those that provide a link to your URL.

☐ Direct traffic, people who type your URL directly into a browser or had your site bookmarked.

☐ Organic search keywords, which guide those who reach your site via a search engine on which you are not running a paid campaign.

☐ The custom campaigns you created, perhaps using an eblast that linked to several product descriptions, or a choice of benefits (say, either 20 percent off or free shipping).

Especially if you're paying for referrals—through display ads, search engine key words, or email campaigns—evaluate how effective each source of your traffic is:

☐ How many pages of your site each visitor sees.

☐ How long the visitor stays.

☐ How many visitors leave after viewing only your home/landing page (the bounce rate).

In traditional sales and promotion, "conversion" usually means the responses to ads that result in sales. In online ad lingo, the term often applies to lesser goals, such as "liking" a page, completing a survey or requesting contact by a salesperson. When online ad salespeople say, "goal conversion rate," be sure you understand how they are defining this goal.

Actual sales made via the website are measured via "e-commerce effectiveness," which may report revenue from a sale, the number of site visitors who make purchases, and how much each visitor spends per visit on average.

Obviously, a careful study of what drives traffic to your site, and what encourages site visitors to get out their credit cards, can help you decide how to modify advertising campaigns and your website design.

One common error that results in high bounce rates: an ad that promises information that is missing from the page the visitor links to (the "landing page"). Too often ads or media stories direct prospects to the home page rather than a page created to provide details about the offer or event.

What's also important: if a page deep within your site gets lots of referrals only from a search engine, then the home page needs to link directly to that page so that site visitors can get to it quickly. Similarly, a page that generates many sales needs to have a very visible link from the home page, to catch the attention of those who are browsing the site.

Which Sites Link to Your Site?

Among the factors that determine how high your site places in search engine results is links—how many sites link to yours.

One way of checking links is with Google's "Webmaster Tools," at https://support.google.com/webmasters/answer/55281?hl=en. This page says to do a search by link:www.*yourdomainname*.com; you may also want to use link:http://*yourdomainname*.com. Remember, this is a search term, not a URL, so it's in the search box that you type "link:" immediately followed by your domain name (or your competitor's,

Example of links Google can show.

or that of any other business or organization you're interested in). For example, *link:www.lindacarlson.com*.

If you don't see as many links as you expect, Google's Webmaster Tools page provides two possible explanations:

☐ Links to a page blocked with robots.txt won't be listed. "A total count of these pages is available in the Crawl section of Webmaster Tools on the 'Blocked URLs (robots.txt) tab,'" says Google.

☐ Links that are broken or invalid won't be listed.

Using Google Analytics

Google Analytics is free, and it's what many consultants use, so there's little reason to pay one of them for information already available to you.

Among the information you can get with this Google service are SEO reports, which appear under "Traffic Sources" via the "My Site" tab:

☐ Queries users typed to reach your site.

☐ Number of impressions of your website's URLs in search results pages.

☐ The number of clicks on your website's URLs from search results pages.

☐ The ratio of clicks to impressions for your website's URLs.

☐ The average position of your website's URLs in search listings.

☐ The pages visitors landed on when clicking on search results listing your site.

You'll also receive a Navigation Summary Report, which identifies which of your pages has broken internal links.

A Blog as Your Site

Want something truly simple? Use a blog as your online site and you can avoid even minor fees.

Without a domain name, the web address for a business

like Tex's Arco will be www.texs-arco.blogger.com instead of texs-arco.com or texs-arco.info; that may be inconsequential if all you want online are the basics: your business name, address, phone number, hours and services.

Although blog software is designed to accommodate several posts, you can make your blog resemble a website by the template you select, and by always revising the initial post rather than adding new posts.

More detailed information is in the section "Blogs," and at the websites of the most popular free blog hosting sites, WordPress, wordpress.com; Blog, blog.com; Blogger, blogger.com; and Tumblr, tumblr.com.

Another economical way of getting an online presence: Facebook. Creating a Facebook page for you as a professional or for your business is free. For information, see "Social Media."

Advertising on Others' Sites

How effective is website advertising?

Banner ads, now common, pull at the rate of .01 percent today, digital designer Joe McCambley told the *New York Times* in late 2013. Read that number again: it's not one percent, or even one tenth of a percent. It means that if a site has half a million visitors, *50 of them might click through on an ad*.

These are averages, of course, which is why it's important to check statistics and be realistic when considering website ads.

What happens when someone does click on an ad and progress to your website or blog? It's unlikely that the first visit to your website will result in a purchase. Remember the maxim repeated in the beginning of this book: *It usually takes six to eight impressions before a purchase decision is made*.

Another key number: 50 percent. That's how much of Facebook advertising revenue came from mobile phones, the company reported for 2013. Industry-wide, holiday season shopping online surged in 2013, and much of that was via mobile devices. This correlates with information shown on the page, "Social Media Advertising Reports," in

> ## Click Fraud Defined
> *Click fraud is the practice of artificially inflating traffic statistics to defraud advertisers. It's done with automated clicking programs (hitbots) or low-paid workers who click links in ads. Often it is done with websites created only to house ads—websites that because of automated buying may not be verified for their quality prior to ads being placed on them.*

"Social Media," where all of the click-throughs for a certain campaign came from mobile devices. So it's important that your ads work well with phones. If response to your online ads is poor, determine how much your target market uses smart phones. More than 50 percent of Americans had smart phones as this was written, but some audiences seldom use them for shopping.

Buying through Networks

Many website ads are sold through advertising networks, or exchanges. These accumulate ad space across thousands of sites in order to sell large, targeted advertising packages to major clients.

If you're thinking about buying advertising via a network, be aware that not all networks or exchanges carefully vet the sites where ads are placed. In many cases, the entire purchase process is automated, and no one has actually seen the sites where your ad will appear.

If you have a limited budget and expect to advertise on only a few sites, consider buying direct rather than through a network or exchange. The reason: click fraud. Originally due to workers in Third World countries who were paid to continually click on certain ads, and software that could be installed on PCs to duplicate such actions, click fraud is now caused largely by "botnets."

In late 2013 the *Wall Street Journal* defined these as "zombie armies of hijacked PCs that are controlled from unknown locations around the world" and "mimic the behavior of online consumers, clicking from one site to the next, pausing at ads, watching videos, and even putting items in shopping carts."

Botnets, which the paper said can be rented or purchased online, work by infecting computers with malware. "Those infected computers are then connected by a command machine, which stealthily directs the network of zombies [to sites set up only to host ads]...A computer user may not be aware of it."

Among reasons that botnets and fraudulent traffic have become more common:

□ The use of ad networks and exchanges, which some accuse of not appropriately vetting the sites where they are placing ads.

□ Paid key word advertising with search engines.

According to the *Wall Street Journal*, as much as 29 percent of online display advertising traffic results from botnets. Translation: if you advertise through a network that does not verify website quality, at least a quarter of each online advertising dollar may be wasted.

Kinds of Ads Available

Classified: The most popular website for classified-style ads is Craigslist, craigslist.org. One reason: most advertising on it is free. Another reason: it's one of the best-read websites overall: in late 2013, it was the 11th most popular website in the U.S., according to Alexa's analysis.

Ads have a simple format, and the size options for photos are limited. Ads also have to be renewed at least once a week, and because so many ads are added daily, revising an ad slightly and re-posting it every few days is recommended. Otherwise, your ad may be buried within 24 or 36 hours by more recently posted ads in the same category.

Craigslist also expects an ad to be posted in only one category and one geographic option at a time.

Text: The short text ads and the similar ads with a single image that usually appear at the top of a search page or along the right side of a website were popularized by Google. It and

Facebook are today the dominant online ad companies.

> Show your ad on Google
> www.google.com/AdWords/Express ▼
> 1 (866) 632 6319
> Promote your business and get
> More customers. Try AdWords Express

Which of these ads appear first on a page is determined—whether via Google, on Facebook, LinkedIn or others—by automated auction. As the Google AdWords web page explains, auctions "determine the ads that show on the search results page, and their rank [position] on the page."

Ads only appear when someone has searched for terms that relate to your ad. For example, because I used "small business" as my key word for a Facebook advertising test, the ad could only appear when someone searched on Facebook for "small business." Whether the ad actually did appear depended on whether I had bid enough compared to other advertisers whose key words also related to a search such as "small business."

The more you agree to pay for each of your key words, the more likely your ad will appear. That is, if anyone is interested in your topic. If people rarely ever search using the key words you've chosen, your ad won't have much chance to be shown, regardless of what you bid.

A search for "most popular key words" will turn up thousands of terms, many of them so general that you're unlikely to be successful with them unless you have a large budget. One free resource is "Using Keyword Planner to get keyword ideas and traffic estimates," on a Google.com support page; you can use it to see how often your possible key words have been used in searches.

Banner Ads: Display ads—horizontal, vertical or square— can be all-text, in your choice of fonts and colors, or they can be a combination of images and text, like ads in print media. As with many magazines, there are standard sizes for banner ads:

728 x 90 pixels
468 x 60 Pixels
392 x 72 Pixels
234 x 60 Pixels

120 x 240 Pixels
120 x 90 Pixels
120 x 60 Pixels
125 x 125 Pixels
88 x 31 Pixels

Source: IAB

Banner Ad Production: Especially when buying an ad on a small site, you'll avoid surprises if you send the site owner a graphics file that meets the site's specifications for the banner (or skyscraper, a vertical banner). If the URL of the landing page is not incorporated in the ad, provide that to the site owner.

You can produce your own banner ad if your graphics software allows you to create a JPEG or GIF. Once you've done that in the dimensions of the banner you plan to buy, create a table in your HTML editor of the appropriate dimensions and type in link tags that will direct site visitors from the ad to your website. (For specifics on HTML tags, use your editor or the online how-to's in Appendix F.) Then name and save your file with the .html extension.

If you're a web-authoring whiz or you're working with one, be aware that while banners that have audio, video, and other sophisticated components work well, they take a long time to load. This means that visitors to a site might scroll past your ad before it's loaded.

Fees for Website and Blog Ads

The websites and blogs that host display advertising charge in different ways.

□ ***Flat rate*** is a simple method. For example, it's what is used by the Washington Newspaper Publishers Association, wnpa.com, which sells space for the print editions and websites of dozens of non-daily papers, papers that may not have IT specialists. It charges $200 per month per paper for a 728 x 90 pixel banner when the order includes at least 20 publications.

More common are:

□ *Pay-per-click*, also called cost-per-action, pay-per-action, or cost-per-conversion, charges the advertiser for each specified action: usually someone clicking on an ad, submitting a form, signing up for a newsletter, registering for an event, or making a purchase.

□ *CPM, cost per thousand*, where the advertiser pays each time the ad appears on a page. Like the advertising billing method used by newspapers, magazines, television and radio, fees are based on the assumption that people who view the web page will see your ad. You pay regardless of whether they do, and whether they take any action, such as clicking through to your website.

Accepting Advertising for Your Site
Running ads can be a secondary source of income, especially if you can avoid ads for competing businesses or those you and your prospective customers find offensive.

If you sell ads direct, you have the opportunity to limit ads to those businesses or services which complement yours: the fabric shop website that runs ads for long-arm quilters, for example, or the concert hall website's ads for instruments, music lessons and nearby restaurants.

If you have a blog, either stand-alone or as part of your web site, another option is a sponsored post. There may be businesses that will pay you to write reviews of their products or businesses, or pay to have their announcements posted on your site. You must disclose that these are sponsored posts. (See "Advertorials.")

Selling ads direct mean you set rates, collect payments and possibly market your site to potential advertisers.

You'll have less control and far less work if you accept ads through such vendors as search engines Google, Yahoo, and Bing.

Signing up with a network (also called an exchange) is similar when it comes to control of what appears on your site, but it can be technically easy: the network will provide HTML and Javascript code that automatically pull banners from its server and place them on your site. You usually will first have to qualify as a network member by showing evidence of a certain number of page views or a desirable group of users.

More Information
"Coupons" for daily deal sites
Google, google.com
Interactive Advertising Bureau, iab.net
International Society of Automation, isa.org, "Selling Banner Ads"

Word-of-Mouth
See "Word-of-Mouth," page 19.

Appendix A: Media Releases

Remember high school journalism class? What makes news starts with the basics: who, what, where, when, why, how and how much. Traditionally, these are presented in an "inverted pyramid," with the most important of the facts first. That's what is most important to the audience of whichever medium you're pitching, not what's most important to you. The less important information follows.

This format ensures that the most important information is conveyed, even if the reader or listener skips later paragraphs—or if an editor decides there isn't room or time for them.

If you've read "Newsworthiness" in "Advertising Explained," page 22, you know that good media releases are written with different "lead" (initial) paragraphs depending on the media to which they are being submitted. To illustrate how this can work, let's assume you're writing about a start-up located in one neighborhood, founded by someone who lives in a different neighborhood, and funded by organizations in yet other areas.

For the daily paper's business page and the business weekly, the release might say:

> *Seattle's first certified fair-trade nut gift packs, packed in 100 percent recycled materials, are being introduced in a 10-foot-wide Belltown storefront by a 30-year-old former software programmer, Taylor Brustad.*

This lead paragraph has:

> *What: nut gift pack, recycled materials, being introduced*
> *Where: Belltown neighborhood of Seattle*
> *Who: young former programmer*

Next, we expect to see more "what," including the business name, as well as "why" (probably because Brustad perceives a market demand and was ready for a career change), "how" (which would include the sources of the nuts and packing materials), and "how much" (the price range). "When" may be answered with about when Brustad learned about fair-trade nuts, when the company was founded, and the store's hours.

For the Belltown blog or any neighborhood weekly, the release might start:

> *A 10-foot-wide Belltown storefront carved from a 1910 structure is the first home of Fair Trade Nuts, which is selling Seattle's first certified fair-trade nut gift packs—in 100 percent recycled materials.*

This sample release shows a subject line, because most releases today are emailed. This very brief description is followed by a slightly longer headline, which tells us what the sale will benefit.

The first paragraph provides more "what," "how much," and "when."

The second paragraph says more about what will be sold, answers the question "where," and tells about the tote bag design and donation.

The third paragraph explains the goal and specifically what the funds will buy.

The next two paragraphs are "boilerplate," information that creates a context but is not vital to this story. The second of them can appear in every release issued by the library and the Friends.

The release concludes with contact information should media representatives want more information, and the three hash marks to indicate the end.

Subject line: Library Book Sale Jan. 24-26

**Buy Books, Fund Computers
at Library's Annual Sale**

Books are a dollar or two, and tote bags are $5 each at the Center City Friends of the Library's annual sale from 9 a.m. to 6 p.m. Friday, Jan. 24-Sunday, Jan. 26.

More than 10,000 vintage and gently-used hardbacks, paperbacks, pattern books and children's books will fill tables at the Center City Armory, said Friends president Lee Smith. The 2,000 cloth tote bags, designed by Briarcliff Middle School seventh grader Quinn Quito, were donated by Bags, Inc.

"We're hoping to raise at least $20,000," said Smith. All proceeds from book and tote bag sales will be used to help purchase new desktop computers for the library's main branch.

Organized in 1990, the Friends are a nonprofit that has raised more than $250,000 for library equipment. The book sale is now its largest fund-raiser.

The Center City Library, centercitybooks.info, established in 1912 in an elementary school cloakroom, has more library patrons than any other public library in this county. Each of its three branches provides more than 40 hours of service each week. Since 2009, "Slim" Baxter has been library director.

For more information: Friends president Lee Smith, bookster@library.info.

###

Advertising with Small Budgets for Big Results 223

Taylor Brustad, 30, company founder and sole employee to date, is a former computer programmer who...

For Brustad's own neighborhood blog and paper, a release might say:

A 30-year-old Wallingford resident, Taylor Brustad, has founded Fair Trade Nuts, which is selling Seattle's first certified fair-trade nut gift packs in Belltown.

When a release is sent to the city of a Fair Trade Nuts's funder, it might start:

A retailer of certified fair-trade nuts is the latest consumer business to be backed by Oregon Venture Angels, the Corvallis organization that funds environmentally and socially conscious small businesses.

For Brustad's college alumni publication, the announcement might say:

Taylor Brustad, B.A., 2005, has founded Fair Trade Nuts in Seattle. The retail operation is Seattle's first to sell certified fair-trade nuts — in 100 percent recycled packaging.

When a release is sent to media or reporters specializing in fair trade or sustainability, it can begin:

Certified fair-trade nuts, packaged in material that is 100 percent recycled, is the specialty at Fair Trade Nuts, the retail store Taylor Brustad is opening in downtown Seattle.

Appendix B: Examples of Periodical Publishers

The U.S. consumer magazine publishers with the highest circulation (listed with the publications in each company that generate the most advertising revenue):

American Media (*Star, National Enquirer, Shape*)
Bauer (*In Touch, Woman's World*)
Bonnier (*Popular Science, Field & Stream*)
Conde Nast (*Vogue, Glamour*)
Hearst Magazines (*Cosmopolitan, Good Housekeeping, O, The Oprah Magazine*)
Martha Stewart Living Omnimedia (*Martha Stewart Living, Everyday Food*)
Meredith (*Better Homes and Gardens, Family Circle, Ladies Home Journal, More*)
Reader's Digest Association (*Reader's Digest, Every Day with Rachael Ray, Family Handyman*)
Rodale (*Prevention, Men's Health, Runner's World, Organic Gardening*)
Time Inc. (*People, Sports Illustrated, Time*)
Wenner Media (*US Weekly, Rolling Stone*)

Among the niche consumer publishers are:

Interweave (16 subscription magazines such as *Quilting Arts, American Artist* and *Beadwork* for art and craft enthusiasts plus special publications)
Equine Network (*American Cowboy, Dressage Today, Horse Journal, Horse&Rider, Practical Horseman* and similar publications for the professional and rider)
Kalmbach Publishing (15 magazines such as *Model Railroader, Discover,* and *Cabin Life* plus dozens of special publications)
Ogden Publications (*Mother Earth News, Utne, Gas Engine Magazine* and *Grit*)
Taunton Press (five monthlies—*Fine Woodworking, Fine Homebuilding, Fine Gardening, Fine Cooking* and *Threads*—plus special publications)

Examples of U.S. trade journal publishers, with representative titles:

Advanstar Communications (*Medical Economics, Veterinary Medicine, Auto Body Repair News, Urology Times*)

Crain Communications (*Advertising Age, Automotive News, Modern Healthcare*)

Edgell Communications (*Hospitality Technology, Greetings etc., Selling Halloween*)

Fairchild Fashion Media, owned by Conde Nast (*Women's Wear Daily*)

Hanley Wood (*Architect, Builder, Multifamily Executive*)

Lebhar-Friedman (*Chain Store Age, Drug Store News, Home Channel News*)

McGraw-Hill (*Architectural Record, Engineering News-Record*)

Appendix C: Examples of Northwest Public Radio Stations

For stations outside the Pacific Northwest, start at npr.org.

NPR Affiliates, Idaho
Boise, KBSX-FM 91.5, KBSU-FM 90.3
Bonners Ferry, KIBX-FM 92.1
Burley, KBSY-FM 88.5
Cottonwood, KNWO-FM 90.1
McCall, KBSK-FM 89.9
McCall, KBSM-FM 91.7, KBSQ-FM 90.7
Moscow, KRFA-FM 91.7
Pocatello, KISU-FM 91.1
Rexburg, KBYI-FM 100.5
St. Maries, KXJO-FM 92.1
Sun Valley, KBSS-FM 91.1, KWRV-FM 91.9
Twin Falls, KEZJ-AM 1450, KBSW-FM 91.7

Unaffiliated
Lewiston, KLCZ (88.9 FM)

NPR Affiliates, Oregon
Ashland, KAGI-AM 930, KSMF-FM 89.1, KSRG-FM 88.3, KSOR-FM 90.1
Astoria, KMUN-FM 91.9, KOAC-FM 89.7
Baker City, KOBK-FM 88.9
Bend, KOAB-FM 91.3
Coos Bay, KSBA-FM 88.5
Corvallis, KOAC-AM 550
Enterprise, KETP-FM 88.7
Eugene, KLBR-FM 88.1, KOPB-AM 1600, KRVM-AM 1280, KLCC-FM 89.7
Florence, KLFO-FM 88.1
Gleneden Beach, KOGL-FM 89.3, KQOC-FM 88.1
Gresham, KMHD-FM 89.1
Hood River, KHRV-FM 90.1, KQHR-FM 88.1
John Day, KOJD-FM 89.7
Klamath Falls, KLMF-FM 88.5, KSKF-FM 90.9
La Grande, KTVR-FM 90.3
Lakeview, KOAP-FM 88.7
Myrtle Point, KOOZ-FM 94.1
Newport, KLCO-FM 90.5
Pendleton, KRBM-FM 90.9
Portland, KOPB-FM 91.5, KQAC-FM 89.9

Advertising with Small Budgets for Big Results   227

Reedsport, KLFR-FM 89.1
Roseburg, KMPQ-FM 88.1, KSRS-FM 91.5, KTBR-AM 950
Talent, KSJK-AM 1230
The Dalles, KOTD-FM 89.7
Tillamook, KTCB-FM 89.5, KTMK-FM 91.1
Warrenton, KCPB-FM 90.9

Unaffiliated
Corvallis, KBVR-FM, 88.7
Fossil, KFSL-LP 99.5 FM
Grants Pass, KAGI-AM 930
LaGrande, KEOL (91.7 FM)
McMinnville, KSLC (90.3 FM)
Paisley, KPAI-LP (103.1 FM)
Portland, KBPS-AM, 1450
Sisters, KZSO-LP (106.5 FM

NPR Affiliates, Washington
Bellingham, KQOW-FM 90.3, KZAZ-FM 91.7
Chehalis, KSWS-FM 88.9
Clarkston, KNWV-FM 90.5
Ellensburg, KNWR-FM 90.7
Manson, KHNW-FM 88.3
Moses Lake, KLWS-FM 91.5
Mount Vernon, KMWS-FM 90.1
Olympia, KPLI-FM 90.1
Omak, KQWS-FM 90.1
Oroville, KPBG-FM 90.9
Port Angeles, KNWP-FM 90.1, KVIX-FM 89.3
Pullman, KWSU-AM 1250
Richland, KFAE-FM 89.1
Seattle, KEXP-FM 90.3, KING-FM 98.1, KUOW-FM 94.9
Spokane, KSFC-FM 91.9, KPBX-FM 91.1
Tacoma, KPLU-FM 88.5, KVTI-FM 90.9
KTWP-FM 91.1
Walla Walla, KWWS-FM 89.7
Yakima, KNWY-FM 90.3

Unaffiliated
Everett, KSER 90.7
Olympia, KAOS 89.3 FM

Sources: npr.org, radio station websites

Appendix D: Sample Release
for Model and Photographer

I, the model or model's guardian, authorize _____

to use photographs of _____
          (Name of individual pictured, and if younger than 18, birth date)

in _____
                    (Medium/media if specified)

I understand I have received/am not due compensation for this use.

Author/Model Name (printed)_____

Parent/Guardian _____
                        (If model is younger than 18)

Signature_____
              (If model is younger than 18, signature of parent/guardian.)

Date _____

I, the photographer, assign all rights to photographs of

_____

to _____

Photographer's name (printed) _____

Photographer's address, email address and telephone number

_____

I understand I have received/am not due compensation for this use.

Photographer's signature _____
 (If photographer is younger than 18, printed name and signature of parent/guardian.)

Date _____

For a more detailed release, which is important if you are paying either the model or photographer, see the American Society of Media Photographers, asmp.org, Business Resources > Tutorial and Guides. Most professional photographers also provide model releases. If you do not receive a release from the photographer, the invoice you receive should specify what reproduction rights you are purchasing and who owns the copyright. If the photographer is not being compensated, one of you should write a letter of agreement outlining rights, and it should be signed by both of you.

Appendix E: Advertising and Promotion Checklist

Use the detailed "to do" list that starts on page 230 as a guide when you're brainstorming, or when you need a new idea or two to jumpstart lagging sales or donations. Of course, you're unlikely to use all of the promotions in any one campaign—and perhaps there are some you'll never use. Because it's unlikely that this list includes everything possible, use it as the basis for your own "to do" list, adding recommendations from colleagues and promotional techniques you've seen others use.

Note that the first items have the most detail. If you choose to advertise on satellite radio, for example, you'll want to use the detailed questions from broadcast radio about stations, message, and implementation.

Remember the tip introduced on pages 9-10: identify which of these you'd undertake if you had unlimited funds, and then think of how you can do something similar with a budget—even a budget of a couple of hundred dollars.

Plan Ahead

There are promotions that can be effective with a few hours, or few days notice, but most work better when you allow lead time to get media releases printed and broadcast, Twitter posts read and re-tweeted, Facebook posts "liked," and emails received and forwarded. Ads of all kinds need time to be written, reviewed, produced and disseminated, with lead times a particular issue when print ads are to be inserted in monthlies, quarterlies or annuals or on websites that limit the number of ads.

If you are a nonprofit seeking pro bono work or an unpaid intern, or a business that wants to use students, figure on even more lead time for your project.

Creative

You want to drive action—a call, an email, a catalog request, and ultimately, a sale or a donation. How you ask for this is what's called "creative" in advertising jargon. Maybe it's obvious: you're scheduling a swimsuit sale, or soliciting vendors for a street market, or opening your consulting practice.

Even then, consider a theme for your promotion: after all, "Get tanked with our Speedos" will probably attract more attention than, "Swimsuit sale this week," and "Have a heart for Valentine's month: donate red cans and boxes to the food bank" is catchier than, "Donate to the food bank in February."

Brainstorming a theme is best started with an "anything goes" attitude. Start jotting down possible slogans or ad titles and leave space to add ideas of how each might be implemented in print, broadcast (even if your only "broadcast" is your voice messaging system), in-store displays, email, on your blog or website or with networking.

A "thank you," fan mail, testimonial or someone's willingness to endorse your business, product/service or campaign can also help you generate a theme. If I were promoting this book and someone told me, "You offer more ideas than I'll ever be able to use," you can bet I'd be using that in advertising and publicity, perhaps with:

"More ideas than you'll ever be able to use—that's what small business owners say about *Advertising with Small Budgets for Big Results*."

You can also imply endorsements, especially with legendary characters in the public domain: "Johnny Appleseed would have loved the new homes at Orchard Acres" and "We're as honest at George Washington when we say..."

Remember that the names and images of deceased celebrities and their characters are managed by their estates, so much as you'd like to say that John Wayne would have appreciated your cancer screening program, or that Snoopy would endorse the doghouses you design, better not. The same goes for current characters in fiction and, of course, anyone who is alive. To tie into pop culture and current entertainment, references such as "gowns inspired by the era of Downton Abbey" are safer than describing a suit as one preferred by Edith Crawley.

For most of us, budget helps determine creative. We look at what photos we already have, or can get through a manufacturer's co-op advertising program, who's available to help us design an ad or poster or voice a commercial, what we can create in-house, and of course, what budget we need for the media time or space we'll buy.

Media

☐ Television

Broadcast publicity (e.g., news programs, talk shows)
What will the news hook (angle) be?
Who at stations will be contacted and how?
Will we send photos, video or samples? Offer demonstration, tour or test drive?
Who of our staff will make the contacts?
Who will represent us on air if an interview is arranged?
Google Alerts set up to monitor publicity?

Advertising with Small Budgets for Big Results

Broadcast advertising
Creative
What's the theme?
What materials do we already have?
Are co-op materials available?
What else can we obtain? Who will get it?

Production
What's our budget?
Are co-op funds available?
Who will coordinate?

Time
What stations?
What programs?
What schedule can we afford?
Are we using a media buyer? If so, who?

PSAs: Are we eligible for them?

Television station website advertising
What is the creative theme?
Who's producing the ad?
What's our budget?
Are co-op funds available?
Can we get station to co-sponsor our event?
Which websites should we consider?
Secondary channel publicity
Secondary channel advertising
Cable publicity/infomercials
Cable advertising
Online television publicity/infomercials
Online television advertising
Public television publicity
Public television underwriting/sponsorships
Public TV fund-raising participation (e.g., on-screen phone banks, providing premiums for donors, refreshments for volunteers)

☐ Radio
Broadcast radio publicity
What will the news hook (angle) be?
Who at stations will be contacted and how?
Who will make the contacts?
Who will represent us on air if an interview is arranged?
Google Alerts set up to monitor publicity?

Broadcast radio advertising
Creative
What's the theme?
Are co-op materials available?
What else can we create? Who will do it?

Production
What's our budget?
Are co-op funds available?
Provide stations with prerecorded commercial or have each station record?
Script or announcer ad libbing?
Who will coordinate?
Sponsor weather, traffic, stock market report?

Time
What stations?
What programs?
What schedule can we afford?
Are we using a media buyer? If so, who?

PSAs: Are we eligible for them? If so, who will create?

Radio station website
Online radio publicity
Online radio advertising
Satellite radio
Public radio publicity
Public radio underwriting/sponsorships
Public radio fund drive assistance (on-air credit for staffing phones, providing premiums for donors, refreshments for volunteers)

☐ Newspapers
Publicity: Examples include

News stories: what is the hard news?
Is there a tie-in to a recent event? Who is to contact editor?

Feature stories: what's the angle? Is there a local/neighborhood resident involved who can be featured? Who will determine appropriate contact, make call or write email/release?

Calendar listing: Deadline? Who to handle?

Product reviews: what columns review our product or service? Who is to handle submission? Must we send a sample? A professional photo?

Personnel changes column: who is to handle submission?

Advertising with Small Budgets for Big Results

233

Photo required?

Special sections: Calendar? Contact person? Ad required to be featured in editorial?

Google Alerts set up to monitor publicity?

Newspapers by audience:
Who will determine which of the following to contact? Who will write release? Who will make contact? Who will be spokesperson if media contact us?

National papers
Metro dailies
Business
Legal
Community/non-daily
Alternative
Special interest

Newspaper ads:
Creative
What's the theme?
Are co-op materials available?
What images do we have? What can we create?

Ad production:
Create ad in-house, use free-lancer or agency, by paper?
What's our budget?
Will newspaper co-sponsor our event/campaign?
Are co-op funds available?
Should we consider premium placement?
Schedule: Which days of the week should our ads appear?

Newspaper website?

Inserts?
In which zones?
Schedule
Creative
Production
Budget

☐ Magazines and Trade Journals
   Publicity
   What hard news, current event tie-ins or features do we have to offer?
   Editorial calendars and deadlines? Contact people? Submission format?

Publication's calendar columns: Do we have events that can be listed?

Product reviews: Prototype or sample to be sent? Image? Video? Offer test drive or tour?

Personnel changes: What level of position is necessary for inclusion? Photo required?

Who will determine which of the following to contact? Who will make contact? Who will be spokesperson if media contact us?

Google Alerts set up to monitor publicity?

Magazines by audience
National general interest
National niche topic
Regional
Local
Business
Parents/Children
Entertainment

Magazine ads
Creative
Deadlines and schedule for production
Budget
Co-op funds?
Magazine as co-sponsor of event?
Creative
Production

□ Website
URL and website host
Text/images/video/key words
Icons and links for social media sites
Sign-up for database
Ads for own products on own site
Links to other sites
Links to our site to solicit from other site owners: who will coordinate?

Creative
What image to portray?
Production
Publicity on others' sites
Which sites to consider? Who to contact their owners?

Search engine page ads

Advertising with Small Budgets for Big Results

Do they make sense for us?
What's our message?
What key words shall we buy?
Landing page: does it exist or must it be created?

Ads on others' sites
Which sites do we want to be on?
Can we afford such ads?
Creative: What is it?
Production
Budget
Schedule
Landing page?

Ads for others on our site
Rates to charge
Sizes to allow
Restrictions on content, placement
Sold direct
Sold through search engines
Sold through networks

☐ Blogs
Our blog posts: who will create?
Offer syndication?
Icons and links for social media sites
Guest blog posts
Soliciting blogs to host us as a guest
Soliciting guests for our blog
Google Alerts set up to monitor publicity?
Blog ads

☐ Eblasts
Soliciting testimonials
Announcing product/service/campaign
Soliciting talk show appearances
Soliciting media announcements
Soliciting speaking appearances (e.g., at professional, civic or alumni association meetings)
Announcing schedule of media and personal appearances
Excerpting from fan mail
Excerpting from sales reports
Excerpting from reviews
Vendor
Database

☐ Social media

Links to website and/or blog
"Follow" invitations

Facebook
Personal pages for key employees: posts scheduled?
Business/product pages: posts scheduled?
Facebook groups
Ads: offer specials to followers?

LinkedIn
Personal pages for key employees
Business page
Groups: Which ones? Who of us to join? What to post?
Ads

Twitter
Company posts: who to post?
Division or product group posts?
Key employee posts
Scheduled in advance?
Promoted posts

YouTube/Vimeo
Pinterest
Instagram
Other?

Out-of-Home

☐ Billboards
Publicity (e.g., regarding creation of unusual board)
Creative
Production
Locations and vendors
Budget
Co-op funds?

☐ Bus cards/transit stations
Creative
Production
Transit mode
Station locations/bus routes
Sign type
Budget
Co-op funds?

☐ Highway signs/Tourist information
Adopt-a-Highway
Tourist services

Advertising with Small Budgets for Big Results 237

- Sidewalk/yard signs
  - Creative
  - Production
  - Locations
  - Frequency of sign updates?
  - Budget
- Sidewalk/window clings
  - Creative
  - Production
  - Budget
- Vehicle signs
  - Creative
  - Vehicles to be signed: Your own? Others?
  - Production
  - Budget
  - Co-op funds?
- Posters
  - Creative
  - Production
  - Postering: What's the law? Who will handle?
- Characters in costume/on street
  - Creative
  - Production
  - Budget
  - Personnel
  - Locations
  - Schedule
- Banners
  - Creative
  - Production
  - Budget
  - Co-op funds/materials?
  - Locations
- Bathrooms
  - Creative
  - Production
  - Locations
  - Budget/trade-outs/sponsorship?
- Lobbies/elevators
  - Creative
  - Production

Budget
Locations/permission

☐ In-store signage/promotion
Budget
Co-op funds/materials?
Creative
Production
Locations
Your store/office, your retailers' stores
Colleagues' stores

Types:
Chalkboards/whiteboards
Table clings/tablecloths/place mats
Table tents
Easels
Business card and brochure holders
Floor clings
Mannequins
End caps/dump bins
Window displays
Shelf talkers
Coupons
Demonstrations/sampling

Personal Sales

Upselling
Sampling
Tracking sources of inquiries
Surveying customers to get testimonial comments: By phone/in person/SurveyMonkey and similar software

Guerilla marketing

Postering without permits
"Ask me about..." buttons/T-shirts worn by staff/street teams
Employees wearing "sandwich board" style signs in public
Leaving flyers in public places: on transit, taped to park benches, offered to passersby
Carrying product packaging wherever we walk

Giveaways

Samples or coupons to return for samples
Self-liquidating premiums

Downloadables (white papers, note cards, clip art, games)
Free classes, kids' programs, demonstrations in your office/storefront
Webinars/appearances via Skype or other programs
Contests
Drawings
Special events (e.g., sponsoring an electronic recycling pick-up)

Identifying Markets, Products, Prices, Distribution Methods and Promotion Options

Use this chart and Appendix E to outline who you want to reach, what you'll offer each, and what you want from each. No project is likely to use all of these tools.

Market/audience	*What you offer this market/audience*	*What you want from this market/audience*
Current customers Prospective customers	Basic product/service VIP level Quantity purchase Long-term contract Sample *These are examples of what a business, nonprofit or agency might offer, not what every operation will offer.*	Purchase: basic, bulk, or standing order Purchase on sale: flash or season-end Wholesale purchase *Pricing options. Some businesses use* Consignment deal *one, some use several, especially for* Barter *different kinds of product (e.g., seconds, leftover seasonal items).*
Opinion leaders		Promotion via social media Endorsement Word-of-mouth *What you want from opinion leaders, including satisfied customers with many contacts, and reviewers.*
Donors	Recognition/publicity/thank-yous *Donor recognition may include special events, announcements of gifts, and thank-you gifts.*	Cash or in-kind donation Commitment to continuing donations *Your goal may be to move a donor to a higher contribution level, to get cash, or to get in-kind help.*

Identifying Distribution Methods and Promotion Options

Use this chart and Appendix E to outline how and where you'll reach
your target audiences/markets. No project is likely to use all of these methods.

Place/Distribution

Direct sales
- Storefront
- Pop-up store/craft fair/farmers market
- Direct response

Online
- Own website
- Online storefront (Amazon, Etsy, eBay, Craigslist, etc.)
- Affiliates
- Crowdsourcing

B2B
- Wholesale (direct)
- Wholesaler
- Distributor
- Party/Commissioned Reps/Affiliates

Promotion

Traditional
- Broadcast
- Print
- Direct mail
- Telemarketing
- Direct sales
- Out-of-home

New Media
- Online broadcast
- Blogs
- Websites
- Email and Twitter
- Social media sites (e.g., Facebook, Pinterest, YouTube)

Among the topics in the book
to check for information on these methods/media:

Advertorial
Alumni Publications
Banners
Blogs
Databases
Email
Ferry System Advertising
Gas Pump Advertising
Maps & Tourist Brochures
Catalogs & Sell Sheets
Magazine Advertising
Newsletters
Newspapers
Out-of-Home
QR Codes
Radio
Social Media
Television
Websites

Appendix F: For Additional Help

Besides the contacts listed under "More Information" throughout this book, you may find the following helpful.

Website design

Online tutorials for HTML are easy to find with a search engine and a phrase such as (no surprise) "online HTML tutorial." HTML is not a language, only a system of tags, so it can be written in a word processing program and then pasted into your website. Here's an example from the University of Washington Press website:

```
<h1>Company Towns of the Pacific Northwest</h1>
<h2><!-- SUBTITLE --></h2>
<h3 class="uc">Linda Carlson</h3>
<ul class="smallPrint">
```

For help, I usually start with tutorials provided by colleges. One example:

□ "An Introductory HTML Tutorial" by Tom O'Haver of the University of Maryland at College Park, inform.umd.edu/ UMS+State/UMD-Projects/MCTP/Technology/handouts/html. html.

Your library and bookstore will have more comprehensive and more recently updated resources such as those from:

□ For Dummies Store, "Web Development," dummies.com/store/ Computers-Internet/Internet/Web-Development.html, which lists both beginning and advanced website design guides.

□ Idiot's Guides, "Computer & Technology," idiotsguides.com/ static/quickguides/computertechnology/social media explained, which lists guides for website design, blogging, social media, Skype and crowdsourcing.

Community colleges, community centers and other adult education programs often offer how-to workshops, some as short as a day or two. Free online courses are offered by major universities through Open Culture, openculture.com/freeonlinecourses. Select "Computer Science & Artificial Intelligence" to see what's currently available. (Coursera.org and edX.org also provide free online courses, but as this was written, the topics were more appropriate for those pursuing programming. Through Open Yale Courses, oyc.yale.edu/, neither business nor computer courses were being taught in 2013-14.)

Advertising agencies and media buyers

The American Advertising Federation, aaf.org, has chapters in several parts of the country; you can use its directories or network at its meetings to introduce yourself to advertising professionals in your area. What will take careful thought is determining which of the agencies or free-lancers are a fit with your business or organization.

Some will be too edgy for you, some too stodgy, some flakey, and worst of all, others unrealistic given your budget. Research what's possible given your budget and timeline before you begin interviewing agencies so that you can be explicit about what you can afford. Don't let agency execs intimidate you or the creatives condescend to you. Look at dozens of examples of what each agency has done, and check with previous and current clients regarding client relations, deadlines and budget overruns.

Although much media buying is automated today, be aware that a good media buyer may be more of a negotiator with media salespeople than a client schmoozer. In decades past, the best media buyers were sometimes the loudest screamers, determined to get the best deals for their clients. Don't be put off if a buyer appears brusque.

Graphic designers and illustrators

Whenever you see something you like, find out who designed or illustrated it. In many cases, illustrators are represented by agents who can quote fees and provide more samples.

Among other places to network: the Graphic Artists Guild, graphicartistsguild.org, and AIGA, aiga.org, both with several chapters and online portfolios of members' work, and the Society for Experiential Graphic Design, segd.org, also with several chapters. As with advertising agencies, identify the kind of work you like and check with many former and current clients.

Free-lance help, interns and work-study students

Many sections of this book suggest contacting appropriate departments of local schools and universities regarding instructors, students or recent grads who might take on part-time or project work. Openings can also be posted in colleges' student placement offices and with departmental internship coordinators. Low-income college students may be eligible for work-study positions, in which the federal government pays half or more of the wages. See U.S. Department of Education, ed.gov, "Federal Work-Study Program."

Glossary

If CMYK, PDF, JPEG, GRP, native files, and pixels sound like Greek when you're asking a printer for quotes or reading a rate card, the explanations that follow will help. They provide information you'll need if you're creating pieces to be printed, placing advertising yourself, or when working with someone with limited experience. This glossary will also help when you're asking for estimates and evaluating quotes. NOTE: Cross references to text sections appear within quotation marks: e.g., "Magazine Advertising"; cross references to topics within this glossary appear by name only, e.g., Descender.

Acrobat: The Adobe software used to create files in Portable Document Format (PDF). PDFs are opened with the free Adobe Reader, a different program. PDFs can be created with various levels of quality, the highest appropriate for printing and the lowest appropriate for websites and email. Generic PDF converters may not be able to provide the highest resolution PDFs. Print media rate cards often specify what level PDFs are acceptable (see the sample in "Magazine Advertising" and PDF later in the Glossary).

Application files: Software such as QuarkXpress, Adobe InDesign, Photoshop, Illustrator, and font files. Printers and media salespeople may ask that application files be submitted along with PDFs.

Apron: Extra blank space at the binding edge of a foldout which allows a page or card to be folded and tipped in (that is, glued in, between the pages of a signature, or between signatures) so that all the text or illustrations on the foldout can be seen. Likely to be required on material preprinted and then submitted to a magazine or catalog for insertion.

Ascender: The parts of letters that rise above the height of lower-case letters, like the upward-extending parts of the l, h, or t. Contrast with descenders, the parts that extend below the baseline, as in

Advertising with Small Budgets for Big Results **245**

the "tail" of the letters y, g, or p. When type is leaded tightly (for example, 9 point type on 9 points of leading space), the descenders of one line may overlap the ascenders of the next. (See Descender for an example.)

B2B: Business-to-business sales, e.g., by a manufacturer to Amazon. com, or by a farmer to a restaurant or grocery, sometimes through a wholesaler or distributor.

B2C: Business-to-consumer, sales by a business directly to an end user, e.g., by a craftsperson via Etsy.com, or by a farmer at a street market.

Bad break: A word broken incorrectly at the end of a line: when a short last line of a paragraph appears at the top of a column or page, or a short first line of a paragraph appears at the end of a column or page; a subhead that appears at the bottom of a column or page; or a hyphen break at the end of the last line on a page. Starting a new line between or after initials in a name also creates a bad break.

Binding: Folding, trimming and attaching pages of a pamphlet, magazine, catalog or book with adhesives, sewing, stitching, plastic or metal coils, metal prongs, or snaps. The bindery is also where perforating, embossing, die cutting, and other specialty work is done.

Bleed: An image or text that extends ("bleeds") over one or more edges of a page. When you ask for quotes on a printed piece with bleeds, specify how many bleeds it will have: for example, "bleeds one side" or "bleeds four sides." A full-bleed image extends (that is, bleeds) over all edges. Most printers require that artwork extend at least an eighth of an inch (sometimes a quarter inch) past the trim line to ensure the margin is completely covered with ink. Because paper is wasted with bleeds, jobs with them cost more. Also describes ink that has spread incorrectly.

Blind embossing: A printing technique in which a bas-relief design such as a logo is created without foil or ink.

Block style: When all lines of text, including the first, are set flush left. Most of this glossary is set block style.

Blueline or Blues: The final one-color print-on-paper copy of a publication before it goes to the press, and the last chance to fix anything that needs fixing. With digital reproduction, there is no film and thus no blueline; instead, you check the laser print.

Boldface: Thicker, visually heavier or darker type. In desktop publishing programs such as InDesign, the stroke menu can be used to further increase the thickness of type. In this glossary, the terms are set in boldface italic and the definitions in what is traditionally called "roman," and now often referred to as "regular."

Brightness: A technical measurement of the light reflected by paper, expressed in the U.S. by the 0 to 100 scale of the Technical Association of the Pulp and Paper Industry. A higher number means brighter paper. You see this number on the copy machine and printer paper packages you buy, often between 85 and 93.

B-roll: Used today to describe video footage provided with publicity releases. The Content Marketing Institute describes it as, "Additional video footage, still photographs, animation or other graphic elements" in addition to "talking heads."

Callout: A reference in text to a numbered figure or table (e.g., "see Figure 1").

Camera-ready art or CRA: Material (that is, text with or without illustrations and photographs) ready to be imaged onto film. Until electronic preproduction, CRA for offset reproduction was prepared as pasteups or Photostats. Today camera-ready art is submitted electronically, often as PDFs.

Caption: Text accompanying a photo or illustration.

Caret: The copyediting or proofreading mark that indicates the insertion point for additional text: ^ (usually handwritten).

Centerspread: The facing pages in the center of a signature. If you're printing something like a catalog, this is the only place your image or text can extend across the gutter (center margin).

Character: Single letter, number, symbol, or blank space. A Twitter post has 140 total, which means that spaces and punctuation count. So does every character in an online text ad, such as on Google or Facebook.

Click fraud: When pay-per-click ads are repeatedly clicked for malicious purpose, either to increase income to the sites hosting the ads, or to increase costs to the advertiser.

 *Clip art:* Stock illustrations used instead of commissioned artwork, like that on left. Once sold on large sheets from which the desired image could be cut, or clipped; now sold as digital files or individually on stock photography sites. Some clip art is free; some must be purchased. Not all clip art is available in the high-resolution graphics files needed for good-quality reproduction, especially if it is scanned from vintage advertisements or books.

CMYK: Four inks—cyan (blue), magenta (red), yellow, and black (key)—are used with four-color process printing. In digital printing, Pantone Matching System (PMS) ink colors are usually converted to CMYK. This can cause color variations between digitally printed jobs and offset jobs, where PMS colors can be matched. This could be an issue if you are combining pieces printed both ways in one promotion and need colors to match: for example, if you want the color of your logo to match on a catalog which has pages printed offset (because you use thousands of those pages) and a catalog cover printed on a digital press (because you want different covers for customer groups as small as 500).

Because computer monitors display colors in RGB format (red/green/blue), it is impossible to accurately proof CMYK or PMS colors with a digital display or with prints made with a laser or inkjet printer. For CMYK, you or your designer should provide the printer with a printed example of the color to be matched. If PMS colors are specified, provide paper swatches with the comps.

Color separation: In a multicolor print job, each component color requires its own monochrome image. A film negative is made from each of these monochrome images for offset printing. A two-color job requires two separations; a four-color job requires four if process color (see CMYK) is being used. A multicolor job using several PMS inks but no full-color images would have a separation for each PMS color.

Column: A block of type (usually) almost always narrower than the width of the page. The space between columns is called a ditch.

Comps: Comprehensive layouts, the second visual step in the creative process, after thumbnails (rough miniature sketches). If working with an advertising agency or designer, you should be shown both thumbnails and comps. The comp of a book, catalog, ad, or other promotional piece is an early draft that shows color, fonts, and at least rough images. Low-resolution stock photos and greeked text are common. A comprehensive proof shows material as it will look when printed. Today comps are often presented electronically, as either JPEG or PDF files.

Condensed type: Typefaces with tall, narrow characters that allow more characters per line (in contrast to expanded typefaces, which permit fewer characters): Franklin Gothic Medium Condensed vs. **Franklin Gothic Demi**. Desktop publishing programs such as InDesign allow designers to further reduce space between letters and between words: Palotino Linotype condensed with InDesign (vs. Palotino Linotype).

Continuous tone/contone: Images with a range of tones from white to black that may have every shade of gray represented, as in traditional photography. In offset printing, continuous-tone images are converted (screened) to halftones for reproduction.

Copyright: Exclusive legal right to reproduce, publish, sell, or distribute literary, musical, or artistic work. Can include advertising and website text. Anything to be copyrighted should include a copyright notice with the symbol © or the word Copyright, the year of first publication, and the name of the copyright holder. For current copyright law: "Copyright Basics," copyright.gov/circs/circ01.pdf.

Crop: To reduce the size or change the dimensions of an image by removing part of one or more sides rather than reducing the size of the entire image, as shown below.

Crop marks: Lines on the camera-ready art that show where cuts will be made for the final trim (see Bleed).

CTR: Click through rate for website or search page advertising: what percentage of those who see an ad click on it and continue through to the landing page.

Dash: A typographical line longer than a hyphen (which in typeset text should not be used to create it). Short ones are en dashes; long ones are em dashes. Hyphen: - En dash: – Em dash: —

Delimiter: A character that is used to separate items of information, important when information is transferred from one format to another. A mailing service may ask that a mailing list be exported from a database in tab or comma-delimited format. Website advertising reports may be available for export with delimiters.

Descender: That portion of a letter—the tails of lower case g, j and p, for example—that extends below the baseline. When type is leaded too tightly (see Ascender), descenders and ascenders can overlap: Too tightly leaded

Designated Market Area, DMA: Nielsen-trademarked term that refers to a geographic area where the same television programming is available.

Die-cutting: Cutting a shape out of paper. Done with standard dies that the printer or bindery has in stock (e.g., an oval) or with a custom die, such as a company logo, which because it must be manufactured increases the cost of the project.

Digital: Describes type and images that exist on computers rather than on paper, and are transferred electronically or with such storage devices as flash drives.

Dingbat: A printing symbol such as a bullet, heart, box or diamond: ✓ ✓ ⚲ ☐ ♥ 🎁 🚋

Direct mail: Promotional material sent via postal mail to prospective customers. Direct mail is usually sent at Standard (bulk) rates, which are significantly lower than first class postal rates, but require permits, indicia, pre-sorting and delivery to a bulk mail processing facility.

Direct response advertising: Any kind of advertising that solicits immediate orders, e.g., "Call now...," "Return this card for 10% off..."

Dot gain: Spread of ink past the specified dot size, making tones darker or colors stronger, or as at right, images muddy or blurred. More common with highly absorbent inexpensive papers such as newsprint typically used for catalogs than with hard, coated stock, the reason paper should be specified before a screen is selected for an image. A photo to be printed 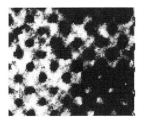 on newsprint is prepared with a coarser line screen (fewer lines per inch, or lower lpi) and thus fewer dots per inch to compensate for dot gain.

Dots per inch (dpi): A measurement of the resolution of a laser or inkjet printer. A higher dpi yields crisper images and type (but see above regarding dot gain). Sources differ on how dpi compares to lines per inch (lpi): some printers and designers recommend that images be created as TIFFs with dpi that is at least double the lpi that will be used when a halftone is made for printing. Following this recommendation, a photo would be created at no less than 600 dpi if it were to be screened at 300 lpi. Other sources recommend a much greater difference: a 600 dpi for an image to be used in a newspaper, which may have an 85 line screen (lpi); or a 2400 dpi for an image that will appear in a glossy magazine, which may have a 150-200 line screen (lpi).

Double bump: To print twice, sometimes necessary because the stock (usually a cover) is heavily textured and requires two applications of ink for good coverage.

Doubletruck: Two facing pages of a publication printed on the same sheet of paper and used for an image, usually an advertisement. See Centerspread.

Drilling: The print industry term for punching holes, as for pages to be inserted in ring binders.

*D**rop cap*: An oversize initial capital sometimes used at the beginning of a magazine story or book chapter. It will be the height of several lines of type.

Drop ship: Shipping of products from the manufacturer to a wholesaler, distributor, retailer or end user. Usually increases the overall freight costs from the point of manufacture but eliminates the labor and cost for fulfilling large initial orders from the company warehouse. However, with drop shipping, you may not see the finished product before fulfillment of orders has begun, so you will not immediately know if there are errors in the product or packaging.

Dump bin: A floor display, often a self-contained shipping carton that is assembled as a display unit. A smaller version is the counter prepack.

Duotone: A two-color halftone. Often used for special effects or when the budget does not permit full-color images. Technically, a halftone (grayscale image) with a second color overlaid on a portion of the image.

Eblast: Email message to a large group, usually with an automated program, either in-house or through an email blast vendor.

Embossed: Printed or stamped with a design or type created from a die. The design or type may be blank, covered with foil or printed.

EPS: Encapsulated PostScript, a common file format for exporting Adobe Illustrator files. It uses PostScript coding and so can be output to a PostScript printer, but it cannot be used instead of a JPEG or TIFF image for printing.

Expanded face: A font with especially wide characters, usually more rounded and heavier of stroke. Often used for titles or chapter headings, and in advertising and logos. For example: **SHOWCARD GOTHIC.** Desktop publishing programs allow type to be increased in width, and extra space to be added between characters to create the impression of an expanded face: **Palotino Linotype Bold** expanded with InDesign vs. **Palotino Linotype Bold.**

Fair use: Often claimed when copyrighted material is used without authorization from the copyright holder. Whether a use is legally "fair" is determined by four factors: purpose and character of the use, including whether it is of a commercial nature or is for nonprofit educational purposes; nature of the copyrighted work; amount and substantiality of the portion used in relation to the copyrighted work as a whole, and effect of the use on the potential market for or value of the copyrighted work. In general, avoid unauthorized use of copyrighted material.

File transfer protocol (FTP): How large electronic files, usually for full-color ads or catalogs, are sent via the Internet from one computer to another, or from one server to another. For receipt of files, most printers and book manufacturers have FTP portals, which have specific addresses and passwords. For an example, see the Martha Stewart Living rate card in "Magazine Advertising."

Flat fee: One-time compensation for a writer, illustrator or photographer in exchange for all rights. Paid in lieu of royalties. Does not affect copyright ownership.

Flush: Even with. *Flush left* means that type is set block style with all lines except paragraph indents even with the left margin.
                     Flush right, demonstrated with this sentence,
                      occasionally used for titles and display type,
                     means the text block aligns with the right margin.

F.O.B.: Freight on board, free on board. Refers to where goods will be delivered without freight charges. If the manufacturer's quote specifies F.O.B. Ann Arbor, you will pay for delivery from Ann Arbor.

Foil: Tissue-thin material with metal or pigment that is pressed onto the cover of a book, annual report or brochure with a heated die (see Embossing).

Font: Complete set of characters, including numbers, punctuation and bullets, in a given type face. Traditionally each font included one size and one style; for example, 24 point Times Italic. All the sizes and styles were called a font, or type, family, with typeface variations including roman (regular), bold and italic. Light, semi-bold, bold italic, book, black, extra-bold, condensed and expanded faces could also be included. Today style is usually denoted by a "face" such as bold or italic. When a print job is submitted in native or PostScript files, the submission must include all the fonts including dingbats, decorations and symbols. In desktop publishing some of these will be in the glyphs file. A job submitted as a PDF does not require submission of fonts.

Font metrics: Spacing attributes of type, one reason that a given font such as Times Roman is unlikely to match the font of the same name on two different computers, unless both were loaded from the same release of the same software. It is why an electronic file must be accompanied by its fonts when sent to the printer unless submitted as a PDF. It's also why you cannot ask one printer to replace a paragraph that another printer typeset.

Font size: The size (height) of a character in a particular font as measured in points from the lowest descender to the highest ascender. Because there are 72 points to an inch, a character in 36 point type is theoretically a half-inch high—but no single character has both an ascender and descender.

Four-color printing, four-color process: Creating full-color material during the printing process with the four process ink colors, CMYK. Offset printing requires a separation and plate for each of the four.

Ganging: When artwork for related jobs using the same paper and ink is grouped together on a plate and thus on the press. For example, ganging business cards and postcards and cutting them apart after printing. Ensures that ink colors on all pieces match, eliminates press make-ready for second job, and can reduce waste of paper.

Gatefold: Technically, a wide sheet with foldouts on either side of the centerspread. Also describes an extra-wide page that has one foldout. Covers sometimes have a gatefold (commonly on magazines that sell the inside cover for advertising). May also be used to accommodate an extra-wide image such as a map, chart or photograph.

General/national advertising rates: Newspapers usually charge higher rates to national companies and units of franchises. Locally-owned businesses qualify for the lower "local" rate.

Generation: Each successive impression. With traditional offset printing, the comprehensive is the original, the negative the second, and the plate the third. The printed copy is at least the fourth generation. This is the reason to start with an original photo when creating a new brochure rather than scanning the old brochure.

Advertising with Small Budgets for Big Results 253

With direct-to-plate printing, the number of generations is reduced, the opportunity for error is reduced, and the quality of the type and images should be better.

Ghosting: Unwanted images on the printed piece that should be corrected after a press check.

GIF, Graphics Interchange Format: Bitmap image format introduced by CompuServe used on websites: lacks the quality for printing.

Gigabyte: A unit of electronic storage, 1024 megabytes.

Gloss ink: Ink with extra varnish, which creates a glossy appearance when dry.

Gloss, glossy print: A finish available on paper and with coatings such as varnishes (in contrast to matte, or flat). Glossy prints are photographs made on shiny paper. When photographs are printed for use in reproduction, they are usually glossies.

Graininess: Undesirable print quality characterized by unevenness, particularly of halftones. Typical of printing done from copies or previously printed material rather than originals. See Generation.

Graphics: Anything in visual form (in contrast to text), including photographs, illustrations, and charts. See Images.

Grayscale: Grayscale images, usually photos with as many as 256 shades of gray. Color images are often converted to grayscale for reproduction in books, especially paperbacks.

Greeked text: Meaningless blocks of characters used to mock up layouts in the design process. When pages in a desktop publishing program are reduced significantly in size, and the type is too small to be legible on the screen or in a printout, it's also said to be greeked.

Gripper, gripper margin: On a press, grippers clamp the paper and control its movement. Gripper margin is the narrow space where the paper is clamped and no ink can be laid. For a printed piece to have a bleed image, the sheet must be trimmed inside the gripper margin. This wastes paper and is one reason bleeds typically increase printing cost.

Hairline: A thin stroke, or in the case of a hairline rule, a line.

Halftone: Images such as black and white photographs converted for printing with one color with a line screen that breaks the continuous spectrum of blacks, whites and grays into either black or white dots. A higher concentration of black dots results in a darker shade. Images screened and then printed in two colors are duotones.

Hard return: In word processing or desktop publishing, the equivalent of a carriage return, a manual keystroke that ends the current line and starts a new paragraph. Creating them in HTML requires a tag.

Hickey: Spots or other imperfections on the printed page due to dirt or debris on the press; should be caught on a press check and corrected.

High resolution: When an image is reproduced with such high quality that there is a significant amount of detail or a high level of grey scaling. Such images take up more electronic space, and take longer to send via email or load on a website, the reason email and websites use JPEGs. Converting a JPEG to a TIFF will not improve resolution. In printing, the higher the dpi or the line screen used to create an image, the greater the resolution possible. The memory required by high-resolution images is one reason large jobs are often transferred to the printer via FTP.

Hits: The number of times a program or item of data has been accessed. Each download of the home page of a website is considered one hit to the site. Hits also refer to the number of page and/or graphic files requested by visitors.

House stock: Papers that a printer inventories in large quantities; less expensive than similar paper that must be ordered for a job.

HTML: HyperText Markup Language, how text for websites is coded, or tagged. Not a computer language. Visible on websites when right-clicking with a mouse (on a PC) and selecting "view page source."

Images: Illustrations, photographs or other graphics. For print production, best prepared as TIFFs. If a job is submitted in any electronic form other than PDF, images must also be submitted and electronically 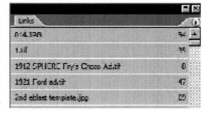 linked to the computer files for the publication. Printers say that missing links are among the most common problems with electronic files. Software like InDesign allows links to be checked prior to submission of a job (above, initial links to images in this book).

Imposition: Process of arranging individual page images so that after they are printed, folded and trimmed, the resulting pages will be in the proper order. An important issue when catalogs are printed in signatures, or when you are printing one or both sides of a sheet to create a four-page piece.

Impressions: Number of homes or individuals exposed to an advertisement or group of advertisements. In Internet parlance, the total number of times an advertising banner has been shown on a web page. To be counted as an impression, the banner has to successfully load on the user's browser.

InDesign: A commonly used desktop publishing program included in Adobe Systems Inc.'s Creative Suite.

Indicia: Postal permit number and type, placed where a stamp would be. Ordinarily used for bulk mail, or direct mail. See "Permit Imprints," pe.usps.com/text/qsg300/Q604d.htm.

Index.html: Home page of a website often has an extension using "index," e.g., http://www.website.org/index.aspx.

Inkjet printing: The plateless printing system used in digital printing that produces images directly on paper from digital data. Streams of very fine drops of dyes produce images on paper. Most office printers are inkjet printers.

Italic: Type that slopes. There are true italic faces, and with desktop publishing software, roman (regular) type can be inclined to simulate italic: *Palotino italic face* vs. *Palotino italic simulated* with InDesign.

JPEG: Joint Photographic Experts Group, graphic file format created by digital cameras and used in websites. A JPEG (or JPG) does not offer the same potential for resolution as a TIFF, and so is not recommended for printing. Converting a JPEG to a TIFF will not improve resolution.

Knockout: When ink is masked, or blocked, from being applied to part of a surface, to expose the color of the paper. Often done so that a lighter color later will print accurately (e.g., red might be knocked out of a background so that a yellow image or type will print yellow, not orange). In the example, red was knocked out to create white type, later outlined in black, and to provide a space for an image.

Justify: Type with spacing adjusted between words so that each line is flush, or aligned, both left and right, as in this glossary. See Flush.

Landing page: Where a link leads a viewer. This can be from an online ad, or from a live link in a blog, website, email or QR code.

Large print: Usually 18 or 20 point type, large enough for use by some with visual impairments. More information: "Best Practices and Guidelines for Large Print Documents used by the Low Vision Community," provided by the Council of Citizens with Low Vision International, an affiliate of the American Council of the Blind, cclvi.org/large-print-guidelines.html.

Laser printing: Office printer that, like a photocopy machine, uses an electrostatically charged drum and toner to produce an image on paper.

Leading: Space added between lines of type. Pronounced "ledding," it is expressed as a baseline to baseline measure. Nine point type leaded at 12 points will be written 9/12, phrased as "set 9 on 12." The extra space comes between descenders of the top line and ascenders of the next line. Type set 9/18 will have more space between lines. Type leaded too tight will be hard to read. The text of this book is set 11/14. This glossary is set 10/12. The name "leading" refers to the narrow metal strips which separated lines of metal type in early typesetting. See Descender.

Legal: Paper measuring 8½ x 14 inches.

Letterpress: Today primarily used for high quality short-run jobs such as invitations and personal stationery. The primary method of printing everything for 500 years starting with Gutenberg. Replaced for long-run and large jobs by offset lithography in the mid-1900s. Also defined as relief printing, letterpress originally used engravings and type created by hot-metal typesetters such as the Linotype.

Line art: Images created with a single color and without halftones, usually a black and white drawing. Most clip art is line art. See Clip Art and illustration at right from a vintage children's book.

Lines per inch (lpi): Measures resolution of a halftone or line screen. The higher the lpi, the finer the screen and the sharper the image. See Dots per inch.

Low-resolution: Low-res images can be transmitted electronically faster than those with high resolution, but lack clarity, especially when enlarged; may look blurred. Images such as stock photo previews are provided in low resolution for layout purposes; a high-resolution image must be purchased for the production of your ad, brochure or website.

Make-ready: The same as setup; includes all tasks required to prepare a press (or other equipment) for a specific printing or bindery job. In offset printing, includes washing the press, mounting plates on it and adjusting their registration and the quantity of ink reaching the printed piece. One reason that jobs printed in black ink on house stock are less expensive is that make-ready is decreased.

Margins: Unprinted space between the main body of text or illustrations and the edge of the paper. Top margin is also called head. Gutter is the term for the margin between two facing pages.

Mask: Used to block a portion of an image and therefore isolate the remaining part (for example, to remove a distracting background). Masking can be done electronically, with programs such as Photoshop. See Knockout.

Masthead: Name, ownership and editorial staff information for a publication, often appearing on second page of a newspaper and on contents page of a magazine. Valuable source of editorial contact information for submitting media releases (as contrasted to the subscription contact information, which for magazines is usually a service bureau in the Midwest, or the advertising bureau contacts, which may be for commissioned sales reps).

Matte: A dull finish, the opposite of glossy. Papers and coatings can be matte or gloss.

Media: Plural for medium, any device that packages and transmits information. Includes printed publications, tapes and records, films and television, computerized data vehicles and such online content as social media sites (for example, Facebook, Twitter, and LinkedIn).

Media release: Announcement in journalistic style, ideally well enough written that it can be published with little revision. Best written in inverted pyramid style, with information most important to the editor or reader first. Also news release. See Appendix A.

Mock-up: Pre-production sample. May use text in suggested type fonts and sizes or greeked text. May include specific instructions; for example, with brochures, will show direction of folds. Made with specified paper, it is used to determine weight of final piece for postage cost.

Moire: Undesirable pattern in printed images resulting when halftones and screen tints are made with improperly aligned screens.

Native advertising: Paid messages on online sites (search engines, blogs, Twitter and Facebook pages) that mimic "regular" content. As then *Wall Street Journal* columnist Farhad Manjoo commented in late 2013, they "derive their power from being given equal placement with the unsponsored content you actually want to read." Manjoo continued in his "High Definition" column, "The widespread adoption of native advertising...[results in] only the faintest visual distinctions between content that carries a commercial message and content that doesn't."

Native file: Files in the desktop-publishing documents in which they were created. Many printers ask that clients submit both native files (e.g., QuarkExpress or InDesign) and PDFs.

Negative leading: Type leaded at fewer points than the point size of the type: e.g., 12 point type leaded at 10. Extreme negative leading causes descenders in one line to overlap ascenders in next line. More common in logos and titles than in text. See Descender.

Negative letterspacing: Reducing space between characters by kerning or tracking, to create a special effect (often in a title) or to squeeze words into a small space, e.g., Advertising with Small Budgets for Big Results vs. Advertising with Small Budgets for Big Results.

Oblique: The slanted version of a type font, done to simulate italic. Common with sans serif fonts, which may not have italic faces. With desktop publishing software, fonts without oblique faces can be slanted manually. For example: Arial, *Arial.* See Italic.

Opacity: Characteristic of paper that prevents "see-through" – i.e., prevents what is printed on one side of a page from showing on the other side.

Opaque ink: Conceals the color below it, whether the color of the paper or a previously printed ink. By contrast, translucent inks combine with underlying color to create other colors: if a flyer is printed in yellow and then the title is overprinted in blue with an opaque ink, the title will appear blue. If the title is overprinted in translucent blue, it will appear green unless a knockout was used to prevent yellow from printing where the title will be. See Knockout and Mask.

Organic: Website visits that do not result from paid search or referrals.

Overprint: Superimposing new information on previously printed sheets (e.g., adding black text to newsletter blanks with the masthead preprinted in color) or blocking erroneous information in a previously printed job. Can mean creating a third color by printing one color over another, usually on a one-color press.

Overrun: When more copies are printed than ordered. May be deliberate if printer expects a high error rate. Most printing contracts allow the printer to deliver (and be paid for) 10 percent less to 10 percent more than the quantity ordered. Also, printing extra copies because there are other uses for the material.

Page: One side of a leaf; a 32-page book has 16 leaves of paper.

Pamphlet: Traditional definition is an unbound booklet of 48 or fewer pages with a self-cover; today the term can refer to a publication that has more pages, saddle-stitching and a cover of heavier paper. Does not refer to periodicals or books, although a short book might be formatted as a pamphlet.

Pantone Matching System (PMS): Ink matching system used to specify colors by number and formula. Most current digital presses cannot match PMS colors. Paper PMS swatches can be attached to comps so offset press operators can match printed output to the colors specified. If an exact match is required, the bid request should 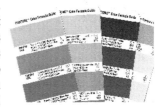 specify this; it may increase the cost of job. Color monitors, laser and inkjet printers, and photocopiers cannot accurately represent PMS colors.

Paragraph style: Word processing, desktop publishing, computerized typesetting and web authoring software have style tags (see next page for menu with original specs for this publication) that eliminate the need to separately specify font, face, type size, leading, indentations, rules and the space above and below a paragraph.

Parent sheet: Paper cut from rolls by paper manufacturers into such sizes as 23 x 35 inches to be sent to printers for use on sheet-fed presses. If waste can be reduced by designing a print job to use most of a parent sheet, the printing costs will also be reduced. This may mean printing two or three copies of a piece on one parent sheet (two-up, three-up). Printing other pieces on the parent sheet can also use paper that would otherwise be wasted. See Ganging.

Pass-along readership: Periodicals' media kits cite "circulation" figures (newsstand sales and number of addresses receiving a copy of the periodical) and "readership" figures ("total readership" and "pass-along readership"). Readership figures, always larger than

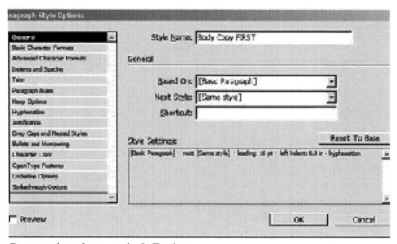

Paragraph style menu in InDesign.

circulation figures, are based on estimated number of readers per copy. For example: "PW's print edition boasts 15,000+ subscribers with a pass-along rate of four readers per issue." Unlike circulation, readership figures cannot be audited.

Perforating: Bindery process in which a line of tiny holes is punched in paper, often to facilitate tearing off a coupon.

Periodical: Publication that appears more frequently than annually, such as a magazine, journal or newsletter. Many carry an ISSN, which is similar to an ISBN in that it identifies the publisher. ISSNs are not required for a publication to qualify for U.S. Postal Service periodical mailing rates. For more information: usps.com, ISSN International Centre, issn.org, and Library of Congress, loc.gov.

Permission: Written clearance for publication of material from the owner of the relevant rights. Also see Rights.

Pica: Equivalent to 12 points in the American print measuring system, or one-sixth of an inch (an inch being 72 points). Until desktop publishing became common, picas and points were the measurements always used in printing.

Pixel: Usually, smallest single component of a digital image. Can be used as a unit of measurement, especially when referring to resolution; e.g., 2400 pixels per inch. The more pixels used to reproduce an image, the more closely it can resemble the original.

Plagiarism: Crime of using someone else's concepts or words without permission and without acknowledgement. If you suspect your material is being used by others, type phrases from it into a search engine like Google Books as an initial step in uncovering both plagiarism and piracy.

Point: The smallest unit of the American print measuring system used today, 1/72nd of an inch.

Portable Document Format (PDF): Originally made only with the Adobe Systems Acrobat Distiller software, PDF allows documents to be transferred via email, FTP and such physical devices as CDs. Can be read on any device with Adobe's free Acrobat Reader software regardless of operating system or platform. Generic PDF creation software is not supported by all vendors. Different print jobs require different levels of PDF. See rate card examples in "Magazine Advertising" and "Newspapers" for examples of specifications. Printing jobs submitted as PDFs require consultation with your printer regarding the appropriate specifications. See Acrobat, page 244.

Press check: Evaluation of print job quality, usually by production manager or graphic designer in the printing plant to check for such possible problems as registration, bleed-through and inadequate ink coverage.

Process color: See CMYK.

Public domain: Text and images not protected by copyright. May be material on which copyright has expired, material never copyrighted or material not eligible for copyright. The fact that material is in the public domain does not always eliminate the need for permission to use it or the need to pay for that right; if a copyright-free image is acquired from an archive, library or stock photo company, for instance, permission to use that image must be obtained, and a fee may be charged.

Quotes, straight or curly: Quotations are set off with "curly" quotation marks in typeset material; a single curly quote is the same as an apostrophe, a straight quote mark is used to indicate feet, and double straight quotes are used to indicate inches: "curly" vs. "straight."

Rating: Used in broadcast commercial sales as an estimate of a program's audience size, expressed as a percentage of the total population in the market area. Indicates the potential audience of a single commercial on a specific program.

Reach: Broadcast advertising sales term, an estimate of unduplicated (unique) number of households or individuals reached during an advertising campaign. Salespeople will also cite "frequency," how many times the same people are reached during a campaign. May be expressed as "reach at least 20 percent of the households three to five times during the campaign." Internet advertising salespeople will also cite "reach" and "frequency" estimates.

Registration: When two or more printed areas are exactly aligned. Important in jobs printed in multiple inks, and in all jobs with embossing, debossing and die cuts. When images don't align, the printing or die cut is "out-of-register" (at right, the black outline is not registered with white knockout). Publications created on large, fast web presses (newspapers, for example) may have images that appear slightly blurry because of poor registration.

Reproduction: Today the term applies to the quality of text or artwork prepared for publication or already printed, as in "poor reproduction" (e.g., grainy, low-resolution, colors not matched to samples or specified PMS colors, or out-of-register).

Resolution: Measurement of clarity. On a digital image, resolution is defined by dpi, number of individual dots that can be placed within span of one linear inch. If the resolution is not high enough, the printed image will be blurry. Resolution on a monitor may be as low as 72 dpi. Also an issue when small or condensed type is reversed. See Reverse.

Retail/local rates: Lower newspaper display advertising rates for locally-owned businesses. Contrast with General/national.

Reverse: Type or line art that may be the paper color because no ink is applied to that area. With multiple colors of ink, background may be printed, and then type is reversed out (not printed) with a later application of ink. Reverses can be combined with knockouts. The knockout ensures that the second color will print accurately, and not be distorted by the background color.

Reversed type is also often outlined with black or a color. Reversed type in small sizes can be hard to read because ink usually spreads at least slightly, and when it spreads into the areas of reversed type the ink is more noticeable. When color is applied to a reversed, or knocked out, area, registration must be precise. See Dot gain, Knockout, and Registration.

Advertising with Small Budgets for Big Results 263

RGB: Red, green and blue create the images on monitors. All RGB images must be converted to CMYK or PMS for printing. This can be done with software such as Creative Suite. See CMYK and PMS.

Rights: Permission to use material created by someone else—photo, drawing, map, poem or joke, article—is usually sold. Rights include merchandising (such as toys, T-shirts, posters and greeting cards); radio; television; audio; print; and digital, both domestic and foreign. Most of these are described as subsidiary rights. The invoice for material to be used in an ad or commercial, on a brochure or billboard, should clearly state which rights are covered.

Rights clearinghouse: Businesses or nonprofits that broker subsidiary rights for content. One example is the Copyright Clearance Center, copyright.com, described as handling rights for "in- and out-of-print books, journals, newspapers, magazines, movies, television shows, images, blogs and ebooks." Publishers that license their content through rights clearinghouses can specify what content is available for what uses. See Copyright.

Scanning: Creates digital images of illustrations, photographic prints, or text. Images can be saved in many formats, including JPEG for website use and TIFF for insertion in material to be printed.

Score: Line impressed into pages of such publications as a self-mailer or brochure during the bindery process to make copies easier to fold.

Second cover: Books, magazines and catalogs are sometimes produced with different covers. When a book is being used as a giveaway, that version may have a cover with a phrase such as, "This copy compliments of …" If a bulk buyer has licensed book content for a certain market, the second cover might incorporate the buyer's name in the title: "The XYZ Company Guide to …"

Magazines sent to subscribers sometimes have different covers than those sold on newsstands; those with regional editions may have different covers for each area. Magazine concepts being tested may have different covers for different parts of the country, to determine which cover results in the most purchases. Retailers who issue catalogs each month sometimes change only the cover.

Set-off: Unacceptable transfer of ink from one sheet to the back of the next sheet going through the press. Causes include paper that does not absorb ink well, ink that is not absorbed well, and humidity in the press area.

Share of audience: Advertising term for estimated percentage of households or individuals watching or listening to a particular program compared to the number of broadcast sets in use when the program was aired. The higher the share of audience, the higher the cost of advertising for that program.

Share of market: Used to indicate market dominance, a percentage of a market that a given product or kind of product has. For example, the percentage of iPad sales compared to sales of all e-readers.

Show-through: Printing on one side of a sheet that can be seen on the reverse side, a problem caused by lightweight paper, paper that is not opaque, or by ink wicking through paper. See Opacity.

Signature: Single page printed with multiple pages of a publication, signature also refers to the sheet when folded and trimmed into pages for one section of a book or catalog. Number of pages in a signature depends on size of the parent sheet and page size of the printed piece. Newspapers sometimes have four-page signatures (two leaves with two pages on each). Book and catalog signatures are usually multiples of eight. See Imposition and Leaf.

Slander: The oral communication of false statements that are harmful to a person's reputation, which may lead that person to take legal action. The written counterpart is libel. Both should be avoided.

Snipe: Short promotional message, often shown across the top of an ad or brochure as if it's an addition to the original piece. Also used on billboards. See Violator.

Social media: Opt-in electronic media such as blogs, Goodreads, Facebook, Twitter, LinkedIn, and Pinterest that you can use to post announcements and invite comments. Participation is usually free; ads can be purchased on many such sites or posts can be "sponsored," ensuring that they get top billing.

Spec: "Job specs," or specifications, describe how something is to be made. In printing, specs will outline quantity, trim size, page count, type fonts and faces, leading, ink colors, paper stock, binding, any special finishes and delivery instructions.

Spot coating: Varnish or another finish applied to only part of a printed piece to enhance a graphic element such as an image or title. For example, a subtle logo can be made with spot varnish, which creates only shine, rather than with ink.

Spot color: A color other than black used for certain elements of text, such as subheads or graphics.

Advertising with Small Budgets for Big Results 265

Stock photos, stock art: Images from companies that license use of their own photos or images acquired from photographers and illustrators. Other organizations also license images (for example, museums, newspaper archives and libraries). Can be purchased on an exclusive basis, so that others cannot use the same image in the same medium and/or for a certain time period, important if you don't want the picture in your brochure or on your website seen in promotion elsewhere. Fees depend on how a photo will be used, and in how many copies: fees for a photo in a text with a press run of 5,000 will be less than fees for an image used on television. Fees for exclusive use are higher.

Tabloid: Small format newspaper publication, usually half the size of a broadsheet, typical of special sections. Also refers to a standard paper size, 11 x 17 inches.

Tear sheets: Often replaced by links to a printed or broadcast piece or a PDF of a printed piece, requested by manufacturers when providing samples to reviewers. Tear sheets document what a reviewer said; can be used as the source of testimonial comments for publicity. Often required for reimbursement through cooperative advertising programs.

Template: Page layout information, now usually saved in a desktop publishing or word processing program, with text area, type fonts and faces, margins, running heads, page numbers and other design element specs saved along with type and paragraph styles.

TIFF: Tagged Image File Format, a standard graphic image usually generated by scanners or software such as Photoshop. A format capable of high resolution and thus the standard format for graphics to be printed on paper.

Tip in: Individual sheets such as an order form can be tipped in, or glued, into a book or catalog after binding. Also a correction method: if incorrect text or images were printed on one page, the page can be cut out and a replacement tipped in.

Trim, trim size: Finished size of printed piece after binding and trimming. A bid or estimate should specify trim size for at least three reasons: to ensure that the finished size of a mailer meets the requirements of desired postal rate; to ensure finished piece fits into an envelope, either outgoing or incoming, if you're enclosing a Business Reply envelope; and to ensure that brochures fit into the racks they'll be distributed in.

Typeface: Characters that form a "family" in a given style of a type design, such as all the characters in Helvetica bold, extra bold, light or italic. Contrast with font, which is the type name, such as Helvetica, Times Roman or Bodoni. See Font.

Type size: Described in points, although letters in different fonts called the same size will seldom be the same physical size. This is especially true of horizontal measure, because styles such as "thin" or "light" will be narrower, and those called "extra bold" will be wider. Some fonts have shorter ascenders and descenders than others, too. Each of the following is 24 points:

Aa, Aa, **Aa**, **Aa**, Aa, *Aa*

Before desktop publishing, each size type was created separately, and only certain sizes were available. Now other point sizes can be selected, and standard sizes can stretched or condensed in the software's "character styles."

-Up: A suffix indicating how many copies of the same cover or artwork are printed on a parent sheet. Standard-size postcards can be printed four-up on one letter-size sheet of cover stock.

Upper case: Capital letters.

Violator: Signage that extends beyond the edge of a package or a display (and thus "violates" the edge), such as a starburst with a short promotional message that flares out from a cardboard dump bin.

Work-and-tumble, work-and-turn: When artwork for both sides of a piece (such as a postcard) is arranged on a single image or plate so that one side of a sheet can be printed and then turned to print the other side with the same image. The sheet is then trimmed to create two or more copies of the finished piece. Can easily be done today with the high-quality color printer-copiers used in many offices and in copy shops.

WYSIWYG: Pronounced "wizzy-wig," the acronym for What You See Is What You Get, computer displays that accurately represent what will be printed on a press. Because colors are displayed as RGB and printed as CMYK, they cannot be WYSIWYG.

Index

For additional help, check the appendixes and glossary.

A-frame sidewalk sign 174
Adhesive note ads 138, 143
Adopt-a-Highway 236
Ads on web sites, checklist for 235
Ads with toll-free numbers 75
Advergaming 105, 106
Advertising agency, how to find 243
Advertising, blogs 52
Advertising buying service, alternative papers 145
Advertising novelties 35, 109
Advertorials 35, 36, 54, 125
Aerial advertising 149
Affiliate marketing 43, 51
Affinity credit cards 119
Airport advertising 151
Airport websites, advertising 151
Alaska Marine Highway System 103
Alexa 52, 54, 211
Alliance of Area Business Publishers 147
Alternate text, website images 208, 210
Alternative papers 144
Alumni events, networking at 133
Alumni publications 43
Amazon.com 182
Amazon Local 69
American Catalog Mailers Assn 72, 96
American City Business Journals 147
American Horse Publications 128
Anchorage Brochure Distribution 103
Anderson and Ketron Island ferries 103
Anti-spam language 88
Apparel 45
Arbitron 166

Assn of Alternative Newsmedia 144
Assn of Business Information and Media Companies 128
Assn of Free Community Papers 142
Assn of Magazine Media 128
Assn of Medical Media 128
Atom 185
Automated telephone systems 46
Avoiding spam filters 95

B-roll 246
Bags, newspaper 138, 143
Ballparks 151
Banner ads 217-218
Banners 49
Bathroom advertising 49
Beach marketing 154
Beaver Island Boat Co 105
Bellybands 77
Benches 152
Big Cat Rescue, game tips 106-107
Billboard embellishment 150
Billboard facing 150
Billboards 148, 152
Billboards, tri-vision 150
Billboard sizes 150
Bind-in/blown-in postcards 75
Bing ads on your site 219
Blimps 148
Blog advertising/promotion, checklist for 235
Blog as website 213
Blogger/Blogspot 51
Blogs 38, 50, 182
Blog statistics 54
Blogtalk Radio 165
Book of Lists 141, 146
Botnets, fraud with 215
Bouncebacks 115
Bounce rate 52, 212
Branded content 126

Bridgeport & Port Jefferson Steamboat Co. 104
Brochures, printed in-house 57
Broken links on website 213
Building sign options 175
Bulk mail permit 80, 158
Bumper stickers 55
Bus cards 148
Business cards, letterhead 55
Business cards, networking 132
Business papers 146
Business Reply Mail 80, 158
Business Wire 26
Buttons 46
Buyer's Guide 41

Cable television 200-201
Campus papers 147
CAN-SPAM Act 74, 88
CAPTCHA 210
Cash register tape ads 65
Casual Games Assn 107
Catalina Marketing Corp. 66
Catholic Radio Assn 174
CBS Outdoor 153
Celebrity endorsements 97
Certified Folder Display Service 103
Chalk art 153
Chalkboards 174
Checklist for advertising/promotion 229–239
Chinook Book 71
Cinema Advertising Council 60
City and Regional Magazine Assn 128
Classified advertising, newspapers 140
Classmates.com 114
Clear Channel Outdoor 153
Click fraud, online ads 215
Co-op advertising packets 76
Codes, as tracking devices 115, 129
Commissionable rates 140, 199
Community newspapers 145
Computer and online games 105

Conference giveaways 192
Conferences, promotion 205
Constant Contact 88
Content, free 36
Content Marketing Institute 246
Content providers for newsletters 137
Contests to build database 73
Controlled circulation 82, 121
Cooperative advertising 62, 64
Copyright-free newsletter content 136
Costumed characters 59
Costume Specialists 60
Count station 150
Coupon books 65
Coupons 65, 76, 130
Coupons, in-house, short periods 67
Coupons, cash register receipts 65
Coupons sent to own database 67
CPM billing, online ads 219
Craigslist 140, 142
Crain Communications 147
Creating a newsletter 136
Creative themes, ads/promotions 229
Credit cards, affinity/co-branded 119
Cross-business promotion 168
Crowdsourcing 72
Custom Content Council 126
Custom publishing 125, 137

"Daily deal"sites 65
Database, means of increasing 91
Database, networking to increase 135
Database, newspaper helps you create 136
Denso-Wave QR codes 161
DigiPen Insitute of Technology 107
Direct mail, defined 249
Direct mail, samples 78
Direct mail wraps 77
Direct Marketing Assn 72, 90, 96

Advertising with Small Budgets for Big Results **269**

Directories, effectiveness of ads 74
Direct response advertising, defined 75, 249
Direct response advertising, not on public radio 165
DMA, Designated Market Area 198
Dynamic advertising, games 106

eBay 140
Eblasts 73, 88, 136
Electronic Retailing Assn 42
Elevator and lobby advertising 86
Email 87
Email addresses, "borrowing" 92
Email promotion, checklist for 235
Emails, individual 93
Email Sender and Provider Coalition 96
Email vs. postal mail 89
Encore Media 61
Endorsements 96, 98, 230
Endorsements, networking as source 134
Entertainment Resources & Marketing Assn 41, 107
Entertainment Software Assn 106
Espresso Book Machine 58
Ethnic newspapers 146
Etsy 140
Evangelical Press Assn 128
Exchanges, online ads 53, 215

F.O.B., defined 251
Fabric On Demand 46
Fabric scraps, bags from 48
Fabric with business name 46
Facebook 54, 67, 70, 114, 182, 185, 187, 190, 217
Fan mail, source of testimonials 97
Federal Communications Commission 172
Federal Outdoor Advertising Program 176
Federal Trade Commission 73, 99
Federal Trade Commission and sponsored content 38

Ferry Media 102
Ferry system advertising 102
File transfer protocol (FTP), defined 251
"Flash sale" websites 68
Flat rate billing, online ads 218
Floating billboards 153
Followers, social media 183
Food truck advertising 180
Footer, website design 209
Free-lance help 243
Frequency discounts 138, 197
Fringe days and times 167

Games, creating your own 107
Gas pump advertising 108
Gender-specific messages 49
Gilt Groupe 69
Giveaways 108, 239
GLBT readership 145
Gobo 154
Goes viral 39
Google 53, 182, 189, 217
Google+ 187
Google ads on your site 219
Google AdWords, automated buying explained 217
Google Analytics 163, 210, 213
Google Offers 69
GoogleSearch 208
Graphic designers 243
Gross Rating Points 197
Groupon 68
Guaranteed circulation 142, 145
Guemes Island ferry 103
Guerilla marketing 87, 151, 159, 238
"Guides Concerning the Use of Endorsements and Testimonials in Advertising," 38

Handhelds, website design for 209
Hearst Integrated Media 126
Help A Reporter Out 25
Hempfest giveaway, innovative 112
Hewlett-Packard banner paper 49

Highway department roadside signs 174, 236

Hits, defined 254

HootSuite 185

Horse-drawn carriages, ads on 56

HSN 174

Hulu, ads on 60

Idaho Film Office 41

Illustrators 243

In-game advertising 105

In-house email databases 91

In-kind help/compensation 64, 113, 130-131

In-store advertising 116, 154

In-store coupons 65

In-store displays 116-117

Independent Free Papers of America 142

Indicia 80, 158

Indiegogo 8

Indoor Billboard Advertising Assn 50

Infomercials 36, 41

Insertions as factor in price 123

Inserts 114, 115, 138

Instagram 182, 188

Interactive Advertising Bureau 220

International Game Developers Assn 107

International Society of Automation 220

Interns 243

Invoices 118

Iron-on designs 48

Ivy League Magazine Network 44

Kantar Media SRDS 128

Klout 54

Labels 48

Lamar Advertising 153

Landing page 89, 212

Large print, visually handicapped, defined 256

Lead generators, contests as 62

Lead time, importance of 229

Legal papers 146

Lighthouse International 209

LinkedIn 182, 187, 190, 217

Links in eblasts 89

List rental 82

LivingSocial 69

Local Media Assn 145

Loss leaders, "Daily deal" sites 68

Loyalty programs 119

Luggage carts 151

Magazine ad costs 123

Magazine ad production 122

Magazine advertising/promotion, checklist for 233

Magazine reader demographics 126

Magazines 120, 224

MailChimp 88

Mailing list cost 82

Mailing list formats 82

Mailing list quality 82

Mailing lists, purchased 80

Mailpiece design analysts 158

Malware and click fraud 216

Maps, ads on 129

Media kit, magazine 122

Media release 17, 20-24, 114, 221

Meredith Xcelerated Marketing 126

Microsoft Tag 163

Military papers 147

Mobile billboard 150, 153

Model releases 122, 228

Montana Film Office 41

Motorist information signs 177

Movie theater advertising 60

Multiple impressions, importance of 214

Naming privileges 130

National Etailing & Mailing Organization of America 72, 96

National vs. retail ad rates 138

Navigation Summary Report 213

NCOA 81

Near Field Communication 163

Advertising with Small Budgets for Big Results — 271

Network, sustaining 134
Network ads on your site 219
Networking, introducing 132
Networks, online ads 53, 215
New England Business Media 147
News America Marketing 67
Newsletters 38, 131
Newspaper advertising/promotion, checklist for 232
Newspaper Assn of Idaho 145
Newspaper inserts/preprints 142
Newspaper rates, general vs. local 138
Newspapers 137
Newspaper website advertising 144
Newspaper wraps 77
Nielsen Audio (Arbitron) 166
Nixies 84
Nonprofit ad rates, newspapers 140
NPR 171
Nth select 86
NY Waterway 104
Ohio Game Developer Assn 107
Online ads, cost estimates 218
Online coupons 65
Open rate, newspaper ads 139
Opt-in 73, 89
Oregon Film 41
Oregon Newspaper Publishers Assn 145
Organic, defined 258
Out-of-home advertising, checklist for 236
Outdoor advertising, defined 150
Outdoor Advertising Assn of America 148

Package insert programs 115
Package stuffers 115
Packing slips 118
Page rank 54
Pageviews 54
Pandora Internet Radio 165
Pantone Matching System (PMS),

defined 259
Parent Institute 137
Pay-per-click billing, online ads 219
"Peel off ads" 143
Personal sales, checklist for 238
Photography release 122, 228
Picture Permit Imprint Indicia 158
Pin-back buttons 46
Pinterest 67, 182, 187, 190
Pixel, defined 260
Plum District 70
Point-of-purchase 116
Political ads 139
Polybag outserts 77
Portable Document Format (PDF), defined 261
Postal mail 75, 156, 157
Postal standards for newspapers 142
Poster production, budget 159
Posters, URLs for more info 160
Poster services 160
Precancelled stamps 158
Premium placement 140
Prestige Media 104
Pride of Cassville 105
Prime Consulting Services 44
PR Newswire 26
Pro bono help 229
Production specs 122
Product placement 36, 39-40, 106, 108
Programs, concert and theater 61
Promotional Products Assn International 35
Public broadcasting stations 130
Publicizing giveaway for PR value 113
Public radio stations 171, 226
Public radio audience demographics 171
Public radio station website ads 173
Public service announcements 140, 168

QR code 50, 65, 122, 160, 161, 163
QVC 174

Radio, audience demographics 166
Radio, buying time 166-167
Radio, independent broadcast 163
Radio, network-affiliate 163
Radio, online 163
Radio, paid programming 164
Radio, pay-to-play 165
Radio, public 164, 226
Radio, satellite 163
Radio ads, producing 169
Radio ads, samples 170
Radio ads and social media 169
Radio advertising/promotion, checklist for 231
Radio Locator 174
Radio station promotional events 168
Rate cards, magazine 122
Rate cards, newspaper 138-139
Rating, defined 261
Reach 197, 261
Readerboards 176
Reader response cards 75, 120
Readership estimates 126
Register Tape Network 66
Register Tapes Unlimited 66
Remnant advertising, TV 200
Rest area signs and brochures 177
Rich Site Summary 185
Ride-alongs 138, 143
Rooftop signs, vehicles 180
Rubber stamps 48
Run of station 167

Sagacity Media 44
Sales reports, import into databases 73
Samples 109-112
Self-liquidating premiums 109, 113
Serious Games Assn 107
Share of audience, defined 263
Share of market, defined 264
Shoppers (printed) 141

Shopping bags 48
Shuttle buses 151
Sidewalk advertising 153
Signs, company vehicles 181
Signs, three-dimensional 176
SilverPop 88
SiriusXM 165
Site map on website 208
SkyMall 59
SkyVector 151
Skywriting 149
Snipe 149
Social media, defined 264
Social media, saving time 183
Social media, syndicating 185
Social media promotions, checklist for 235
Social media site advertising 189
SocialOomph 185
Southern California Media Group 61
Spadeas 77
Special interest newspapers 146
Special Interest Publications 125
Special publications, newspapers 138, 141
Special sections 36-37, 138, 140
Sponsored content 36, 38, 125
Sponsored posts on your site 219
Sponsorships 39, 130
Spoonflower 46
Spotify 165
Statement and package stuffers 76
Statements and envelopes 118
Station Index 203
Steamship Authority 103
Stickiness 52, 89
Sticky note/peel-off ads 77, 143
Stock photos 122, 137
Street furniture advertising 150
Street projections 154
Street teams 59
Surveys 98
Swag/goodie bags 131, 193

Taxi cab advertising 180
Technorati 51

Television, evaluating 193
Television advertising/promotion, checklist for 230
Television air time, buying 198
Television audience decline 193
Television Bureau of Advertising 203
Television buys, extras 200
Television commercial production 195
Television, attire for 196
Television ratings lingo 197
Television viewing 39, 194
Text ads, online 216
Time Inc. Content Solutions 126
Tote bags 48
Tourist information 237
Tourist Oriented Directional Signs 177
Trade-outs 108
Trade journal advertising/promotion, checklist for 233
Trade journals 120, 225
Trade shows 203
Transit advertising 150
Truth in Advertising 99
TSA checkpoint bins 151
Tumblr 51
TweetDeck 185
Twitter 67, 106, 114, 182, 185, 192
Twtrland 183

U.S. Census Bureau reports with direct mail 81
U.S. postal rates 79
Uline 48
Underwriting spots 165, 172
Unenveloped letter-size mailpieces 157
URL 208

Vehicle signage 179
Vehicle wrap 181
Video trailers 206
Vimeo 182, 189
Vinyl clings/decals 153
Visually handicapped 209

Voice mail 46
VT/NH Marketing Group 72, 96

Wall mural, advertising as 150
Washington Filmworks 41
Washington Island Ferry Line 104
Washington Newspaper Publishers Assn 145
Washington State Ferries 102
Website, ads on yours 207, 219
Website, advertising yours 207
Website, checklist for 234
Website, creating 207
Website, testimonials on 99
Website advertising 138
Website advertising effectiveness 214
Website authoring basics 208
Website design, resources for 242
Website visitor counter 211
Website visitor traffic sources 211
Weekly reach 54
Window clings 176
Wooden Horse Magazine Media News 25
Word-of-Mouth Marketing Assn 55
WordPress 51
Work-study 243
Wraps/Spadeas 138, 143

Yahoo ads on your site 219
YouTube 189

274   *Advertising with Small Budgets for Big Results*

Your Turn!

Use this page or the *Advertising with Small Budgets for Big Results* Facebook page to make general comments, write compliments or criticism, point out errors—whatever!

Please describe yourself (check as many as apply):

☐ Work in small business
☐ Work/volunteer in nonprofit
☐ Work in government

☐ Have no formal marketing/advertising/PR training or experience
☐ Have formal marketing/advertising/PR training but no paid experience
☐ Have done some marketing
☐ Have spent __ years in some aspect of marketing

What's most helpful in this book?

_____

_____

_____

What you wish it also had:

_____

_____

Comments on format, illustrations, examples, glossary?

_____

_____

This book is most appropriate for:

_____

☐ Check here if your business and/or professional association has a budget for speakers and you'd like Linda Carlson to contact you regarding a brainstorming session or how-to presentation.
☐ Check here if you are interested in a quantity purchase of this book or licensing content from it.

Name, phone, and email address (if you wish to be contacted):

_____

_____

Send to: Linda Carlson, P O Box 99642, Seattle WA 98139, lindacarlson@ earthlink.net.

Made in the USA
San Bernardino, CA
19 September 2014